# Ancient Egypt and Us

The Impact of Ancient Egypt on the Modern World.

— By Adrian Kerr —

To MJ + KEN

BEST WISHES

Adrian

Library of Congress Cataloging–in–Publication Data

Kerr, Adrian R J,

Ancient Egypt and Us.

ISBN-13 978-0-615-27359-4



1.History-Egypt, 2 Archaeology- Excavation 3 Egypt – Kings, 4 Tombs-Pyramids-Temples

Printed in the United States of America

First Edition 2009

## Acknowledgments

I am greatly indebted to Jean Huston and to Lauren and Jay Kerr for their help and advice and my wife Louise for her encouragement and support in preparing this volume.

## Ozymandias

I met a traveller from an antique land,
Who said: Two vast and trunkless legs of stone
Stand in the desert. Near them, on the sand,
Half sunk, a shattered visage lies, whose frown
And wrinkled lip and sneer of cold command,
Tell that its sculptor well those passions read,
Which yet survive stamped on these lifeless things,
The hand that mocked them,and the heart that fed.
And on the pedestal these words appear:
'My name is Ozymandias, King of Kings;
Look on my works,ye Mighty, and despair!'
Nothing beside remains. Round the decay
Of that colossal wreck, boundless and bare
The lone and level sands stretch far away.

*Percy Bysshe Shelley, December 1817*

*The word Ozymandias represents a transliteration into Greek of part of the throne name
of Ramesses 2, User Maat Re Setep en Re.
Shelley's sonnet paraphrases the inscription on the fallen colossal statue at the Ramesseum.*

# Contents

# *Prologue*

My first contact with Egypt was when my family emigrated to live in Bombay, India in 1954. On the outward journey our ship, The Batori passed through the Suez Canal and stopped off at Port Said, it was my first experience of what seemed like endless desert sands and bright blue sky. A few years later I visited Cairo and I was completely entranced by the oriental culture. One memory that stays with me was the practice at that time for men to wear the traditional red Fez. It was as a school boy, at the age of fourteen, that I was introduced to the history of Egypt, and first became aware of this intriguing ancient civilization *'from an antique land'* which had disappeared thousands of years ago and yet still had a remarkable and probably unique hold on modern minds. Shelley's poem *'Ozymandias'* written in 1817 was influenced by the arrival in Europe of this bust (below) of Ramesses 2 (British Museum, London). The process of the rediscovery of Ancient Egypt by the West was a long slow one, starting with the early European travelers such as Sandys and Greaves in the 1600s, Sicard, Pococke, and Norden in the 1700's through to the major collecting activities of Napoleon, Salt, Drovetti, Bankes, Belzoni, Lepsius, and Budge in the 1800's.

However, the translation of hieroglyphics, by Young and Champollion in the 1820s, was the major breakthrough needed to allow the chronology of Egypt to be slowly unraveled as accurate king lists and reigns began to be pieced together. The fine artistic work of members of the French Commission and that of the Lepsius Expedition plus the brilliance of the lithographs of David Roberts, gave the Victorian world wonderfully accurate and beautiful images of the monuments and temples still standing. They also showed a tantalizing glimpse of the magnificent colors that could still be observed after four thousand years. This led to a surge in tourists, facilitated by a low cost fast trans-Mediterranean steamer service to Alexandria, a train to Cairo and then relaxing paddle steamer up the Nile. Thomas Cook in November 1869, almost single handedly opened up Egypt to Victorian mass tourism with his pioneering package tours and dedicated modern, for their time, ships. In 1873 his clients numbered two hundred and in 1881, he alone was transporting eight hundred tourists a year to Luxor. By 1900 his clients were enjoying waiter-served lunches inside each of the major temples on his trade mark china and table linens.

Control of wholesale antiquities collecting began to be established with the pioneering appointment of Mariette in 1858 as the Director General of the newly created Egyptian Antiquities Department, ably followed by his countryman Maspero in 1881. Archaeological excavation, based on scientific methods, was first introduced and quickly published by Petrie, from the 1880s onwards.

A few years later, the first comprehensive and accurate history of Ancient Egypt was written by Breasted. His magisterial work published in 1905 was based on a marathon journey to visit, record, and translate all the major historical inscriptions in collections outside Egypt and all those still at that time surviving in Egypt and Nubia. In effect, by single handedly translating every known piece of ancient Egyptian writing, he could draw up the first mostly accurate list of kings and their reigns. New discoveries since then have gradually added to this knowledge, probably climaxing for the public at large in the discovery by Carter, in 1922, of Tutankhamen's almost intact tomb in the Valley of the Kings. This so far still unique event set the world alight with a fascination not seen since the late nineteenth century. Interest was reignited again in the 1960s, when following a world wide appeal and successful funding, UNESCO organized the rescue of the endangered Nubian temples. Particularly notable was the raising, piece by piece, between 1964 and 1968, of the outstanding Abu Simbel temple, built by Ramesses 2, above the rising waters caused by the then new Aswan high dam. This was followed by the relocation of the magnificent but partly flooded temple of Philae to the higher nearby island of Agilka between 1977 and 1980.

My study of the history and archaeology of ancient Egypt, and its neighbors in the Middle East, has been driven by the desire to better understand what it is about this civilization that has created the hold it has on us. We still look in awe and study a once lost civilization that lasted over three thousand years from c3500BC to Roman times. This is three times the duration of the Western Roman Empire itself and is by far the longest civilization in human history.

My historical journey has led me to visit and revisit the magnificent tombs, temples, palaces and ruins of this past civilization as well as to examine at first hand the many remarkable historical artifacts now housed in the magnificent Egyptian collections of museums throughout the world. My enthusiasm for ancient Egypt has manifested itself in a series of illustrated lectures focusing not on the detailed history but the main personalities, achievements and particularly on examples of the direct impact that Ancient Egypt continues to have on our lives today. This current work has grown out of these talks to audiences who share in the fascination of an ancient culture which still speaks to us and influences our lives today.

The human race has long been fascinated by achievement and those who have made the first steps. We remember who was the first to sail across the Atlantic, to fly, to reach the South Pole, to scale Everest, and to step on the moon Then there are the leaders in science who invented the printing press, defined gravity, made the first mass produced car, and in health and medicine, the first nurse, the first pain killer, and so on. It is much harder to identify firsts when they occurred five thousand years ago, but in many cases we can use the archaeological evidence to give us approximate dates, and in exceptional circumstances, we can actually identify the specific individuals who made or recorded the discovery.

This volume demonstrates how our modern religions, literature, art, architecture, medicine, cosmetics, warfare, mathematics and science all have their roots in ancient Egypt. It is interesting to remark that hieroglyphic writing first appeared over five thousand years ago and yet classes to learn this language, dead for over fifteen hundred years, are still thriving. That tells us that the fascination with ancient Egypt is still as strong as ever.

Fort Myers, 20th December 2008

'Chronolgy and geography must accompany history to make it all intelligible'
*Sir William Wynne, Cambridge 1812*

*Map of Ancient Egypt and Nubia showing the main cities and sites.*

# Introduction

There are certain aspects and themes of the history of ancient Egypt which need to be introduced at this point to assist the reader through the unfamiliar chronology and terminology commonly used.

**Ancient Egypt Time Line** How does the ancient Egyptian civilization fit into our comprehension of the huge expanse of history? Of all the ancient civilizations, Egypt's is the most challenging because of its extreme longevity compounded by its remote chronological distance from the present day. To fully grasp the contribution ancient Egypt has made to our modern society it is important to be able to place ancient Egypt in context. The time line below shows ancient Egypt in relationship to familiar and less distant civilizations such as ancient Greece and Rome

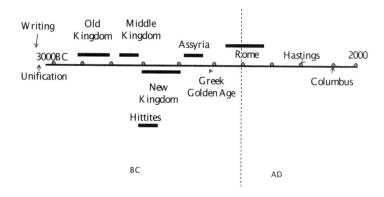

It does emphasize that events such as the first crossing of the Atlantic by Columbus in 1492, which we consider to be very distant, can be considered to be a relatively recent occurrence when compared to the time of the first king of a united Egypt c3200BC.

**Kingdoms and Dynasties** We are indebted to the Egyptian priest Manetho for the earliest detailed history of Egypt. He was born in the northern delta city of Sebennytos during the time of the early Greek Egyptian Ptolemaic dynasty, probably late in the reign of Ptolemy I. Ptolemy I had taken Egypt and created a new dynasty when his lifelong friend and king, Alexander the Great, died in Babylon without naming an adult heir. Manetho is believed to have become the chief priest of Re at the massive temple complex of Heliopolis, on the northern outskirts of what is now Cairo. He wrote exclusively in Greek and around 250BC compiled parts of the history of Egypt and produced a list of the Egyptian gods, kings and dynasties up to the conquest of Egypt by Alexander. He had available to him at that time a number of king lists to work with but it is believed that his main source was the Turin Royal Canon papyrus as his lists of king's names and the lengths of each reign fit quite well.

His great work 'Aegyptiaca' is now lost to us but copies of some of the sections made by later Roman period authors such as Josephus, Africanus, Eusebius, and the Alexandrian Pope Theophilus have survived. Manetho conveniently divided Egyptian history into three Kingdoms each divided by intermediate periods. Within each of the Kingdoms and intermediate periods he collected groups of kings into what he called 'dynasties', from the Greek meaning governmental power, of which there were thirty one. However, he did not use dynasty in the way we do today implying a royal bloodline change. Manetho created a new dynasty when he detected some form of discontinuity. Sometimes it was indeed a genealogical change in bloodline, but it could also be a geographical change, for example when a ruler moved his palace or capital or when burial locations or practices changed. Confusingly he refers to each successive king as the 'son' of the previous ruler, this does not always mean a blood son, as he uses the term merely to imply continuity. Beside each period below, is a guide to the approximate year and duration of each plus a key word or two to help distinguish each phase of the civilization. It is worth emphasizing that there is still wide interpretation of the dates in the early years becoming less so by the time of the New Kingdom.

| | | | |
|---|---|---|---|
| EARLY DYNASTIC | 3,200-2,584 BC | DYN. 1+2 — UNIFICATION |
| OLD KINGDOM | 2,584-2,160 BC | DYN. 3-6 — PYRAMID BUILDERS |
| 1ST INTERMEDIATE | 2,160-2,066 BC | DYN. 7-11 — CENTRAL POWER FAILS |
| MIDDLE KINGDOM | 2,066-1,650 BC | DYN. 11-14 — EXPANSION INTO NUBIA |
| 2ND INTERMEDIATE | 1,650-1,549 BC | DYN. 15-17 — THE HYKSOS |
| NEW KINGDOM | 1,549-1,064 BC | DYN. 18-20 — THE EMPIRE |
| 3RD INTERMEDIATE | 1,064-656 BC | DYN. 21-26 — ASSYRIA, ISRAEL |
| LATE PERIOD | 656-332 BC | DYN. 27-31 — BABYLON, PERSIA |

**Population** Although there were formal government 'cattle counts' every one or two years, there was no comprehensive annual population census gathering until the Ptolemaic period. Hence our estimate of the population of Egypt throughout the various periods is rather approximate. Population estimates are based on a range of factors, from the numbers of villages and towns known to exist at a given time, to the records of the amount of land a soldier would be given to farm, in place of payment, and from that estimating how many people that land could support. Butzer's population estimates are:

| | |
|---|---|
| EARLY POTTERY PERIOD | 100,000 TO 200,000 |
| PRIOR TO UNIFICATION | 400,000 -600,000 |
| LATE OLD KINGDOM | 2 MILLION |
| LATE NEW KINGDOM | 3 MILLION TO 4 MILLION |
| LATE PTOLEMAIC PERIOD | CIRCA 7 MILLION |

The rapid growth in population is ascribed to the irrigation and water retention development in the huge Fayum Oasis area southwest of Memphis. The work was mostly completed during the Middle Kingdom and the expansion of agriculture it supported gave a boost to the population of the north. It is estimated that by the end of the New Kingdom the world's population had grown to around 48 Million, implying that roughly seven percent of the world lived in Egypt at that time. In comparison, the population of North America comprised around five percent of the world's population throughout the twentieth century.

**The King Lists** Precise records of the very early kings of the separate two kingdoms have been lost. The oldest record we have relating to the early rulers of the unified kingdom are fragments of what was once a seven feet long and two feet high free standing basalt tablet or stele called the Royal Annals. The stele stood on its longest edge and was inscribed on both sides; it probably was originally erected in the capital Memphis. The text is dated to some nine hundred years after unification and provided a king list up to that time c2500BC. The largest remaining fragment of this stele is called the Palermo Stone which had been in Sicily since 1866 and probably arrived there as ship's ballast; it is now in the Palermo Museum. Another large piece was found in 1910 and is now in the Egyptian Museum, Cairo. A smaller piece (right) is in the Petrie Museum London and there are three other smaller pieces existing. The early part of the Royal Annals records the names of many hundreds of kings prior to unification but these are thought to be mainly mythical. The records of the post unification kings are given in some detail, including their names, the length of the reign and the important events that occurred in each regnal year

Unfortunately the sections of the stele which would have shown the kings from the first two dynasties are largely missing. Typical events worthy of record by the royal scribes were the height of the Nile's inundation, the cattle count census for taxation, typically every one or two years, festivals held, palaces built, ships constructed, statues made, trading expeditions and military campaigns won. The rulers of the Sixth Dynasty are recorded on the sarcophagus lid of Queen Ankhes En Pepi called the 'South Saqqara Stone' circa 2150 BC.

There are other stone king lists that were created at later dates. One such was constructed in the temple of Amen Re at Karnak. The so called Karnak King list was situated by the jubilee Festival Hall of the great king and empire builder Thutmosis 3 dating from around 1440BC. This list, now in the Louvre Museum, Paris, also identifies Menes as the first king of the first dynasty and credits him with unifying Egypt. However, the Palermo stone, which is substantially older, lists rulers who predate Menes. It seems to indicate that the unification of Egypt occurred earlier than Menes's rule and that he reunited the nation after a period of fragmentation.

An even later notable stone king list comes from the Seti I/Ramesses 2 period c1280BC. The Great Temple of Seti I at Abydos, dedicated to Osiris, contains a western corridor leading to the chapel. Here can be seen to this day, a wonderful wall of finely crafted reliefs. King Seti I stands behind his young son prince Ramesses proudly gazing at a list of seventy six of his ancestors, right up to his own time. However the order of some kings is incorrect and some names are glaringly omitted for political reasons. We shall learn why in Chapters 8 and 9. The tomb of Thunery, the royal scribe to Rameses 2, contained a stone tablet recording fifty-eight cartouches of kings from the 1st to 19th Dynasties found in 1861AD. It is called the 'Tablet of Saqqara' or 'Royal lists of Saqqara'.

Arguably the most important king list is also from around this period, or perhaps later, and is written not on a temple wall or stele, but on a delicate papyrus. The 'Turin Canon' papyrus, written around 1250BC and found in 1822AD by Drovetti, is now only five feet long and during the years since its discovery has broken into many fragments. It contains the names and reigns of all kings from the unification by Menes to the time of Ramesses 2 and was probably the main source for Manetho's work.

As we have seen, establishing the precise date of early events in Egyptian history is inexact as the royal scribal records refer to events in each of the king's regnal years, absolute dates are never used. As a consequence, the precise dating of events is probably only accurate to within 50-100 years during the Old Kingdom. It is only during the New Kingdom, fifteen hundred years later, that it is possible to be accurate to better than five years. By the Ptolomeic period world chronology has become more accurate and dating improves to within a year or so. The chronology used in this volume is consistent with that most commonly used by Egyptologists today (see the Bibilography).

**The kings with five names** The early kings were known only by their so called Horus name, it identified the king with the heavenly falcon or hawk god Horus. As time progressed following unification, the number of names they used expanded to emphasize their legitimacy and to underscore their royal lineage and their divine patronage. By the Middle Kingdom, kings were comonly using five formal names in their official records. Historians use numbers to refer to kings bearing the same name for example, Thutmosis 4 meaning the fourth king to bear the Thutmosis name. This is a practice borrowed from the naming of European monarchs from the past, for instance George 3 of England and Louis 15 of France. This has now become so accepted that we even refer to the number of the ruler during their life time, for example Elizabeth 2 of England. However it certainly was not the practice in ancient times to ever use a ruler's numbering.

The king's five names were 1. Horus name, 2. Nebty name, 3.Golden Horus name, 4. Throne name or Prenomen - this was the name given to the king when he ascended the throne and was the most important, 5. Personal or Birth or Son of Re Nomen this was given to him at birth. Temple inscriptions could on occasion list all five names when referring to the ruler; however it was more common to see the king identified only by his two most important names. Therefore historians normally identify a specific ruler by reference to these two i.e. the Throne name and the Personal name. (Full details are given in Appendix 2)

We know from the Amarna letters (Chapter 9) that when the king of the Hittites wrote to his 'brother', the king of Egypt Amenhotep 3, he addressed him not by his Personal name Amenhotep (Amen is pleased) but only by his Throne name Neb Maat Re which distinguished him from all others with the Amenhotep Personal name. Ramesses 2 used only his Personal name, Ramesu, and his Throne name, User maat re Setep en re, in the inscriptions on his Abu Simble temple.

**King or Pharaoh** The word used for the ruler of Egypt throughout this work is king (Egyptian nsyt or nisu) rather than Pharaoh, mainly because it was the original title used by scribes from the earliest days. The much later title of Pharaoh is a Hebrew/Greek corruption of the Egyptian word per-a'a meaning the 'great house', the name for the palace where the King resided. To make a modern comparison, its use is similar to referring to the president of the USA as the 'white house' meaning the occupant of the president's residence. The first recorded use of the title Pharaoh, specifically meaning the king, not his palace, was relatively late in the history of Egypt. It was first used in an address to the New Kingdom ruler Akhenaton c1350 BC by a foreign ruler. By examining the subsequent ancient records it can be seen that the title Pharaoh then became as commonly used as the title king or majesty. Towards the end of the ancient Egyptian civilization, it had actually become the most commonly used title for the ruler.

During the height of the Egyptian Empire, foreign rulers, when communicating with the Egyptian king would always commence with reference to him as 'Great King' as he was widely regarded as the most powerful ruler of the known world. By 950BC, towards the end of the last phase of ancient Egypt, their vassals in the Middle East, namely Palestine and Syria, were in almost constant rebellion against either Egypt or the other great power at that time, Assyria. The early books of the Old Testament describe, and provide an excellent second source for, events in Egypt during this period. The first king of Egypt mentioned by name in the Old Testament is the invasion led by 'Pharaoh Shishaq' (Egyptian Shoshenq 1), the founder of the 22nd Dynasty and a contemporary of kings Rehoboam and Jeroboam (1 Kings 11.40 and 2 Chronicles 12.2 ).The Egyptian inscriptions of Shoshenq 1 confirm that he did in fact lead a major campaign into Palestine around regnal year twenty and boasted of capturing 'fifty cities'. Jerusalem was besieged but this time managed to hold out against the Egyptian army.

**The interaction between Greece and Egypt.** Many of the names of the cities, gods, kings and artifacts from Ancient Egypt are known to us today by the names the ancient Greeks gave them and not by their original Egyptian names. The Achaean Greeks were descended from the migration of Indo European peoples originating in northwest Asia and modern Russia. They had tamed the horse by c3000BC and had progressively moved south and settled in the northern Mediterranean lands. The great Greek city states of the Mycenaean period were the subject of legendary Homer's epic poem the 'Illead' and their ten year war with Troy. This early Greek civilization peaked c1200BC and was then catastrophically overrun and almost totally destroyed around 1150BC by another massive wave of Indo European migration called by the Egyptians the 'Sea Peoples', described in Chapter 10. Mycenae itself, never recovered and became 'lost' until the Lion Gate was excavated and restored in 1841. Later Schliemann excavated the whole city in 1874. The new Greeks (Dorian) abandoned literature and the country entered the four hundred year period referred to as The Greek Dark Age.

By c800BC the new Greece began to emerge. Seeking a basis for literature, it adopted the Phoenician alphabet (see Chapter 4) and over the next two hundred years began to expand from the major city states (polis in Greek) of

Athens, Sparta, Corinth and Thebes. They spawned semi independent colonies all along the Mediterranean coasts including Turkey, Lebanon, North Africa, Spain, France and Italy. Greece began to completely dominate the Mediterranean world both

militarily and linguistically as the population of the combined city states and colonies grew from an estimated eight hundred thousand in 800BC to twelve million by the time of Alexander. As these inquisitive sea faring Greek traders expanded southwards c700BC, they came into contact with the decaying south Mediterranean power, Egypt. By this time Egypt had lost its Asian Empire and was struggling to maintain its independence from the new Asian super powers of Assyria, Babylon and later, Persia. The Egyptians began to rely on the well trained Greek troops to bolster their exhausted military. The experienced Greek mercenaries possessed superior hoplite armor, and dominant naval expertise along with state of the art trireme warships (above).

Egyptian texts record the extensive use of Greek mercenaries from 670 BC onwards. By 560BC the Greeks had become so important in supporting the Egyptian state that they were permitted to set up Naucratis in the Delta on the west branch of the Nile. Naucratis was a Greek colonial city with free trade rights, it was the first, and for much of its early history the only, permanent

Greek colony in Egypt. It acted as a symbiotic hub for the interchange of Greek and Egyptian art and culture. The ruin was first excavated by Petrie in 1884 and has since become a significant archaeological site. It has produced some of the earliest Greek writing in existence, in the form of pottery inscriptions.

The Egyptians supplied the Greeks with grain, linen and papyrus, while the Greeks traded silver, timber, olive oil and wine. Naucratis soon became a source of inspiration to the Greeks by exposing them to the wonders of Egyptian architecture, medicine, mathematics and sculpture. Egyptian artifacts

began to flow along the Greek trade routes throughout the Mediterranean. Although some Greek art and ideas came to Egypt, their absorption into a largely Xenophobic Egyptian culture (see Chapter 13) was very modest. Naucratis was not only the first Greek settlement in Egypt but also Egypt's most important harbor in antiquity until the founding of Alexandria, two hundred and fifty years later and the shifting of the Nile led to its decline.

The Greek historian Anaximander of Miletus born c610BC is accredited with creating the 'first' map of the world (reconstructed above) showing the three continents of Europe, Asia and Libya (Africa) surrounded by the great world ocean. The river Nile is shown accurately separating Africa from Asia.

The first known Greek writer on Egypt was the geographer and historian Hecataeus of Miletus who was born c550BC and wrote his 'Ges Periodos' or 'World Survey', which included a comprehensive account of Egypt. Unfortunately it is now largely lost to us and only 374 fragments survive. However, Hecataeus did leave us with a substantially more detailed version of the Anaximander world map (reconstructed right)

identifying mountain ranges and a more accurate geography of the Mediterranean coast.

**Herodotus** from Halicarnassus, was a Greek historian who lived c484-425BC and is regarded as the 'Father of History' in western culture. He was the first historian to collect his materials systematically, test their accuracy where possible and arrange them in a well constructed and vivid narrative which became 'The Histories', which has survived intact. The original purpose of the book was to explore the origins of the Greco-Persian Wars which were raging throughout his lifetime and were dominating the Greek world.

He reported on the various places and peoples he encountered during his travels around the lands of the Mediterranean and the Black Sea. It is important to bear in mind that many of his narratives and stories are not accurate; he  admits this and states that *'he is only reporting what has been told to him'*. Herodotus (left) is correctly recognized as a pioneer not only in history, but in ethnography and anthropology. Book 2 of 'The Histories' called after the muse Euterpe, gives an account of his travels in Egypt c450 BC. It described the geography and fauna of the country, particularly the crocodile, cobra, and the hippopotamus which all seemed very strange to the Greeks. He speculated on the source of the Nile, finding it hard to believe it rises in reportedly snowy mountains so far south where the climate is generally so much warmer. Herodotus described the gods and religious practices of Egypt, especially where they differed from the Greeks. He described the Egyptian culture, medicine, funeral rites, food, mathematics, writing and boats. Egyptian funerary practices and the process of mummification particularly fascinated him and were consequently described in quite some detail.

Based on his travels, Herodotus produced this, the most detailed map yet of the 'inhabited world'. However the section of Book 2 that most interests historians is his account, in classical Greek, of the kings and history of Egypt as related to him by the 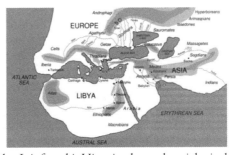 priests of the Egyptian temples. It is from his Histories that we have inherited the Greek names for the Egyptian kings such as Menes, Nitocris, Mœris, Sesostris, Pheron, Proteus, Rhampsinitus, Ahmosis and Thutmosis.

He devoted a chapter to Cheops (Egyptian Khufu) and the construction of the Great Pyramid, most of which is highly inaccurate and based on hearsay from the priests, as the true history had been lost two thousand years beforehand. He provided a list of Khufu's successors; Chephren, Mycerinus, Asychis, Anysis, Sethôs. Although it is not known if he actually visited the Lahun Labyrinth, he gave an accurate description of what was the largest temple and government complex existing in Egypt at that time. It has now almost entirely gone, as it was built from mud bricks and located too close to the water table. When Herodotus describes events closer to his own time he naturally becomes much more credible, listing correctly in order twelve late period kings including Psammetichus, Necôs, Psammis, Apries, and Amasis 2.

**Greek, Egyptian and Arabic names.** The Macedonian Greek Dynasty of the Ptolemies ruled Egypt for three hudred years (332-30BC) and used their own Greek words to replace the unfamiliar, to them, Egyptian names. As well as the kings of Egypt being recorded in Greek so were their monuments and artifacts. Many are still commonly known in English by their ancient Greek names.

| Greek Word | Greek Origin | Egyptian |
|---|---|---|
| PYRAMID | PYRAMIS- TRIANGULAR CAKE | MR |
| OBELISK | MEAT SKEWER | TEKHENU |
| HIEROGLYPH | SACRED WRITING | |
| SPHINX | 'THE STRANGLER' | |
| PHARAOH | | PER-A'A |

Even more confusing to us is that today place names are referred to in either Greek or Ancient Egyptian or modern Arabic. The following are a few examples of the more important locations.

| Greek | Ancient Egyptian | Arabic |
|---|---|---|
| AIGYPTOS (=EGYPT) | KM.T (=BLACK EARTH) | MISR |
| THEBES | WASET , NIWT RST | LUXOR |
| | IPET ISUT | KARNAK |
| THINIS | TJENY | GIRGA |
| HELIOPOLIS (SUN CITY) | I'WNW (PLACE OF PILLARS) | CAIRO SUBURB |
| HIERAKONPOLIS | NEKHEN | KOM EL AHMAR |
| ABYDOS | ABEDJU | UMM EL-QA'AB |
| APOLLINOPOLIS (CITY OFAPOLLO) | BEHDET, DJEBA | EDFU |
| SYENE | SWNET OR ABU | ASWAN |
| NOT KNOWN BY GREEKS | AKHETATEN | EL AMARNA |
| TANIS | DJAN'NET | SAN EL HAGAR |
| PHILAE | SWENET | |
| LATOPOLIS | TA SENET | ESNA |
| TENTYRA | TA YNT NETERT, IUNET | DENDERA |
| MEMPHIS | MN NFR PPY | MIT RAHINA |
| AVARIS | HUT WARET | TEL EL DABA |
| OMBOS | NUBT | KOM OMBO |

In this volume the city name in most common use today is the one referred to followed, if appropriate, by the ancient Egyptian name.

# — CHAPTER ONE —

## *Origins and Early Kings*

---

Early humans established settlements across northern Africa as they migrated out of their early origins in north east Africa. The remains of the earliest human discovered in Egypt were found north of Luxor at Dendera (ta ynt netert) and are dated to around 55,000BC. The grassy plains of the whole of northern Africa, and what is now the Sahara desert, at that time had supported Stone Age hunter-gatherer life for tens of thousands of years.

However, from around 20,000BC the last great ice age was ending, the northern hemisphere began to warm, the great ice sheets began to recede and sea water levels rose. The climate of northern Africa also adjusted and was to permanently change North African habitation. However, around 13,000BC the gradual warming of the earth suddenly went into reverse for around 1,000 years. The ice sheets stopped receding, earth's temperature cooled and rains which used to fall in the Sahara region moved south. Elsewhere, northern America was plunged into a new short ice age and the newly established Clovis people, living mainly along the east coast, almost died out and moved westward to survive. Sabre toothed tigers and woolly mammoths could not adjust to the climate change and became extinct by around 10,000BC.

In northern Africa the reduction in rainfall led to the Sahara becoming more arid and less able to support both humans and animals. The hunter-gatherer Stone Age clans and tribes migrated over time progressively eastwards and settled around the oases in what is now the Western Desert on the Libyan and Egyptian border. There is also evidence of wild grain harvesting along the Nile, dated to c9500BC from early stone sickle blades.

Elsewhere in the Middle East agriculture was becoming established. Jericho, near the river Jordon, had become a settled community by 9,500 BC and is considered to be the world's oldest permanently inhabited town. Excavations down to the earliest layers of habitation at Jericho show that by 8,500BC Jericho's 2,500 inhabitants were planting domesticated wheat and barley, hunting wild animals, and building mud brick houses as well as erecting the first known rough stone town wall for protection.

Stone Age agriculture was also becoming established in the Sahara and the Western Desert. Excavators have discovered the remains of farming settlements, dating to around 7,000BC, goats and sheep were by now being imported from south west Asia. Agriculture, both animal and crop, was taking hold in the east Sahara, however, rainfall in the region was becoming so sparse that the central Sahara was being transformed into desert and humans were being forced to move further east to reach a permanent source of water. By 6,000BC rudimentary rowed and single sail ships were depicted in Egyptian rock art, and hammered copper tools were appearing.

**First astronomers.** Nabta Playa was a large permanent settlement sixty miles west of Abu Simbel and the Nile. By c6500BC deep year round wells were being used to replace rainfall and numerous stone huts have been found constructed in straight rows. Food during this period included fruit, legumes, millet, and sorghum and there is evidence of imported goats and sheep along with many large communal hearths.These people appear to have lived a more sophisticated existence than the Nile dwellers at this time. They sacrificed cattle, worshiped a cow god, possibly a forerunner of the important cow-eared god Hathor, and constructed an arrangement of large megalith stones that is considered to be the oldest astronomical configuration, dated to c6200BC. The orientation is fashioned to align with the stars in Orion's belt and accurately points to the summer solstice. A later astronomical stone circle (right) is considered to be the worlds earliest and predates the Stonehenge circle by 2,000 years. The constant migration of peoples east to the Nile led to the development of a more centralized society and the history of Egypt properly begins.

**The Nile** is one of the planet's few rivers to run from South to North. It is the earth's longest river covering a distance of four thousand six hundred miles. It starts just south of the equator, as the White Nile, and is joined by the Blue Nile at Khartoum fed by melting snows in the mountains of Ethiopia. It is then joined by the Atbara between the 5th and 6th Nile cataracts bringing with it vast quantities of suspended silt. The Nile then flows another two thousand five hundred miles north before spreading out into a broad delta named after the shape of the inverted Greek letter D. It then slowly enters the Mediterranean Sea by two principal mouths, the Rosetta in the west and the Damietta in the east. Erosion has created limestone and sandstone cliffs on either side of the river. These cliffs typically rise to a height of a few hundred feet but reach nine hundred feet where the Nile swings sharply north-east at Qena south of Luxor. Because the river typically flows to the east of the valley ninety percent of the cultivable land lies on the west bank.

**Annual inundation.** In antiquity, the peak river flow occurred each year from mid June at Aswan in the south, to early October at Memphis in the north. The river burst its banks by up to thirty feet and flooded a broad strip of land up to twelve miles in width. This annual event was called the inundation or 'akhet'. It was seen by the Egyptians as the coming of the God Hapi bringing fertility to the land. When the waters receded,

they deposited a rich layer of fertile silt on the land, ready for crop planting. This created a rich agricultural green ribbon stretching a thousand miles. This dark ribbon (opposite-bottom) is a dramatic contrast to the stark endless desert on either side. The winter growth season or 'peret' was followed by the spring/summer harvest season 'shemu'. In some cases the rich soil could accommodate two crops a year.

The Egyptians carefully measured and recorded the height of the life giving flood at the various Nileometers along the length of the Nile. One of the earliest to be constructed and the most important because it was the furthest south and gave

the earliest warning, was the Nileometer on Elephantine (Abu) Island at Aswan (left). Other important Nileometers were strategically located from south to north at Philae, Kom Ombo, Edfu, Esna, Dendera and Memphis, and were even kept in good condition by the Greeks and Romans. The height of the waters determined the amount of silt left behind and quantity of crops that could be expected. The Nileometer measurements were carefully recorded and then used to set the tax rate for the year. The Palermo Stone records from the reign of king Nynetjer c2700BC, reported a height variation of almost three feet over a five year period. Herodotus the Greek traveler and 'first historian', coined the expression *'Egypt is a gift of the Nile'* when he visited Northern Egypt in c450BC. He observed that *'. . . they get their harvest with less labor than anyone'*.

**Agriculture and pottery.** Between 5000 and 4000BC, small scale agricultural villages had become well established along much of the Nile and these had coalesced into what was to later become a total of forty two counties or districts called 'sepats' which the Greeks called Nomes. Each Nome was headed by a governor called a Nomarch and each had its own patron god and temple.

The Nile Delta was especially fertile and supported many early small scale village cultures. These were descended from prehistoric Semitic eastern peoples who had migrated west to the Nile and gave Egypt its Semitic language but not its gods which were unique to the Nile. Polished red or brown black-topped pottery (right) characteristic of this period known as Badarian, came into common use by around 5000-4500BC.Examples have been

discovered in the mid Egyptian towns of Asyut, Dendera and the southern religious center of Hierakonpolis and by trade had reached the Asiatics by 4000BC. Later around 4000-3500BC the geometric spatial designs adorning early Naqada style pottery became common. The beginnings of early writing started to appear in their images. Petrie in 1894, was the first to classify three distinct periods of Naqada pottery covering the period from 4400-3000BC. It was the country wide spread of Naqada 2 southern culture with its characteristic buff-colored pottery (right) that started the unification process.

**World's first calendar.** Sometime around 4500BC the need to make simple records of commercial transactions and labels resulted in the development of what was to later become hieroglyphic writing. At first it was not wide spread and was limited to commercial activities, in larger settlements, such as the delivery or sale of oil and linen. It is believed that it was at this time that the Egyptians established a momentous breakthrough in record keeping, associated with the movement of the stars, which was to lead to the invention of the calendar. It was driven by the need to be able accurately to predict the start of the annual inundation. Astronomers of the Delta used precise observations and mathematic calculation to match the start of the inundation with the exact day that the rise of one of the brightest stars Sirius (Sopdet), the Dog Star, rose at exactly sunrise. It is believed, from modern celestial calculations, that the Egyptian calendar was established as early as 4242BC when they started to use the heliacal rise of Sirius as the start of their new year. Their calendar year consisted of exactly 365 days; it was divided into twelve thirty day months plus five feast days at the end. Each month was sub divided into three weeks, each of ten days. The leap year concept was a much later Ptolemaic and Roman invention, hence the Egyptian calendar year was a quarter of a day shorter than the solar year, and the months therefore moved slowly through the seasons on a 1460 year cycle. However, divergence from one year to the next was so slow as to be imperceptible to the general population. Breasted believed that *'The creation of this convenient and practical, though artificial, calendar was an achievement unparalleled in any other ancient civilization'*. This remarkable calendar was to become the basis of our time recording to the present day.

By c3500BC wooden temples were being constructed in the major religious centers along the Nile and in the Delta. These temples were dedicated to the local gods specific to their region and varied between towns. The foundations of the oldest wooden temple have been found at Hierakonpolis, near Esna, which had a population then of between 5,000 and 10,000. This early temple, dedicated to sun and hawk god Horus, consisted of a wooden hut surrounded by short walls. Only the holes of the posts bearing totems, flags and insignia of the gods remain.

'Cradle of Civilization' It was at this time that trade between Egypt and its neighboring countries became sufficiently commonplace to leave us with records of its pattern. The term *'Fertile Crescent'* was coined by Breasted in 1900. He used it to describe the rich soil of the moon shaped region (right) of early civilizations in the Middle East. These all grew up grouped around the three major rivers; the Nile, Euphrates and Tigris. Egypt's earliest trading partners were most likely Canaan, where Egyptian pottery of this era has been found, and Nubia in the south

Around the time that Egypt was developing its own culture and unique hieroglyphic writing, a similar process was occurring in the other major river based civilization at the south eastern end of the Fertile Crescent. On the lower Euphrates (modern Iraq) the Sumerian civilization was developing its own writing. Its first examples were used to keep accounts

and were based on its own form of pictograms. The 'Kish tablet' (right) is dated to c3500BC. Sumerian pictogram-based writing later developed into its unique cuneiform or wedge writing (left) produced by using a wedge shaped stylus. Sumerian cylinder seals of this period have been discovered in Egypt's Naqada sites, demonstrating that even in these early times the two civilizations were in contact with each other. Further afield, Egyptian pottery from this period has been found in Afghanistan, over two thousand miles away to the east.

By c3500BC the gemstone Lapis Lazuli was being traded to Egypt from its only known source in the ancient world, Badaksan in north east Afghanistan. Ivory was relatively plentiful, from imported southern elephant tusks and the numerous hippopotami which inhabited the Nile. A beautifully carved ceremonial ivory knife with a gold foiled handle was excavated by De Morgan, dating to this period. Of particular historical interest, is this ivory handled ceremonial flint stone knife (right) with the handle made

from a hippopotamus tooth. The ten inch knife is now in the Louvre Museum, Paris, it was found near Abydos at Gebel el Arak and is dated to c3300BC. The back of the handle shows a warrior in clearly Mesopotamian clothing and two lions in the style of that area. Clearly the two cultures were influencing each other even then. There is much debate as to the likely trade routes, the most probable two being by sea from the Persian gulf to the Egyptian Red Sea coast and then across land to the Nile, and by sea from Byblos (modern Lebanon) to the Delta. The silver for the jewelry items found in Egypt from this period can only have come from Anatolia (modern Turkey), six hundred miles north of Memphis, again demonstrating the very long trade routes that were in use in such early times.

**First board game.** By 3500BC, the Nile society was becoming more sophisticated. Technology was advancing, for example, the glazing for making decorative ceramic beads was becoming commonplace. Jewelry was being made from imported Lapis Lazuli, musical instruments, such as clarinets and lyres, were being made and Senet, (right) the world's oldest board game was in use.
The Senet game board is a grid of thirty squares, arranged in three rows of ten. Senet has two sets of pawns at least five of each, and in some sets more.

Senet was a race game for two players, with moves determined by tosses of a throwstick or early dice. The example above is one of the finest sets of the game made; it has been dated to the time of Amenhotep 3 and is now in the Brooklyn Museum, New York. This wall painting from her Valley of the Queens tomb, (left) shows Nefertari, the wife of Ramesses 2, playing the Senet game.

**The kingdoms of the north and south.** The oldest fully developed Egyptian hieroglyphic writing has been dated to around 3300BC. It records the commercial delivery of oil and linen. From this time forward there are surviving written records of events, so by definition, this date marks the 'formal' start of Egyptian history. The population of the country had by now reached an estimated half a million people and the Nomes, each with a capital city, had grouped themselves into two discrete kingdoms along the Nile. The northern 'red' kingdom was centered on the fertile Delta region and was heavily influenced by Libyan and Asian migrations; its main towns were the capital Pe near Buto and Sais both in the northwest Delta. Red was the distinctive national color and its treasury was known as the 'Red House'. The king wore the flat red crown; the national symbols were the bee, the papyrus tuft and the cobra. There is a written record of twelve very early kings of the north, seven of them are named, but unfortunately there are no records of their reigns. The southern 'white' kingdom was more 'Egyptian' than the north. The king wore the tall white crown; the symbols were the vulture, the lotus flower and the sedge plant. The treasury was called the 'White House' and the government capital was at Nekheb, modern El Kab, south of Esna. The king's palace was across the river at the early religious city of Hierakonpolis (Nekhen). Both kingdoms by now recognized the hawk god Horus as the patron of their king and the winged sun as their king's creator. Seth was worshipped at his cult temple at Naqada, north of Thebes.

At this time Egyptians buried their dead in simple shallow graves in hot dry sand, well into the desert. From the earliest pre-historic times they had discovered that this natural desiccation process preserved the bodies for the next world. The wrapped body was placed in the fetal position in rectangular pits along with their important personal possessions and weapons in readiness for the afterlife.

**The Scorpion king.** The first recorded ruler of the south is king Scorpion named from the hieroglyph of a scorpion beside the white crown on the so

called 'major' ceremonial war mace head (left), now in the Ashmolean Museum, Oxford. It was found during the 1897-8 excavation season by Quibell in the ruins of the temple of Horus at Hierakonpolis. This relief shows Scorpion holding a plough to ceremoniously break ground by a body of water to create a new irrigation canal. The limestone mace head shows another scene which shows his Nome armies and has been interpreted as the king defeating his enemies in the north, the culturally more sophisticated delta peoples. It is important to note that he does not appear to claim permanent control of all Egypt. A second smaller 'minor' mace head is badly damaged but shows king Scorpion wearing a red crown being protected by Horus holding a rope. There are no other records of this period and it is possible that king Scorpion may have achieved only temporary unification of the north and south kingdoms. Excavations at the same site have also discovered ivory and wood labels bearing the Scorpion king hieroglyph.

**Unification under king Narmer c3100BC.** What has been called the world's first document, the Narmer Palette (overleaf) is now a treasure in the Egyptian Museum, Cairo. This was also discovered in the Horus temple at Hierakonpolis by Quibell in the same 1897-8 season that he found the two Scorpion ceremonial mace heads. The Narmer Palette was a ceremonial siltstone flat shield-shaped object around thirty inches high. It was used for mixing cosmetics to be applied daily to the cult statues of Horus kept at the temple. The palette is inscribed on both front and back and shows a number of historically significant scenes and incorporates early royal hieroglyphs. It is so called because above the kings head are two hieroglyphs, one of a catfish (n'r) and one of a chisel (mr) which when together give the king's name Narmer. On the right hand side he is seen wearing the tall white crown of the south, smiting his defeated  northern enemy, either a leader named Wash or an area called wash, with his ceremonial mace in the standard victorious pose of Egyptian kings. The king's chief adviser, his 'sandal bearer', stands behind him. Narmer is protected by Horus to his right, holding a rope joined to six papyrus flowers representing the killing or capturing of six thousand northern prisoners, perhaps from Delta or Libyan tribes.

On the reverse (left) side, he is now wearing the southern red crown with the hieroglyphs of his name in front at eye level. Ahead of him are four standard bearers. Some Egyptologists interpet these as symbols of kingship; others believe they represent Nome militia army standards. In front of him lie the decapitated bodies of his enemies laid out for his inspection. Below this is a most enigmatic scene showing two beasts which have their long necks entwined. A Sumerian cylinder seal from Uruk dated to this period c3000BC shows similar mythical creatures which have the body and head of a lion and the neck of snake. The implication is that Narmer has finally defeated the northern kingdom and permanently unified the whole country. There is, however, an alternative interpretation that the palette represents not the single act of unification but a series of events that occurred in the year he dedicated this item to the temple. The final scene shows the king as a bull taking a walled city.

A ceremonial stone Narmer mace head was also found at the temple of Horus, and hand drawn by Quibell in his 1900 excavation records. Now in the Ashmolean Museum, Oxford, it displays a complex series of scenes. Narmer (right page) is shown seated on his throne wearing the red crown and Heb Sed jubilee cloak with his four Nome standard bearers in the top register. He is being offered tribute in the form of bound prisoners, oxen and goats during a jubilee celebration. Some archaeologists, Petrie, believe that sitting opposite to him in a wedding bower is his new wife, a northern princess. This so called 'wedding scene' is still debated; however, the implications are that Narmer has made an important strategic marriage to the northern princess Neith Hotep. This action would have been carefully planned to link the two royal houses and bind the country together. It created

a new single royal family with a defined blood line which would lead to the first Egyptian dynasty. This was an important political and symbolic process which was repeated throughout Egyptian history. It has been adopted by many civilizations since and is still common practice today for not only royal families but also political dynasties.

Narmer made another very important strategic move to unite the country. Although his family's traditional capital had been in the vicinity of Hierakonpolis in the south of the country, he saw the political wisdom of moving the capital of the newly united Egypt to a new neutral location between the North and South. The exact location of his new palace and capital called 'White Wall' (inbw-hdj) has been lost, but was probably just north of Memphis near Abusir. White Wall was so called because its mud brick buildings were plastered and then painted white. Memphis was soon to become the permanent government capital of Egypt and remain so for over two thousand years.

It is believed that Narmer had a short reign of around ten years. He was buried in his sun-dried mud and straw brick tomb in Abydos, the traditional ancient royal necropolis of the southern kingdom, although an ivory fragment with his name shortend to nar, was found further south at Naqada.

**Royal jubilees then and now.** In his so called 'wedding scene', Narmer is pictured wearing the Heb Sed jubilee cloak. The Heb Sed was an early tradition of ancient Egypt kingship. After he reached the milestone of thirty years since being declared crown prince or thirty years actually on the throne, the king had to demonstrate to his people that he was virile enough to continue to lead the country. He did this by completing a formal Heb Sed race around fixed ground markers in full view of the priests and officers of his court. We will see more reference to the Heb Sed in Chapter 3. The tradition of a monarch celebrating his or her jubilee has continued to this day. For example in England, the monarchs still traditionally celebrate their twenty five and fifty year jubilees with extensive national celebrations involving military processions, feasting, and gifts to the populace. Its traditions are rooted in similar celebrations first performed five thousand years ago in Ancient Egypt.

**King Aha (Menes).** The period we now enter is referred to as Early Dynastic, the 1st Dynasty kings were listed in order on a mud seal found at Abydos in 1985. The names of these early kings of the unified Egypt bore the hieroglyph of their chief royal god Horus perched above their own personal name in a frame called a 'serekh' the base of which represented the royal palace. On the left is a serekh of the later 2nd Dynasty king Re Neb from the Metropolitan Museum, New York. Historically we know very few details of the reign of the next king of the unified country named Horus Aha Meni or Menes. He was possibly the son of Narmer or some believe he was actually Narmer under a different name. Aha Menes is attributed by Manetho as being the first king of Dynasty I. He came from the central town of Thinis, north of Abydos. He had clearly established a strong permanent unification and had for the first time

consolidated the three key pillars of Egyptian regal success. Firstly, as king he had established absolute earthly power. Secondly as a god it was *'he that brings the inundation'* and so he controlled the kingdom and temple wealth. The third pillar he established was the series of national irrigation projects. These boosted food production allowing him to establish strategic grain stores to be used in times of famine or if needed to feed a militia. Extensive royal mud brick grain stores can be seen in the surviving west bank mortuary temples at Thebes; particularly well preserved are those at the Ramesseum. Thus the king had the combined resources of all of Egypt under his absolute control.

One of his first priorities was to generate additional income for his extensive new building projects, irrigation systems, and foreign trade expeditions. His royal scribes initiated the practice of setting tax periods and 'cattle count' census gathering at two yearly intervals during the king's reign. This later changed to annual taxation intervals heralding in the scribal discipline of systematically recording in chronological order the main events of a king's reign. The formal recording of the king's regnal years had thus begun.

King Aha Menes was buried in the ancient royal cemetery of Abydos. In respect of the separate cultures of the two parts of his now united kingdom, he initiated the practice for all future kings of the Old Kingdom to construct a second empty tomb or cenotaph. This was built in the north at Saqqara on the west bank of the Nile beside the future capital Memphis. There are only three artifacts bearing the name of king Aha Menes which have survived. One is a fragment of pottery now in the British Museum, London with the name Aha. The second is an ivory jar label with the name Hor Aha Meni found at his mother's tomb at Naqada in 1897, the third is an ivory label fragment from Abydos showing the earliest hieroglyphs of a courtier along with the king's name Aha.

It was following unification, that the king of Egypt adopted the 'uraeus'. This was a symbol of the cobra god Wadjet from the northwest Delta city of Buto (per wadjet). From then onwards the king was recognized by the wearing of the uraeus on his headdress and crown. This conveyed legitimacy to the ruler by denoting divine authority. The vulture god Nekhbet, patron of the south, was added and both can be seen in reliefs and on royal statues of both kings and gods from this time forward. The first golden uraeus belonging to a king's mummy was discovered in 1919-20 on the dusty floor of a room in a kings

rock-cut tomb under the pyramid at Lahun which belonged to Senusret 2. Initially it was believed that there was only one royal uraeus and it was passed from one king to the next. However only two years later probably the best known uraeus (right) was found in Tutankhamen's lost tomb in The Valley of the Kings. It was still attached to the Nemes royal headdress of his fabulous death mask now in the Egyptian Museum, Cairo, and there accompanying the cobra on the headdress was the golden vulture.

**King Djer and the lady's arm.** Menes son Djer succeeded to the throne around 3,000BC and was later buried at Abydos and recorded two military campaigns into the Sinai Peninsula. The mines at Wadi Maghera there were an important source of copper for tools and weapons; there was also a nearby turquoise mine at Serabit el Khadim. He also conducted a campaign against the Libyan tribes as he attempted to secure his western border. He led the first recorded campaign south into the land of Nubia. The Egyptians called the land south of Aswan Nubia, they divided it into two parts. North Nubia stretched from Aswan at the 1st Nile cataract south to Wadi Halfa and Buhen at the 2nd cataract it was known as Wawat. South of the 2nd cataract stretched south Nubia, modern Sudan, it was also known as the land of Kush. Nubia was independent at this time and was soon to become very important strategically to the growing kingdom. Nubia was a major source for gold, which was the economic driving force of the ancient world. Control of the the Nubian Nile valley was also important as it was the main trading route for African luxury imports such as ivory. The activities of king Djer in Nubia are recorded in a rock inscription at Buhen. Most unusually, his wife Herneith is also mentioned in the text. A tablet from the reign of Djer is the first recorded reference to the Egyptian calendar mentioned above.

When Petrie was excavating the royal cemetery at Abydos in 1902 he found the tomb and burial chamber of Djer. His mummy, and that of his wife, had been robbed in antiquity and were missing, but the robbers left behind, in a hole in the wall of the tomb, the bandaged mummified arm of a lady. It belonged to Herneith and was identified by the inscriptions on her four exquisite gold and semi precious stone bracelets, still on her arm. It was in horror that Petrie later learnt that the curator of the Cairo museum, Emile

Brugsch, had discarded the arm and linen and kept only the bracelets, thus destroying the earliest evidence of royal mummification. Petrie later remarked *'A museum is a dangerous place'.*

**King Djet.** After a reportedly long reign Djer 'went to his destiny' and his son Djet became king. This (left) beautiful serekh stele of Djet (Louvre Museum, Paris) is a masterpiece and probably the mostly finely crafted, and elegant, tombstone stele, showing a serekh that has survived; it was found in his Abydos tomb. The god Horus perches above the serpent hieroglyph for 'dj' representing the king's Horus name. Below the serpent is the stylistic representation of his royal palace. Djet recorded his notable expedition to the Red Sea and a Sinai military campaign on this stone stele. Petrie recovered the oldest ivory comb, it bore the serekh of Djet and was found in his Abydos tomb

**King Den.** His son Den, c2900BC, reigned for around twenty years and recorded his enthronement and Heb Sed jubilee on a notable ebony label found in the burial chamber of his Abydos tomb. The most important position after the king was his chancellor or prime minister, who is often referred to using the later Turkish equivalent 'vizier'. We know that Den's vizier was Hemeka. He was responsible for the running of the state, collecting taxes and implementing

construction projects, the most important being the construction of the king's tomb which was normally commenced shortly after the king came to the throne. Den's mastaba (Arabic for bench) style tomb (right) was innovative. Although its walls were conventialy built of traditional sun dried mud and straw bricks, it was the first to

have had a floor lined with slabs of hard to work granite shipped down the Nile all the way from the Nubian border town quarries at Aswan; this was an unprecedented expenditure in manpower

**Human sacrifice.** Egyptian Kings believed that they would return to life if their bodies were kept intact by the mummification process. When they came back to life they desired to have their servants and courtiers with them. Inside the extensive underground rooms of Den's tomb, excavators found the bodies of between one and two hundred members of his court who had been sacrificed at the time of his death. This unpopular practice was short-lived and human servants were later replaced by small blue glazed faience 'ushabti' figures representing them in the afterlife. Similar human sacrifice was discovered by Wooley in 1923 at the Royal Cemetery of the city of Ur in Sumer this was at the south eastern end of the Middle East's Fertile Crescent (modern south Iraq) and was dated to around the same period c2700BC.

**The first female king.** Den's son **Anedjib** may have been too young to rule at his father's death as Den's Great Royal Wife **Meryetneith** succeeded him as the first recorded female king, there was no word for a ruling Queen in the Egyptian language. She ruled for up to twenty-six years before her son finally succeeded to the throne at which point he set upon a program to strike out her name in an unsuccessful attempt to erase her memory from the records. We know little else about his reign. There were only a handful of recorded female kings in Egyptian history, and they were to use Meryetneith's reign as the precedent.

**First Sinai reliefs.** The son of Anedjib was **Semerkhet,** he succeeded to the throne and constructed the first fortress on the island of Elephantine in the Nile opposite Aswan to protect the southern boundary from raiding Nubian tribes. He has left us with the first Egyptian carved stone relief drawings with inscriptions at the Sinai copper mine of Wadi Maghera, a practice which was to become common for future rulers. The relief of Semerket is similar to that on the Narmer Palette, it shows him smiting the kings enemies, in this case Bedouin tribesmen, with his ceremonial mace. This traditional scene was to be repeated on the walls of palaces and temples by almost every Egyptian ruler for the next two and a half thousand years.

**King Qa'a** succeeded to the throne and was buried at Abydos. By now northern Nubia (Wawat) had been largely pacified and he began the gradual process of controlling this strategically important region.

**2nd Dynasty.** The reign of the next king, **Hetep sekhemy** was recorded as lasting for thirty eight years. It was the start of the rather obscure 2nd Dynasty. Manetho's initiation of a new dynasty implied there had been a change in the ruling family or another significant discontinuity. In this case it was most likely the change in burial location; kings were now being buried not at Abydos but at Saqqara, close to the capital at White Wall. The Saqqara tomb statue of priest Hetepdief gives the names of the first three kings of the 2nd Dynasty; very little specific information is known about the next two rulers Reneb and Nynetjer. General events in their reigns were recorded on the Palermo Stone, for example the Nynetjer Nile innundation levels mentioned above.

**Civil War.** It appears that during the rule of Nynetjer internal pressures were building up within the five hundred year old kingdom, it seems the north was trying to break away. The next king, Peribsen, bears not the traditional Horus name but the Seth name. Seth, the god of disorder, was a competing (northern) god to Horus and may imply that the north was now gaining the upper hand in the civil war which had broken out. However it appears that the south eventually won the prolonged civil war and the new king of the reunited kingdoms was named Khasekhemwy.

**Khasekhemwy** 2611-2584BC was an important ruler whose reign lasted either for eighteen or twenty seven years. We know his wife was Nima ethap, who became the mother of the next king Djoser. Khasekhemwy's reign marks a significant milestone in our narrative for a number of reasons. He regained control of north Nubia after the civil war by leading a military campaign there and starting colonies around the major gold mining sites as well as fortifying trading posts. He also built forts at the two important religious centers of Hierakonpolis and Abydos to consolidate internal control. On a stone vase the following inscription was found *'the year of fighting the northern enemy within the city of Nekheb'* (el Kab, opposite Hierakonpolis). Clearly the civil war had continued into his reign. He is unique in Egyptian history, having both the symbols of Horus and Seth on his serekh. Some Egyptologists believe that this was a diplomatic gesture to unify the two factions. He also changed his name from Neferkare to Nebwhyhetep imef meaning 'the two lords are at peace' in recognition of peace finally coming to his country. After his death Seth was dropped from the royal serekh permanently.

**The first stone tomb.** Khasekhemwy returned to Abydos for the site of his tomb, the last to be built there. After this time, Saqqara became the permanent royal necropolis. Khasekhemwy's architect made two truly significant breakthroughs. He chose to construct his mastaba tomb not out of traditional mud brick but out of quarried small blocks of limestone. This is the world's first masonry building and is dated to c2600BC. This tomb is also remarkable because it marks a major change in size. Previous early tomb burial chambers were square or rectangular with sides of typically thirty or forty feet. Khasekhemwy's burial chamber was of gigantic proportions. It measured two hundred and thirty feet long and fifty six feet at the widest part and it contained fifty eight rooms. In one room Petrie, in 1900, discovered

the king's gold scepter, which was missed by tomb robbers in antiquity, as well as several beautifully made small stone pots (left) with gold leaf lid coverings, a variety of copper tools and pottery vessels filled with grain and fruit.

His burial is also notable as it marks the last time human sacrifices were made to support the king in his next life. At his nearby ruined Abydos mud brick mortuary palace, called Shunet el Zebib, is one of the oldest surviving examples of the traditional royal niched style palace brick façade. His son Djoser is to take this concept further and construct niched façade walls made from stone. Khasekhemwy also built in stone in the south at both Hierakonpolis and El Kab.

Another innovation of this remarkable king was the earliest practice of erecting stone statues of himself. Two seated statues have survived both discovered at Hierakonpolis by Quibell in the 1897/8 season. Both show him wearing the white crown and Heb Sed jubilee robe. That on the left is in limestone (Ashmolean Museum, Oxford) and records a military campaign by the king against enemies in the Delta during the civil war; it claims an almost unreasonable number '47,209' of slain victims.

The second statue of Khasekhemwy, on the right, is in green siltstone (Egyptian Museum, Cairo). These two are the earliest surviving lifesize royal statues from Ancient Egypt.

Manetho ends the 2nd Dynasty after the death of king Khasekhemy despite the fact that the next two rulers were his sons. We are about to enter the period known as the Old Kingdom, or 'Pyramid Age'.

— Chapter Two —

# Early Religion-Gods, Myths, and Temples

Like all the early peoples it was from their surroundings that the early Egyptians derived their Gods. Commonly it was the animals they came across in their everyday lives that they began to worship. They saw in them unusual powers that humans did not possess, some spirits were benevolent helping humans in their day to day lives, and some were malevolent, intent on inflicting bad luck or worse. Some of these spirits were only recognized by a local community, some by whole regions and a select few were worshipped throughout the entire country.

When the farmers of early Egypt gazed into the night sky some saw in the heavens a vast cow with its head in the west and its stomach covered in stars. Others saw a giant female figure standing in the east bending over the earth supporting herself with her outstretched arms in the west. They believed that the sun was reborn every morning and sailed across the sky in a celestial boat or barque. The high soaring hawk Horus (left at the Edfu temple) seemed to move like the sun across the sky and this led them to believe that the sun itself was a hawk. So it was, that the sun disk with its out-spread wings became the most common symbol of their religion for all time.

## Gods of the earth and sky.

Each region had it's own royal family of deities, the four most notable being at Heliopolis, Hermopolis, Mephis and later Thebes. The Heliopolis royal family of deities consisted of of nine gods, this group was called the Ennead, Greek for nine. According to the Heliopiolis creation myth, the most prevalent in ancient Egypt, they were responsible for the creation of life and the earth. Egyptians believed that below the earth a Nile-like river flowed, allowing the setting sun to be carried by the celestial boat, to appear again in the east, with the help of a scarab beetle, the following morning. They believed that this river ran into the huge sea which surrounded the earth. The Greeks copied this concept and called the sea Okeanos, hence our name ocean. At the beginning of time only this sea existed, later earth in the form of a mound appeared made by the creator god Atum Re. Atum Re produced four children; Shu and Tefnut became the air and water, Geb became the earth and married Nut who became the sky. Geb and Nut produced four children, the most important of all the family of gods, they were Osiris, Isis, Seth and Nephthys which led to the most celebrated myth of Egyptian religion. In total the Ennead comprised the inner family circle of the gods. Other local versions of this story claim Re

-ANCIENT EGYPT AND US -

as ruling the earth and Hathor as defender of the human race.

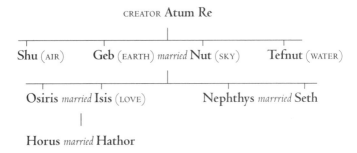

CREATOR **Atum Re**

**Shu** (AIR)    **Geb** (EARTH) *married* **Nut** (SKY)    **Tefnut** (WATER)

**Osiris** *married* **Isis** (LOVE)    **Nephthys** *marrried* **Seth**

**Horus** *married* **Hathor**

Other principle gods and their forms were; Bastet (cat), Bes (dwarf), Khnum (ram), Maat (truth/order), Mentu (war), Serapis (bull), Sekhmet (lion) Thoth (Ibis), Sobek (crocodile), Anubis (embalming), Ptah (Memphis) and Amen (Thebes).

**The legend of Osiris and Isis** is one of the most celebrated of the ancient world. It spread first to Greece and then to Rome where there was an active temple dedicated to Isis (left) until Christianity was adopted and Paganism was then banned in c391AD. The legend was recorded on temple walls throughout Egypt. The best preserved and most complete example is to be found in the ambulatory passage between the inside and outer walls of the Ptolemaic (Greek) Horus temple at Edfu (below).

Although the Egyptians naturally had their own names for their gods we use the Greek forms of their names as these are more commonly known. For example Osiris was Asar, represented with green skin, Horus was Heru, Isis was Aset, Anubis was Anpu, Thoth was Tehuti, Seth was Sutekh and Hathor was Het heru. Osiris had become god

of the earth and protector of mankind. His faithful sister and wife was Isis and his evil brother was Seth. Seth was jealous of the love between Osiris and Isis and plotted their downfall. Seth contrived a battle with Osiris and then killed him, cutting up his body into thirteen pieces and casting the pieces into the Nile to be consumed by crocodiles. Isis heard of this and recovered all but one of the pieces of her beloved husband and prepared the body for burial with the help of the god of the underworld and embalmment, Anubis the jackal headed god.

Anubis (at right from a Theban book of the dead) momentarily helped Isis and Nephthys bring Osiris back to life as he lay on the embalming table being mummified before passing to become the living king of the underworld. Isis thus became pregnant by Osiris and later gave birth to their son Horus. When Horus grew to become  a man he sought out his evil uncle Seth and engaged him in battle to revenge his father. Both were mutilated but Seth was defeated and Horus assumed the earthly throne of his father Osiris. Horus however lost an eye in the battle but this was later restored to him.

**The eye of Horus in use today.** The 'Sacred eye of Horus' was called the 'wedjet' and its hieroglyph (left) is meant to represent a human eye. The teardrop markings below are those of the Peregrine falcon's eye, the animal with which Horus was usually associated. The eye was considered to be a strong lucky charm; this 'wedjet' amulet was found on the mummy of Tutankamun. To either side stand the royal cobra and vulture: it was intended to protect the king in the afterlife and to ward off evil spirits

The Osiris-Isis legend described above is in fact the one which became common from the Middle Kingdom onwards. The earlier version found on the Palermo Stone c2500BC and the Old Kingdom pyramid texts, c2400BC, is slightly different in detail. It tells that Osiris was killed by an extravagantly jeweled wooden sarcophagus secretly made to his measurements by his brother Seth jealous of Osiris's position as king. A celebration was held where the valuable coffin was offered to whoever could fit inside. A few tried to fit inside the coffin, but without success. Osiris was encouraged to try, but as soon as he lay down, Seth slammed the lid down locking him inside. It was then sealed with lead and thrown into the Nile. Upon hearing this, Isis set out to look for him, she learned that the coffin had floated down the Nile into the Mediterranean and had reached Byblos (in Lebanon) and became caught in the trunk of a cedar tree. Lebanon is famous for these trees to this day. She also learned that the cedar tree had been used as a pillar to suport a palace for the king of Byblos. Isis managed to recover the coffin and buried it in Egypt. Seth however found it, he removed the body and dismembered it into thirteen parts, scattering them across the land of Egypt. Each part represented one of the thirteen full moons each year. This early legend now becomes similar to the later version.

**RX symbol.** Eastern Mediterranean sailors still frequently paint the 'wedjet' symbol on the bow of their vessels to ensure safe sea travel. Often worn in the form of a necklace or earring, the 'wedjet' is still in use to this day in Greece, Turkey,

North Africa and parts of the Middle East, it is still called the 'eye of Horus' or the all seeing 'evil eye'. In the west, the simplified version of the decorative cursive eye hieroglyph has become simplified as the 'RX' symbol of the pharmacist and can be seen every day on prescriptions and prescription packaging.

**Re the sun god.** Not all of the gods who appear in the early myths and legends become more than just that. Many of them continued merely in this role without a temple or form of worship. Others became the great cult gods of Egypt, foremost of these was the sun-god Re. Worship of Re was centered at the most important religious center of Egypt the temple of Re at the city the Greeks called Heliopolis, the city of the sun. The Ancient Egyptian name was 'per re' the house of Re or 'i'wnw' meaning place of pillars after the extensive numbers of temples and obelisks there. The first traces of the temple date to c2900BC,at its peak around 1300BC, the temple of Re at Heliopolis employed 13,000 priests and was over twice the size of the future temple complex of Amen at Karnak which itself is the largest temple complex in the world today. Heliopolis (Old Testament On) was burnt and almost totally destroyed by the Persian king Cambyses 2 when he conquered Egypt in 525BC, it never recovered and its remains today lie buried beneath the northeast suburb of

Cairo by the airport. Here the solar orb god Re was linked to the creator god Atum, the symbol of his presence at Heliopolis was the obelisk. The shape relates back to the emergence from the sea of the first primeval mound, the pyramid top of the obelisk is believed to be a representation of the sun's rays falling on the earth. At Edfu the sun god was represented in the form of the hawk Horus as we have already seen.

The Egyptians referred to the sun god at dawn as Kheper.Its hieroglyph was the beetle shown (above) from the walls of the tomb of Ramesses 9 KV6, in the Valley of the Kings. Shown right is the large red granite scarab and pedestal from the reign of Amenhotep 3. It is the largest surviving scarab representation and is located beside the sacred lake at

Karnak. The sun god myth recounts that it was Kheper, the common scarab or dung beetle, that rolled the sun at the end of the night journey to its rising point in the east each morning.

**Thoth.** The god of wisdom was Thoth; he was worshiped at Hermopolis across the Nile from El Amarna in mid-Egypt and was represented by the Ibis bird.

**Hathor.** The most commonly worshipped sky god variety was Hathor, the

daughter of Horus. She became the god of females, love and fertility, and is represented with the face of a woman and the ears or horns of a cow often wearing a sun disc. There are two surviving temples dedicated to Hathor. The

largest and most complete is the stunningly beautiful Ptolemaic/Roman temple at Dendera, featuring finely carved stone pillar Hathor capitals, later defaced by the Coptic Christians. A much older, but well preserved, small temple dedicated to Hathor, (right) is found on the south side of the upper platform at Deir el Bahri opposite Luxor, in Hatshepsut's mortuary temple complex. Hathor was also

worshipped and represented at temples elsewhere, for example as the fun loving Neit and as a cat at Bast and as the lioness Sekhmet, the god of storms and terror, but also healing, at the capital Memphis.

**Isis and Osiris.** The best preserved temple dedicated to the worship of Isis is the Greek Ptolemaic island temple of Philae (left) saved from the rising Nile waters by being moved stone by stone to a higher island, Agilka, nearby. Partly because of its unique setting in the middle of the Nile it has been said to be one of the most beautiful temples in the world. Consequently, it is one of the most commonly visited.

Osiris was one of the most popular of the gods and was particularly favored by kings when they built their mortuary temples. They would add their own face to the traditional Osiride statue. Osiris is easy to identify as he is always dressed in the long white cloak of the dead with his arms crossed holding a crook and flail. Although the original home of Osiris was at a temple in Dedu (Greek Busiris) in the Delta, the most famous extant temple is at Abydos where legend claims his head was buried.

This beautifully simple 'Great Temple' was started by Seti 1 and completed

by his son Rameses 2. On the wall in a small room off the unusual L shaped temple is one of the best preserved king lists. It is notable for its extremely fine wall reliefs created at the request of Seti 1 to display his ancestors. Seti is seen proudly displaying the king list to his young son, prince Ramesses 2,

standing in front wearing the traditional side hair-lock of youth. To the rear is the unique and enigmatic Osirion. This is a miniature temple to the god built deliberately below ground, which during the inundation would become flooded perhaps echoing the creation myth.

**Ptah.** The great god Ptah was the patron deity of the capital Memphis. He was the patron of the craftsman, builder and artist. Many kings over the years added to the huge temple complex called the Great Temple of Ptah dedicated to him there. However the capital's government buildings palaces and houses have now almost totally been lost as they were mostly built in mud brick. The stone built temple buildings themselves have not survived either as they have been gradually quarried for their fine limestone and sandstone and used in the construction of local sugar factories and nearby modern houses.

The exceptions are three marvelous colossal statues of kings which have survived the ravages of time. Originally a pair of giant sixty five foot polished sandstone colossal striding-statues of Ramesses 2 flanked the Ptah temple. Only one (right) remains, it is now exhibited lying on its back the way it was found, its lower legs having been lost. Also at the temple site is a marvelously imposing re-erected colossal striding-statue of Amehotep 2. It was later claimed by Ramesses 2 as his own by inscribing his name on it as he did with many staues of previous kings during his long reign. However, the facial features are clearly those of Amenhotep 2. There is also a unique giant 13 feet high alabaster sphinx with the face of Hatshepsut. A later smaller Temple of Ptah was built at Karnak by Thutmosis 3 on the site of an earlier Middle Kingdom temple. It lies just to the north and outside of the wall of the huge Karnak Amen complex.

**Sobek and Horus at Kom Ombo.** Kom Ombo (left) is unique in that it

is the only surviving double temple, one side of the temple is dedicated to the crocodile god Sobek, god of fertility. The other side is dedicated to the falcon/hawk god Horus in the form Haroeris, also known as Horus the Elder. The original temple dates back to the time of Thutmosis 3 but has now gone. The current temple is extraordinary in that everything is perfectly symmetrical along the main axis, it was started by Ptolemy 6 Philometor (180-145BC) at the beginning of his reign and added to by other Ptolemys, most notably Ptolemy 13th (47-44BC) and Cleopatra 7th c 50BC who built the inner and outer hypostyle halls. Much of the outer parts of the temple built by the Roman emperor Tiberius (14-34AD), have been destroyed by the Nile, earthquakes and later builders who used the stones for other projects. Some of the reliefs inside were defaced by the Copts who once used the temple as a church. The temple has a spectacular aspect being located on a high promontory looking down on a sweeping great bend in the Nile. It also boasts a deep intact Nileometer and a unique set of reliefs. Tucked away at the back of the temple is the earliest display of surgical instruments used during this period, they bear a startling resemblance to instruments commonly used today. The temple was the main focus for crocodile worship; a few of the three hundred crocodile mummies discovered in the templex are on display.

**Amen** originally was a minor god identified with the air. He was usually depicted wearing a cap with tall twin feathers relating to the wind. Amen was the patron deity of Thebes and only rose to supremacy in the New Kingdom at the religous center of Karnak. He became linked to the sun god as Amen Re.

**Temple design.** Although each temple was unique, there were a number of features which comprised a typical design so familiar to visitors today.

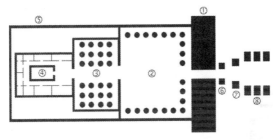

The feature that could be seen from a great distance was the massive, usually stone, pylon (1) or entrance tower with two giant flagpoles. These were built into niches reaching half way up the battered (inward sloping) pylons and were used for flying religious pennants or flags. The pylon entrance originally had giant doors made of cedar wood, but in later years made from bronze or covered in gold foil. Passing through the pylon gateway the temple opened up into a colonnaded forecourt open to the sky (2) and then a hypostyle, multi columned, hall (3). Beyond this was a small roofed chamber or sanctuary (4) often comprising three cult chapels containing furniture, offerings and the religious statues. The temple was surrounded by a stone wall (5) up to forty feet high and often highly decorated with reliefs on the inside surface. In front of the pylon stood twin colossal statues of the king (6) up to sixty five feet high, a pair of obelisks (7) and an avenue of human faced sphinxes (8). A landing stage for the boats that carried the images of the gods to the temple lay at the start of the sphinx avenue.

In the rear of the sanctuary was the holy of holies in which stood a shrine cut from one piece of granite on which was placed a statue of the god itself. Often it was two to six feet high and made of wood covered in gold, silver and precious jewels. The god was served by the priests of his cult, only they could enter the inner temple, supplied in perpetuity from estates donated and maintained by the kings. Essential daily offerings consisted of luxury items; such as expensive oils, honey, cosmetics, and luxurious clothing along with every day needs such as fine food and wine, even dancing and music. The local populace was kept outside the temple complex by a massive brick temenos wall and could only participate by joining in the annual feast days held outside the temple in commemoration of the god's special day. *'In no land ancient or modern has there ever been such attention to the equipment of the dead'* wrote Herodotus.

**The Ba and the Ka.** The ancient Egyptians believed that the human soul was made up of three parts, the deceased body itself and two very important elements which remained with the mummy after death. One was the 'Ba', in some regards this is the closest to the western religious concept of a soul.

It also made an individual unique, similar to personality, and was the part of a person that the Egyptians believed would live after the body died. It is often depicted as a human-headed bird (right) flying out of the tomb each morning ultimately seeking to join with the 'Ka' in the afterlife.

The Ka was the Egyptian concept of life force which distinguished the difference between a living and a dead person, death occurred when the Ka left the body. It resembles the concept of spirit in other religions. The Egyptians believed that the Ka had to be kept alive through food and drink. For this reason these offerings were presented to the dead typically on the anniversary of their death. The Ka was often represented as a second image of the individual, and is shown on the left as a pair of up stretched arms. Once the Ba and the Ka were re-united the individual could continue to live forever in the afterlife in the spiritual form called the akh or 'effective being'.

**The 'Book of the dead'.**

The land of the dead was where the sun set in the west. Hence most, but not all, mortuary temples, tombs and pyramids were built on the west side of the Nile. The land of the living was where the sun rose in the east, here the kings palaces, cult temple complexes and government centers were constructed. Ironically almost all kings' residences were constructed in mud brick and have mostly been lost. The Egyptians were extremely superstitious people and relied on spells and good luck texts to protect them from evil as they progressed from death to the afterlife. Most of the surviving oldest writings are funerary texts written on the stone tomb chamber walls of the early pyramids discussed in Chapter 3.

By the time of the much later New Kingdom, these pyramid texts had evolved into personalized papyrus scrolls. It became common for even people of modest means to pay a year's salary for a scribe to compose a long papyrus scroll containing hundreds of good luck spells and beautifully colored scenes to protect the deceased from such things as snakes,beetles crocodiles and evil spirits. Although today it is commonly called the 'Book of the dead', this is misleading because the texts are not about death but about eternal life which every Egyptian hoped to attain after physical death. The misnomer stems from the early 1800s when these papyri were presented to collectors who could not yet translate the language and were told by the tomb robbers only that they came from the place of the dead.Many of these delicate highly colored papyrus scrolls have miraculously survived to the present day. One of the most beautiful and best preserved was drawn up for Ani around 1240BC and purchased by Budge in 1895 under questionable circumstances. It now resides in the British Museum, London. The one written for Hunefer, (below) around the same

time, shows Hunefer's heart being weighed by the god Anubis holding a heart amulet. The deceased's heart is being weighed against the feather representing truth or Maat, the god Thoth with an Ibis head, was traditionally the author of the Books of the Dead and is seen here recording the proceedings. If the dead person had lived a good life and his heart was lighter than the feather, he was allowed to pass into the afterlife. If it outweighed the feather the owner had led a life of evil and Thoth's monster Ammit, with the body of a baboon and head of a crocodile, sitting expectantly, then had the right to devour it. The owner could therefore not pass on to the afterlife. Vignettes such as these were a common illustrations in Egyptian books of the dead.The afterlife was located in the world the deceased had lived in, though on a higher plane, the individual could then enjoy the best the world had to offer but without the discomforts.

**Maat, truth and order.** Egypt was by nature, a fundamentally conservative civilization; the population lived in an uncertain and volatile world. There was constant uncertainty over when the inundation would start, how long it would last, would there be a plague or a war and so on. The general population believed that there was an ancient pact between mortals and their gods. Those on earth must follow the rules, the established practices and the authority of their king and priests, particularly with regard to keeping the peace and paying taxes. In exchange the gods would control the stars and seasons, manifested in the annual inundation, and would keep them safe and secure. The Egyptians called this status quo Maat which embodied order, truth, law, morality and justice. Maat, on the right, was represented by the female god of the same name. She is normally shown holding a scepter in one hand representing law and order, and the ankh guarantying life in the other. She wore a single ostrich feather in her head band and occasionally was shown with wings on each arm. It is not surprising that the rulers and priesthood both took advantage of this concept, which worked very much in their favor, hence they continually reinforced the importance of Maat.

When things went wrong with the kingdom the ruler and priests would blame it on the population having deviated from Maat. When a king was deposed the reason was offered that he had not honored Maat. In Ani's book of the dead, above, Ani offers Maat a list of thirty eight examples of how he has followed her principles and forty two examples of evil he has avoided. In this way he hopes to persuade her that he should be allowed to proceed to the afterlife.

## Mummification.

A mummy is a corpse whose skin and flesh have been preserved by either intentional or accidental exposure to extreme cold, very low humidity, or lack of air when bodies are submerged in bogs. Mummies of humans and other animals have been found throughout the world, both as a result of natural preservation through unusual conditions, and via artificial means to preserve the dead. In 1991 'Otzi the iceman' was discovered in the Schnalstal glacier in the Italian/Austrian Alps. The body has been dated to c3300BC and is the oldest mummy found in Europe. He died at the age of forty five from an arrow wound in his shoulder possibly received during a raid, he became accidentally mummified by the extreme cold. The English word mummy is derived from the Medieval Latin mumia, derived from the Persian mumiyyah meaning bitumen. It was mistakenly believed that the blackened skin of the mummy, due to oxidization of the embalming oils, was caused by the use of bitumen once thought to be used extensively in the Egyptian embalming procedures. In the 1500s and 1600sAD mummies were highly valued by private collectors and especially European apothecaries who ground up the linen bandages and sold the powdered mummy as a cure for stomach ailments. Sanderson alone reported that he shipped 600 lbs of mummies to England in 1585 to be sold *'as agents to reduce stomach bleeding'*. Sadly many hundreds of mummies were broken up and sold to dealers for this purpose until export restrictions were introduced from the 1850's onwards.

Although mummification existed in other cultures, eternal life was the main focus of all Egyptians, which meant ensuring that the body was preserved for eternity. Egyptians believed the body in the  afterlife still contained the person's Ka and Ba, without which it would have been condemned to eternal wandering. The earliest known Egyptian mummy is called 'Ginger', (above) it dates back to c3300BC and is on display in the British Museum, London.

Although it is unclear whether this particular mummification was intentional it was buried with pottery vessels, so it is believed that the mummification was a result of artificial preservation techniques. Examination of pre dynastic burial pits has shown that in this very early period maintaining the corpse intact was not important, heads, legs and feet have been found separated from the torso. It is only later that maintaining the integrity of the corpse became paramount.

The dry hot desert sand provided a natural process for the preservation of the dead which the use of tombs by the wealthy changed. To preserve the body Egyptian priests developed the process of artificial mummification. The early process was rather basic, it was only later that organs were removed, with the exception of the heart. The heart was believed to be the center of intelligence  and would be needed in the after life. The internal organs were usually stored in four canopic jars (left). The lids for the four jars had different heads, each was associated with one of the four children of Horus. The baboon head protected the lungs, the human head protected the liver, the jackal head protected the stomach or spleen and the hawk head protected the intestines. Internal organs contained much water so that removing them allowed the body to be better preserved. In the New Kingdom, embalmers would break the bone behind the nose, and scoop or with hooks, pull out the brain through the nasal passage and then discard it. The embalmers would then replace the brain by filling the skull with thick resin. The word embalm comes from the Greek 'to put into aromatic resin'; the Egyptians called the process Ut.

It wasn't until the Middle Kingdom that embalmers used natural salts to remove moisture from the flesh. The salt based substance was called natron after the location of its main source Wadi Natron in the west Delta. Natron was a natural mixture of salts comprised of sodium carbonate, sodium bicarbonate and sodium chloride; it dried out and preserved the flesh faster than hot sand. Once dried, mummies were anointed with oils and perfumes, which over time oxidized and turned black. The New Kingdom 21st Dynasty saw the mummification process at its peak demonstrating highly advanced skills in embalming, aromatic resin was used to coat or fill the internal surfaces of the corpse and the skin. Often fingers and toes were carefully protected to prevent breakage, they were wrapped with strips of linen that protected the body parts from being damaged. After that, they were wrapped in a sheet of canvas to further protect them. Many valuable sacred charms and amulets were placed amongst the wrappings to protect the mummy from harm and to bring good luck to the Ka of the deceased.

Once preserved, the mummy was placed in a (usually) stone sarcophagus inside the burial chamber where the deceased would rest eternally. The mummy's mouth would then be opened in a formal religious ceremony which allowed the mummy to breathe and speak. This magnificent scene from Hunefer's 'Book of the dead' shows the upright mummy being supported by Anubis before the two mourning figures of his wife and daughter with their hands on their heads. At the extreme left are three priests who perform the ritual, the one on the right is holding the ritual opening of the mouth adze, another holds a calf's leg to the lips. To the  extreme right is the entrance of Henefers's tomb with a pyramid top and in front of the tomb is the dedication stele. The ritual was designed to symbolize breathing and gave rise to the legend about mummies that come back to life. In the west this reached almost fever pitch when this ceremony was observed painted on the burial chamber wall of Tutankhamen's tomb first opened in 1922. The sudden, unrelated, death of Lord Carnavon (caused by an infected mosquito bite) only days after the opening of the tomb was to give rise to the fanciful notion of the curse of the mummy's tomb.

**Mummy collecting and analysis.** Egyptian mummies were in great demand by collectors and museums worldwide throughout the 1800s. However not a single royal mummy had been discovered until late in the century when two New Kingdom royal mummy caches were found. The first cache was found secretly high in the cliffs of Deir el Bahri c1860, then publicly in 1881; and the second in the tomb of Amenhotep 2 KV35 in 1898. Both sets of royal mummies had been collected, and re-wrapped, then buried for safe keeping by the Theban Amen priests of the 21st and 22nd Dynasties following the collapse of the New Kingdom (see Chapter 11).

There is the notorious but unsubstantiated report of an antiquities collector visiting the Valley of the Kings in the second half of the nineteenth century, and illegally removing a royal mummy. On hearing that the authorities had discovered the theft the collector then proceeded to drop the mummy into the Nile to avoid being caught red handed. It is strongly suspected that this was one of the four New Kingdom kings whose mummies are still unaccounted for.

The missing mummy of what turned out to be Ramesses I was discovered in a curiosities museum in Niagara, Canada where it had reportedly been on exhibition from c1860 onwards. It is said to have been taken to north America by James Douglas and sold to the museum. It is believed to have been found by the notorious tomb robbers the abu Rassul family, as part of the first royal mummy cache at Deir el Bahri which only came to the public's notice in 1881. In 1999 the Emory University in Atlanta acquired the mummy and on determining it to be royal, generously returned it to Egypt in October 2003 where it was put on display at the Luxor Museum.

The first X-ray of a wrapped mummy was published by Petrie in 1898, only five years following their discovery by Roentgen. Early X-ray machines were used in the mid 1920s to try, with often misleading conclusions, to examine features of the body without disturbing the wrappings in an attempt to identify the individual. One of the most notorious high profile misinterpretations was in regard to an early X-ray view of the side of Tutankhamen's head. A lump of dried embalming resin was reported to be a 'skull fragment caused by a blow to the head'. This speculation mushroomed out of control until even experienced and well respected Egyptologists have gone on record as recently as 2004 stating they believed he was assassinated by Tutankhamen's chancellor Ay who then succeeded him. In 2005 the mummy of Tutankhamen was removed from it's sarcophagus in KV62 in the Valley of the Kings and subjected to a sophisticated CAT scan. The resultant three dimensional X-ray images were able to generate remarkably accurate representations of the body including facial features. These digital images of the mummy of Tutankhamen have now proved that he was not assassinated by a blow to the head, as had been speculated, but in fact suffered a complete break of the left femur. Based on the evidence of the break beginning to heal, it is estimated that he survived the accident and died some days or even weeks afterwards from the infection.

The scenes of him racing his war chariot in his temple reliefs created during his short reign, combined with the fact that his tomb contained his favorite chariots, have led to the not unreasonable hypothesis that his broken leg was a result of a chariot accident. Some have gone further and speculated that the chariot accident could have occurred while leading his army with his general Horemheb in the documented campaign of his final regnal year nine, against the Hittites in Syria.

# CHAPTER THREE

# The Old Kingdom – the Pyramid Age

Manetho starts Dynasty 3 after the death of king Khasekhemwy despite the fact that the next two rulers were his sons. The probable reason for this is that this new Dynasty made a herculean leap forward in tomb design and construction. We are entering the period known as the Old Kingdom, or 'Pyramid Age'. Almost all the major Pyramids were constructed on the west bank of the Nile straddling the capital Memphis, along a fifty mile strip between modern day Cairo in the north, to Lahun in the Fayum region as indicated in the map on the right. We have seen that the technology of building in stone was now developing rapidly in Egypt. Meanwhile the Mesopotamian civilizations were growing up along the Tigris and Euphrates rivers which ran into the Persian Gulf. However, here stone was scarce and where it did occur, it was quite remote from the main population centers. Consequently this led to construction being based almost exclusively on sun-dried mud brick and as a result there is very little remaining of the magnificent Sumerian, Assyrian and Babylonian temples and palaces, which at one time rivaled the grand stone structures of Egypt. The exceptions to this are the miles of beautifully crafted gypsum palace reliefs which lined the inside of the Assyrian palaces at the height of their empire 900-615BC as well as the magnificent colossal winged bulls and lions which guarded palace gateways. The Ishtar blue glazed tile gate at Babylon c575BC has has been reproduced in Iraq in part and and in full at the Pergamon Museum, Berlin. They give a glimpse of the splendor that was once Babylon.

Similarly most ancient Egyptian towns built of sun-dried brick have disappeared. They were either situated near the cultivated area of the Nile Valley and were flooded as the river bed slowly rose over the millennia, or the mud bricks from which they were built were used as fertilizer. Others sites which may have survived are inaccessible as new buildings have been erected over the ancient ones. Fortunately, the dry hot climate of Egypt has preserved some mud brick structures. Examples include the New Kingdom workers village at Deir al Medina, the Middle Kingdom town at Kahun in the Fayum, and the Nubian Middle Kingdom fortresses at Buhen and Mirgissa. The latter survived for over two thousand years only to be submerged under the rising waters of Lake Nasser in 1964. Many other temples and tombs have survived because they were built on high ground unaffected by the Nile flood or were constructed of stone.

**The invention of the arch.** High quality building stone was plentiful and readily accessible in Egypt. Limestone was in abundance on the west bank near to where the pyramids, mortuary temples and tombs were to be constructed. Fine white limestone for the pyramid casing was also available just south of modern Cairo at Tura. Sandstone was quarried further south at Silsila and the much harder red granite was abundant, albeit remote, at Aswan on the border with Nubia.

We have been led to believe that the Romans invented the arch around 450BC. This is a misconception. The use of the brick arch was developed first in Egypt in the 1st Dynasty c2900BC. The oldest surviving example of a stone arch can be seen in the roof of the crypt of King Djedkare in the 5th Dynasty around 2300BC, almost 1,800 years before the earliest Roman arch. There are more surviving examples of true relieving arches being used to protect doorways during the 6th Dynasty tombs at Saqqara and Dendera. One particularly fine example from this period is the mastaba tomb of Adu at Dendera where Petrie in 1898 discovered a brick dome over a well leading to the burial chamber. The Ramesseum precinct granaries c1250BC, exhibit extensive twenty feet wide brick vaulted store chambers. However it was not until around 750BC that true semi-circle stone barrel vaults up to seven feet in width, were in common use but strangely never

developed for monumental architecture. Typically, Egyptian monumental buildings were based on stone post and lintel beam constructions, with flat roofs constructed of huge stone blocks supported by the external walls and the closely spaced columns. The temples therefore appeared rather gloomy affairs with only very limited day light penetrating the lattice stone windows. To compensate, the internal surfaces were a riot of color, the remnants of which can be still seen today. The Greeks, when they first visited c600BC, were in awe of the magnificently tall and beautifully proportioned columned temples like the Hypostyle, meaning multi columned, hall at Karnak above.

The main corridor of the Hypostyle hall consisted of columns which reached eighty feet in height and were thirty three feet in circumference. The hall was already six hundred years old by the time the Greeks first began visiting.

The Greeks were naturally heavily influenced by what they saw and used the same concepts in their own temples designs. The most magnificent still standing is the Parthenon (left) in Athens from c440BC 'the most beautiful Greek temple ever built'. To reduce the apparent bulk of the Egyptian columns, the Greeks made their own columns bulge as they reached mid height i.e.cigar shaped, which gave the optical illusion of a more slender design.

It is fair to credit the Romans for taking the Egyptian arch and developing it to its full potential. They applied it to the construction of beautiful stone and brick aquaducts and soaring domed temple ceilings.The Romans also devleped the use of concrete to span truly giant spaces such as the rebuilt Pantheon temple c125AD in Rome itself. It comprised a dome with a width of 142 feet, the largest Roman dome still in existence as it was converted and preserved as a church by the early Christians in 609AD.It was only matched in size by the much later dome of Florence cathedral completed in 1436AD.

This ultra-conservatism in all matters, not just the lost potential of expanding the use of the arch in architecture, will be revisited throughout this volume. We will see later in Chapter 7 how the lack of development in weapon technology allowed the north half of the country to be conquered by Asian (Hyksos) invaders possessing vastly superior military weapons.

**Djoser.** c2584-2565BC The first builder in stone was Khasekhemwy, he died around 2584BC and his son Djoser succeeded to the throne. At this time a truly remarkable individual named Imhotep rose to become very influential with the royal family. He became the king's chief adviser and was placed in charge of the royal building projects. Imhotep was also talented in medical matters and recorded an extensive array of diagnoses and remedies as we shall see in Chapter 5. His fame continued through the ages and a thousand years later was worshipped as a god in Egypt. Imhotep began the construction of the king's conventional mastaba tomb at Saqqara on the west bank of the Nile opposite the capital at White Wall. King Djoser reigned for nineteen years and initially was content with the mastaba style tomb Imhotep was building out of local limestone. It was faced with beautifully cut and polished white limestone which was transported south by boat from the Tura quarries. However as the reign progressed he, and Imhotep, expanded the original ground plan three times.

Imhotep then demonstrated his genius. He added a slightly smaller mastaba on top of the original, the effect was dramatic. As the reign proceeded, typically every 3-6 years, he added a new mastaba on the top of the last until there were a total of six. He had created the world's first stepped pyramid (right). Inside

fifty years, almost out of nowhere in relation to the hundreds of years single mastabas had been constructed, Egypt had progressed from building modest single story brick tombs to a stone construction of truly enormous dimensions. The base of Djoser's step pyramid measured 397 feet by 358 feet and rose to a soaring height of 204 feet. Imhotep and Djoser had created a 'stairway to heaven' and by far the largest structure the world had yet seen. There is a tantalizing hint that tombs in the shape of a pyramid had been experimented with in earlier times. In the reign of 1st Dynasty king Den, three hundred years previously, the noble Nebtku started to develop a pyramid shape for his tomb but later altered it to the conventional mastaba configuaration.

Surrounding his step pyramid, funerary temple, Heb Sed precinct and subsidiary temples, (left) Djoser built a giant thirty four feet high crenellated stone wall. It was made to look like woven mats and was decorated with attractive palace style niches. It had a staggering total perimeter of over four miles and contained fifteen doorways; only the one at the south east was a real entrance. Clearly this leap forward in scale required an extremely high level of government and labor organization to quarry, transport, raise and set millions of stone blocks.

**The word's first archaeologist.** The unified kingdom had now been in existence for over six hundred years and Djoser, like all of his line, possessed a deep respect for his ancestors. He collected hundreds of clay pots from the early royal cemeteries, which by now had decayed from neglect, and stored them carefully in rooms beside his north burial chamber, ninety feet below the ground level of his towering pyramid. He decorated some of these rooms in magnificent blue faience glazed tiles, representing reed matting, with yellow stars painted onto the ceilings. In other rooms of his extensive underground galleries he decorated the walls with reliefs; the most impressive is that in the south tomb showing him running (right) the Heb Sed jubilee race wearing the white crown. At either

end of the huge open Heb Sed precinct created in front of the south side of the stepped pyramid were found the stone markers which he ran around during the ritual jubilee race. All along one side of this open precinct he constructed a series of beautiful sandstone cult temples dedicated to the major

gods of his kingdom. One highlight of the temple complex is the charming pair of eye holes in the north wall of the sealed Serdab, Arabic for cellar, chamber. These were created to allow his ka to move about freely and so that the the lifesize sculpture of the king (left) could observe and smell the offerings being made to him by his cult priests. The Serdab statue is of painted limestone and is the only one remaining of Djoser. The original is now in the Egyptian Museum, Cairo, a replica is housed in the Serdab at the pyramids's north east corner.

**Wood becomes stone.** Everywhere there can be seen a major artistic transition. Traditionally the king's palaces were constructed from natural building products such as wooden doors, pillars and roofs, reed matting, and mud bricks. Djosers architect copied these earlier styles for his mortuary temple at Saqqara but made use of stone or ceramics as construction materials. He may have cleared an earlier temple complex made from these natural materials to make way for the new stone complex. Visitors pass though the two extremely tall cedar-like entrance doors which appear to have been casually left half open, and then walk through the two rows each of twenty engaged columns made from bound reeds, into the entrance hall behind. It is only on close inspection that it can be seen that the material is not cedar or papyrus but stone replicas.

His masons used simple copper chisels to cut the stone blocks for the pyramid and temples. This necessitated a constant supply of copper ore. Texts found at Wadi Maghera record that Djoser expanded the traditional copper mines in south west Sinai to secure the copper needed. At the same time the Serabit el Khadim turquoise mines in Sinai were also expanded. There were no records of significant military action during his reign although he had achieved full control of the main trading route from the important southern region of Nubia into Egypt at Aswan.

The next three little-known successors of Djoser did not complete their pyramids. **Sanakhte** (Nebka) chose to build his pyramid at Abu Roash nine miles north of Djoser's huge stepped pyramid. Only the foundation and underground sections were completed. From the foundation plan it appears he intended to build a brick pyramid of much smaller proportions. He was succeeded by **Sekhemket** c2560BC who reigned for eight (or possibly fifteen years) and laid out a huge precinct beside Djoser's and planned a seven step pyramid with the same base as Djoser but even higher at 230 feet, however this had not reached more than twenty five feet high before he died.

**Khaba** c2550BC became the next king. He ruled for only six years and planned his tomb three miles north of Saqqara at Al Zawyet al Aryan. It was planned to be a modest five step pyramid with a smaller but square 275 feet base reaching only to 148 feet. It was made of poor quality small stone blocks and may have been mostly complete when he died, however only a rounded mound sixty feet high remains, it is believed he was not buried in it. The last king of the 3rd Dynasty was **Huni**, he reigned for twenty four years and reverted to brick for his pyramid which was located at Abu Roash just south of that of Sanakhte Nebka. It was intended to be a seven step pyramid of unknown height, and was probably not completed despite the significant length of his reign. Today there remains only a sixty foot mound where the pyramid once stood. King Huni brought the 3rd Dynasty to a close. His son Snefru succeded him, Manetho refers to him as king Soris.

**Snefru** c2540BC was the king who uniquely built three giant pyramids; Manetho chose to start the 4th Dynasty with his momentous reign. He came to the throne at a young age and reigned for a remarkable fifty years which is considered to be a golden, mostly peaceful, age. He was the first ruler to use the cartouche rope to enclose his name, and was to become the greatest pyramid builder of all time, measured by the amount of stone he used. He built three of the world's five largest stone pyramids. Our main source of information about the reign of Snefru is the Westcar Papyrus now in the Berlin Museum. The papyrus was written during the Hyksos period c1600BC, but is believed to be a copy of a Middle Kingdom text written some seven hundred years after Snefru's reign. When he came to power he appointed his son Nefermet to the position of vizier and chief of works, this was the beginning of a new tradition. From an inscription he left at Wadi Maghera, Snefru extended the Sinai copper and turquoise mines in anticipation of the huge building program ahead. In year two he imported forty ship loads of cedar wood from Byblos. The wood was earmarked for palace and temple doors and the construction of his fleet which contained ships as long as 170 feet. He carried out a military campaign in Nubia and recorded the capture of two thousand prisoners there. His seals found at Buhen in Nubia support the royal records of a major raid in the region. It is probable that Egyptian permanent settlements in Nubia commenced at this time. He may also have campaigned against the Libyan tribes to strengthen his western border. We have evidence that he constructed a fort at modern Suez to protect the eastern approaches and the route to Sinai.

**Snefru's Meidum pyramid.** His first pyramid was in stone at a new site, Meidum, twenty five miles south of Saqqara. It was a giant seven step pyramid. Later it was extended to eight steps, the largest so far with a base of 472 feet and a height of 302 feet. However, it was built on unstable ground and cracks appeared in the innovative burial chamber. This chamber was the first to be constructed above ground level in the body of the structure itself.

The cracked roof beams were supported by cedar logs which can be seen still in place today. The king felt this defective chamber was unsuitable for his final resting place and chose not to be buried there. He curiously later returned to the site and converted this step

pyramid (right) into a fully cased true pyramid. Unfortunately the casing was not properly keyed into the original outer surface of the steps and later either collapsed or became unstable and easily robbed, the left (east) side shows a missing section of the original step structure which fell out when the outer casing dropped away leaving the unusual shaped 213 feet high three tiered structure seen today.

In the shadow of Snefru's Meidum pyramid is the giant brick mastaba tomb of Snefru's son prince Rahotep, high priest of Heliopolis and general, and his wife Nofret. Inside this partially ruined structure, Mariette found in 1871, a remarkable life-size pair of strikingly realistic painted limestone statues in almost perfect condition now in the Egyptian Museum, Cairo. He is shown (left) with a slight frown and a moustache, rather unusual in Egyptian art, she has a wig but her hair is shown peeking below it on her forehead. The skin tones are typical of the Egyptian differentiation between males with reddish brown skin, versus females with paler cream skin.

**Snefru's Bent Pyramid.** Undaunted, Snefru moved north to a new site at Dashur only four miles south of Saqqara and in sight of Djoser's original step pyramid. This time he started to build the first true pyramid. Here he commenced a structure that would have been an even taller pyramid than his first at Meidum, but once again the choice of the site was flawed. The foundations shifted after about one third of the structure had been completed

and again the burial chamber inside the structure itself developed cracks. The architect tried to support the pyramid from the outside fearing a collapse of the very acute 60 degree structure. The lower section was widened and strengthened and the angle was reduced from 60 degrees to 54. (right)

However the cracking continued and cedar beams were again needed to prevent the cracks expanding. To rapidly complete this second flawed pyramid, the angle was reduced for a third time to only 43 degrees, as a result it rose to a final height of only c345 feet even though its base was 617 feet. This last change in angle of ascent is clearly visible, see the previous page, and gives rise to its name the Bent Pyramid. The last layers of stone were the first to be laid horizontally in pyramid construction. This was the world's first true pyramid, uniquely it had a second entrance located over half way up on the west face. This small entrance was to access a new second burial chamber higher in the pyramid, as the lower chamber had cracked. Unfortunately this second burial

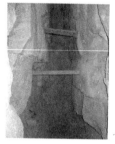

chamber also developed cracks and the walls had to be supported by six cedar beams (left). Although this second pyramid was finished and completely cased, it too was abandoned. Snefru also considered this Bent Pyramid to be unacceptable for his burial. Ironically today this pyramid although odd in appearance, is in fact the best preserved. It has retained almost all of its beautiful white Tura limestone and the magnificent craftsmanship of the precision jointing of the casing blocks can be seen to this day.

**Snefru's Red Pyramid.** Still undaunted, Snefru quickly moved on to his third and final pyramid one mile further north. This time he took a very conservative approach. He was careful to select a site that had a deep deposit of gravel which would take the enormous weight of the structure. He also knew from the Bent Pyramid that a 43 degree angle would work, so he started at this angle and relatively quickly completed it without any further issues. It is known today as the Red Pyramid, as the the inner limestone used for its construction, quarried nearby, had a reddish tinge to it, the outer white Tura limestone casing was completely stripped away in medieval times.

The Red Pyramid had a giant base of 722 feet and matched the bent pyramid height of c345 feet. It was to become the joint third tallest pyramid ever to be built; only the Great Pyramid of his son Khufu and that of Khafre were higher. When compared to the other true pyramids its height is deceptive from a distance, the angle of only 43 degrees gives it an odd squat appearance. The Red Pyramid contains three internal chambers each with a magnificent corbelled ceiling soaring to heights of forty and fifty feet. These stepped ceilings spread the immense weight above the rooms sideways through the bulk of the mass.

In this final effort the foundations were sound and all three chambers remained perfect. After a reign of fifty years the kings body was laid to rest in the burial chamber high up in the body of the pyramid, hoping (unwisely), that it would be safe from tomb robbers. The Red Pyramid (right) is open to the

public and is one of the finest to visit. The three corbelled chambers are an engineering marvel and are visually stunning.

Although he built more than any other king we know very little about the reign of Snefru and there are only a few representations of him that have survived. His rare limestone stele on the left (Egyptian museum, Cairo) was found in the ruins of his mortuary temple at the base of the Bent Pyramid. It shows the hieroglyphics for his name inside a rope cartouche. Below this he can be seen seated on a throne wearing a Heb Sed robe. Underneath is a serekh.

On the right is part of a very rare striding statue of Snefru, also in the Egyptian Museum.

## Khufu's Great Pyramid one of the 'seven wonders'.

Snefru's son Khufu c2470-2447BC (Greek Cheops, Egyptian 'Khnum protects me') had grown up watching his father achieve a feat never to be repeated, the construction of three giant stone pyramids. Not wanting his pyramid to stand in direct comparison with his father's pyramids to the south of Memphis he chose a splendid new pyramid location north of the capital on a high stone cliff on the west bank of the Nile south west of modern Cairo. On ascending to the thrown in his twenties, Khufu appointed the son of his father's vizier and chief of works as his own. His name was Hemiunu. The only surviving statue of him (left) in the Pilizaeus Museum, Hildersheim, Germany, shows a tall, rather heavily built, individual who was to create the only surviving wonder of the world, the Great Pyramid at Giza. His large mastaba tomb is located in a place of honor in the extreme west of the 4th Dynasty Giza necropolis, west of the

pyramid complex that he was responsible for creating. It is ironic that the only representation of Khufu, the creator of the greatest pyramid, is the smallest effigy to a king ever discovered. This tiny three inch ivory statuette, (right) was found by Petrie in 1903 at Abydos and is now in the Egyptian Museum, Cairo. What a contrast to the life size almost perfect statue, above, of the vizier Hemiunu found in his grand mastaba in the shadow of the pyramid he helped to build, The first precise measurements of the pyramid were carried out by Petrie in 1880–82. The volume of the structure, excluding an internal natural shallow mound, is believed to contain roughly 2,300,000 blocks each weighing an average of two to two and a half tons. The Great Pyramid remained the tallest man-made structure in the world for over 3,800 years unsurpassed until the tall spire of Lincoln Cathedral, England was completed c1300AD.

The dimensions of the massive structure are still wonderfully impressive to the visitor. Each side of the base measures 756 feet and the height soared to 481 feet when built, 136 feet taller than his father's Red Pyramid, mainly because the angle at which it rose was the more acute 52 degrees compared to 43 degrees.

**Who built the Great Pyramid and how long did it take?** The subjects of how the pyramid was built, how long it took and who built it have filled libraries across the planet with fantastic theories. Some of these theories have been based on early traveler speculation, some on local hearsay, others have been influenced by occultism and more recently on new-age concepts relating to celestial travelers, nearly all these have now been proven to be historically incorrect. Herodotus can be blamed for the early fiction that the *'cruel Cheops'* enslaved and bankrupted his people to build his pyramid and led his daughter into prostitution to help pay for it's completion. Medievel travellers proclaimed it was not a tomb but Joseph's granary and it is shown as such on the Narthex mosaic c1300AD of St Mark's church in Venice. The nineteenth century cult scientists Taylor and Piazzi Smyth, called *'pyramidiots'* by Petie who disproved their work, propagated fantastic theories relating to divine intervention and the so called 'pyramid-inch'. However, it has only been possible to piece together the full story in very recent times.

During the inundation, the farmers could not work the fields and historians now believe that in lieu of taxation they worked on the king's construction projects, a type of corvee. They were not slaves, they freely left their homes travelled to the work site and lived there in specially constructed workers villages for four to six months. The treasury provided bread, meat and beer as well as clothing. They had access to medical and dental treatment and if they died at work they were buried respectfully in graves nearby. The peasant farmers were used mainly as unskilled laborers. They primarily moved quarried pre-cut blocks, using ropes and water-lubricated sleds on rollers, up from the yellow limestone quarry next to the site ready for the skilled masons to position the blocks. Some were tasked to move the white Tura limestone blocks, quarried on the east bank, south of the later Cairo, down to the river, across the Nile, and then from the specialy built west bank river harbor up the long causeway to the plateau itself.

As the pyramid grew taller, the blocks were then pulled up the direct ramp, from the Gizeh quarry, followed later by a spiral wrap-around ramp which stretched almost to the top. When the mass of the inner yellow limestone blocks were complete, master stonemasons positioned the carefully cut and smoothed white limestone casing blocks from top to bottom filling-in the structure, leaving a gleaming white flat surface on all four sides. Sadly, all of this has been removed for local building use in the fourteenth century AD. The question of how long it took to construct and how many people were needed, are inter-related and have puzzled the world for thousands of years.

In the 1982-3 season, Stadelmann's team recorded the details of Snefru's Red Pyramid blocks and remaining casing stones. They were astonished to find builders' red graffiti referring to the start of construction being in the twenty second year of Snefru's long fifty year reign. Further graffiti were discovered; one dated to two years later, when six layers had been added and a second dated to four years from the start when just under a third of the blocks had been laid. It is truly remarkable that this is the only record of any construction details relating to any pyramid. It is not surprising that this paucity of information has over the ages fuelled speculation as to who was responsible for their construction. For the first time it was possible to accurately establish that the Red Pyramid was built in around eleven or twelve years. Petrie in 1883 had theorized correctly that it was possible for a two and a half ton typical block to be be quarried, brought to the pyramid, raised into position, trimmed and fixed every two minutes. This prodigious work rate was proven by Lehner in 1996 when a small stone pyramid was actually constructed using Old Kingdom technology. It proved that construction was not a miracle of science but the result of a very efficient highly organized state system which was expert at standardizing and then repeating the same operation millions of times over. Using this as a reference it was then straight forward to calculate that the above ground superstructure of the larger Great Pyramid was built in around fourteen years. The whole mortuary temple complex itself could have been completed in around twenty years.

Based on the now established realistic average work rate of one block every two minutes, it can be calculated that in the first year only twenty thousand workers were needed, the second year this dropped to ten thousand as the pyramid narrowed. It is estimated that construction was completed by a core of only five thousand over the following twelve years. The construction of the pyramid was now clearly quite well within the resources of a kingdom comprising over a million souls needing at its peak only 5-10% of the available active work force.

Smith, in 2004, went even further and demonstrated that by using twenty six thousand workers for the first three years the Great Pyramid could have been built in as little as ten years plus three years more for the mortuary temple, massive valley causeway and valley temple. Today the causeway has been completely quarried away so it is hard to visualize what a magnificent structure it was in its own right. It was over a mile long and had to rise one hundred and thirty feet from the river level to the Giza plateau. The stone required was

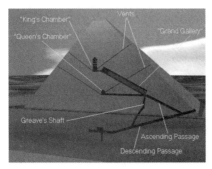

equivalent to one third of that needed for the pyramid itself. As recently as 1842 Lepsius observed that parts of the great causeway still remained and were decorated with reliefs. Not only did Khufu build a much taller pyramid than the Red Pyramid of his father, but the internals of the pyramid (left) were by far the most complex ever to be seen and in parts used red granite, twice as hard to work. Khufu enjoyed a long reign and good health. He recorded the first reference to the southern land of Punt, probably on the the Red Sea coast of Somalia or Ethiopia, and made trading expeditions deep into south Nubia. From here were brought the highly valued dwarf slaves, or pygmies, which became great favorites at court for Khufu and future Egyptian kings. Khufu even had statues made of his particular favorites.

It is generally accepted that a single temporary stone ramp was constructed from the quarry to the south to bring the stone blocks on rollers up to the Giza plateau and then up to the location in the structure where they were needed. This straight ramp stopped at around one hundred and twenty feet, just over one quarter of the height of the completed pyramid, when about two thirds of the stone was in place. An external spiral ramp was then used for the remainder of the construction and then demolished or used in the structure itself. An alternative, unlikely, theory put forward in 2006 by Houdin, proposed that the spiral ramp was internally located forty feet behind the exterior surface, and still remains inside the pyramid.

**Design changes.** Khufu's long reign allowed him to make many pyramid design changes, not unlike the changes Djoser had made a hundred years before. The site was first leveled, apart from leaving a thirty feet high natural rise in the center which reduced the amount of construction stone needed by about ten percent. It was ensured that each corner pointed precisely to each of one of the cardinal points, and then work commenced on the rock cut underground descending passage and the large subterranean chamber. It may have been originally intended as the burial chamber but it was almost too large for this purpose and was left incomplete. Khufu decided that like his father the burial chamber should be constructed in the body of the pyramid well above the ground level. As the pyramid rose, the engineers then had to prepare the ascending passage and the incorrectly named Queens chamber. At this point around a quarter of the pyramid's total blocks had been laid. This chamber was likely to have been planned as his burial place, however there is a minority view that it was intended only to hold his ka serdab (Arabic cellar) statue in the niche in the western wall. A second and last change was made to locate

his final resting place just over one quarter of the way up the structure and approximately in the center of the pyramid. As the pyramid grew taller Hemiunu and the engineers constructed an upward sloping limestone Grand Gallery (left) which was corbelled in seven steps to a height of twenty eight feet and is the most magnificent constructed. There is much debate as to the reason for such a long gallery at this location. The classical explanation is that it was used to store three oblong giant 7 ton granite plugs used later to seal the lower entrance to the ascending passage. However Houdin, in 2006, proposed that it was also used to house a counter weight sled, on rollers, which was employed to drag the massive granite burial chamber roof and stress relieving beams up the external sloping ramp.

The Grand Gallery led to a vestibule containing the three portcullis stones protecting the burial chamber from entrance and robbery. Dropping down to a height of only four feet, the passage then enters the red granite plain burial chamber itself. The massive red granite one-piece 4 ton sarcophagus was brought from Aswan 580 miles to the south. It was then dragged up the external ramp and moved into place as the tomb chamber was built around it. The precise level for the final chamber was probably selected as it represented approximately the half way point in regards to the total number of blocks needed for the pyramid. The roof of the burial chamber was to be flat. It was made up of red granite beams each twenty four feet long, and six feet thick, spanning the burial chamber's sixteen feet width. Each granite beam weighed fifty to eighty tons. Granite was chosen for this purpose because it has a compressive strength 50-100% greater than limestone. There was a very high risk that these and the side wall granite blocks would crack from the immense weight of the remainder of the pyramid yet to be built over them. Khufu had already seen this happen in two of his father's pyramids. To avoid a repeat, a unique construction in place of a traditional corbelled roof was built. They were called stress relieving chambers, of which there were five (right top). They were only discovered in 1837 by Colonel Vyse blasting upwards using gunpowder. In the top two were found red graffiti containing the king's cartouche (right) written by two separate construction or quarry gangs. This is the only written evidence we have that the pyramid was constructed for Khufu.

There have been disputes over the purpose of four very narrow, eight inch square, passages two from the Queen's Chamber and two from the King's burial chamber. These shafts (see the earlier pyramid's internal plan) were once thought to have been used for ventilation during construction, but this idea was eventually abandoned, leaving us to conclude that they were instead used for ceremonial purposes. The consensus opinion now is that that they were designed to allow the king's spirit or ka to rise up and out into the night sky and then to return at dawn. The two passages from the burial chamber point to Polaris on the north and Orion on the south.

**Khufu's funeral.** At the end of the normal seventy day embalming process, the series of nested, highly decorated, wooden coffins containing his mummy were taken by boat across the Nile to his valley temple and from there up the one mile long magnificently decorated stone causeway to the pyramid. The giant causeway took around three years to construct and yet was to be used only once. The coffin progressed into his mortuary temple at the base of the pyramid on the east side to lie in state. All that remains of this temple is part of the floor which was made out of black basalt; because of it's scarcity it was very rarely used in Egyptian construction. His coffin was finally carried up to the entrance on the north face, fifty six feet above the Giza plateau. It proceeded slowly through the tight four feet by three and a half feet descending passage, from there up through the Grand Gallery for the last time and finally it was placed in the red granite sarcophagus installed many years previously. The attendants then used ropes, parts of which can still be seen, to lower the three portcullis stones and seal the chamber. They then retreated back down the Grand Gallery and released the three previously installed giant oblong granite blocks which slid down and acted as plugs to close the lower entrance of the
ascending passage. They then escaped down the almost vertical 'well' using ropes to reach the original descending passage. They sealed the well exit and then left the pyramid via the descending passage. The last task was to close the inverted double gabled pyramid entrance (right) on the north face and carefully install the perfectly matched casing stones over it, thus making it almost impossible to locate its exact location in the enormous expanse of identical white casing stones. Despite these precautions, the tomb robbers gained entrance and bypassed all the barriers, probably only a few tens of years after the king has been laid
to rest, certainly before the Old Kingdom had ended. Probably aided by knowledge from the priests and or designers, they had located the hidden entrance in the north face and digging around the three oblong granite sealing blocks entered the burial chamber breaking a corner of Khufu's sarcophagus (left) and robbing it.

It seems that the entrance was resealed in antiquity perhaps by the robbers themselves and then was subsequently lost in time.

Around 820AD, Caliph Ma'mun from Baghdad, sent an expedition to Giza to enter the Great Pyramid, not to steal the funerary gold and jewels but driven by a prize he believed was even more valuable, the fabled and priceless, but probably completely fictitious, navigation maps allegedly used by the Egyptian fleet to circumnavigate Africa. They tunneled a new entrance, now used by modern visitors, well below the original entrance and cut deep into the pyramid until they met the base of the Grand Gallery. When they arrived at the burial chamber all they discovered was the empty granite sarcophagus. The pyramid has remained open ever since. The final indignity came in the great earthquake of 908AD which dislodged some of the outer casing, starting its wholesale quarrying, and may have cracked the roof beams in the burial chamber and the stress relieving chambers. Others have proposed that the roof beams actually cracked when the pyramid was being completed and point to the two giant limestone gables at the top of the stress relieving chambers, which no longer lean flush, as evidence of movement. It is likely that the removal of the long external construction ramp, which had leaned against the south side of the pyramid, caused settling which then resulted in the roof beam cracks.

**The world's most sophisticated boat.** The Old Kingdom had developed boat building to a peak of high science. Their boats were not only able to easily and swiftly navigate up and down the Nile they could also move huge monoliths over large distances such as the burial chamber roof beams some weighing over eighty tons. Their construction was of such a high technological standard that they were hundreds of years ahead of their time when most of the rest of the world was using simple dugout canoes or reed rafts. Until recently we only had wall reliefs of these technological marvels to indicate their true dimensions and design.

This was until 1954, when, clearing debris from the south side of the pyramid, a young Egyptian archeologist discovered two long rectangular pits. The eastern pit was covered by a roof of forty one huge limestone slabs, (left) weighing between seventeen and twenty tons each. The largest is about fourteen feet long. The three westernmost of these stones were much smaller than the others and have been interpreted as keystones for the pit which measured about seventy feet in length. When one of the slabs was raised, the parts of a great boat were seen, completely dismantled. The 1,224 parts were carefully removed and restored and then painstakingly reconstructed between 1958 and 1968. The completed boat, (overleaf) was 142 feet long mostly made of Lebanese cedar and was found to be of water tight

and fully serviceable construction before it was dismantled. Its displacement was forty five tons with a maximum draft of five feet; it was nineteen feet wide. The separate parts of the boat had numerous holes indicating that the timbers could be stitched together using ropes made of vegetable fibers. Propulsion was by means of ten oars, and it was steered using two large oar rudders located in the stern. There was no mast or sail, hence this boat would not have been used other than for local river travel.

On the walls and roof of the boat pit were many marks and inscriptions, including cartouches containing the year and name of King Djedefre, the son of Khufu. This strongly suggests that some parts of Khufu's pyramid complex were not completed until after Khufu's death. Dobrev believes that the boat pits on the south side of the Great Pyramid were built by Djedefre connected with the establishment of a divine cult for his father.If the boats were indeed used in the funeral of Khufu, it would be natural for Djedefre to have buried them and used his own cartouches. The still unopened western boat pit has been inspected remotely and has been found to contain a similar boat in a disassembled state. On the east of the pyramid are five other smaller boat pits, three associated with Khufu, and two with his wives, all were found empty.To the south east of the complex outside the perimeter wall, are three small step pyramids.Two are dedicated to his wives and one to his mother Hetepheres. Her sealed sarchophagus, along with her exquisite funerary furniture, was found intact, in 1925, but without its mummy. It had been relocated from the pyramid to a nearby hidden underground shaft one hundred feet deep. The contents of which include the oldest examples of intact canopic ceremonial burial jars.

### Djedefre's 'lost pyramid' at Abu Roash.
Djedefre c247BC (enduring like re) was the eldest son of Khufu and as crown prince it was his duty to bury his father. As we have seen, he ordered the completion of his father's pyramid complex, namely the mortuary temple and the two southern boat pits. On the right is one of only four surviving images of Djedefre, it is made from red quartzite chosen to accurately represent the texture of flesh. Traces of paint show his skin was painted red. The head is from a sphinx; it was found in a boat pit south of his pyramid at Abu Rawash and is now in the Louvre

Museum, Paris. During the reign of Khufu the cult of the sun god Re gained momentum. His son Djedefre was the first to bear the Re epithet, furthermore he started the practice of all future kings creating the formal 'Son of Re' title.

Red quartzite had solar significance and its quarry lay close to the temple of the sun god at Heliopolis. On becoming king, Djedefre chose for the location of his pyramid the 3rd Dynasty site used by both king Senakhte Nebka and king Huni at Abu Roash five miles north of Giza. This was one of Egypt's most northerly pyramids and became known as the 'lost pyramid' as it is today mostly ruined (below). The complex included an empty boat pit and a mile long causeway running south to north, not west to east, to reach down from

the very high escarpment to the river valley below. The Abu Rawash escarpment at this point is many hundreds of feet higher than the Giza plateau, and herein lies a clue for its choice of location.

This reason for the move to Abu Rawash and the level of destruction of the pyramid has puzzled Egyptologists for over a hundred years since Chassinat commenced excavation in the early 1900s. He and his sucessors found twenty one completely broken statues, all in red quartzite, which led him to postulate the following fictitious theory. He suggested that Djedefre had killed an older brother to gain the kingdom, he then fell out with his family and the Re priesthood and moved from Giza to Abu Roash to construct his tomb. After his death his family retaliated and destroyed the pyramid and each of his statues in an attempt to erase his memory. The completed pyramid would have been two hundred feet tall, only half the height of his father's four hundred and eighty one feet high pyramid, and about the same as the smallest Giza pyramid that of Menkaure. Here the choice of a highly elevated commanding site showed its brilliance, the top of his pyramid reached a height of seven hundred and twenty two feet above the Nile, twenty five feet higher than the top of Khufu's pyramid; thus he could rightly boast that he had built the highest pyramid in the land. Although the pyramid was much smaller than that of his father, Djedefre compensated in terms of beauty. He was the first to use expensive hard to cut red granite, with its solar significance, to case the twenty lower courses of the pyramid. This imaginative and attractive practice was to be copied by his successors.

Now we turn to the question of was the pyramid ever completed? The first issue is his length of reign. The Turin King list recorded only eight years which might suggest the pyramid was never completed. However the highest known year referred to during his reign appears in the year of his 11th cattle count, found written on the underside of one of the massive roofing beams which covered Khufu's southern boat pit. If the cattle count was conducted every year his reign would have been eleven years, if every two years the reign would be at least twenty two years long. In either case there was enough time to complete construction. This has been supported by excavations over the last ten years of the mortuary temple complex. It has been discovered that contrary to the Chassinat theory, his mortuary temple and by implication his pyramid, was fully completed and moreover it remained in use by his cult priesthood well past the 5th Dynasty over two hundred years later. Another good reason for Djedefre to choose the site was the plateau topography. The pyramid made use of a natural rock outcrop which represented about forty percent of its core; so all evidence supports the fact that, even with a shorter reign of eleven years it was quite possible to complete the pyramid. Then why was it destroyed so thoroughly? Roman wooden mallets found nearby provide the clue. Egypt became a grain province of Rome c30BC and during the reign of Emperor Augustus it proved a convenient source of stone for his construction projects. The Romans however were not able to remove all the stone. We know from local Cairo records that three hundred camels a day were still removing stone from the pyramid as late as the 1850s. Quarrying has left little apart from a few courses of stone superimposed upon the natural rise that formed part of the pyramid's core and only the very impressive sub ground structure remains today.

**The first sphinx.** A remarkably well preserved sphinx (right) with the face of his wife Hetepheres 2 was recovered from Abu Roash, it was the first intact Egyptian sphinx to be found. Dobrev in 2004 used this discovery to support the theory that it was Djedefre who created the head of the Great Sphinx in the image of his father and now god, Khufu.

**Giza's second pyramid of Khafre.** c2437-2414BC. Djedefre's son Baka ruled for only two years, the throne then passed back to Khufu's second son, Khafre, who returned to Giza to construct his pyramid. This was built on a part of the plateau which was twenty feet higher and just to the south west of the Great Pyramid, so although the pyramid structure itself was actually ten feet shorter it gives the impression of being taller.

It is distinguishable by the top section of casing which evaded the stone robbers and still remains, (below) to give a tantalizing impression of what these cased

pyramids would have looked like. In the new style, the lower two courses were cased in contrasting red granite. The causeway and valley temple of Khafre have survived better than those of Khufu, the valley temple in particular has provided a number of outstanding intact statues of

the king now in the Egyptian Museum, Cairo. In 1858 Mariette came across this marvelous statute of Khafre (left) with the wings of Horus mantling and protecting him. It is considered to be one of the finest masterpieces of Egyptian sculpture in the round, and clearly shows the tradition of being shown with a false beard. Unusually, two entrances lead to the burial chamber of Khafre, one that opens c40 feet above ground in the face of the pyramid and an earlier entrance that opens at the base of the pyramid. The original entrance passage is cut into the bedrock, after descending, it runs horizontally to a rock cut burial chamber. Later a new passage was constructed from the original burial chamber to join the later second entrance passage. The later entrance passage is richly clad in red granite, after descending it runs horizontally to the new burial chamber. The most likely explanation for the two entrances is that the pyramid was originally intended to be 100 feet further to the north. But a natural stone ridge was later identified which ran to the valley floor and by using this as the foundation of the causeway, the amount of construction stone needed could be reduced significantly. Hence a new entrance south of the original had to be constructed. An alternative theory is that, as we have already seen with other pyramids, designs were changed and the burial chamber location was moved south during construction. The final burial chamber was not located in the body of the pyramid like that of Khufu, but was carved out the bedrock. Its roof also departs from either the corbelled or flat structures of previous pyramids and is constructed of simple gabled limestone beams. Khafre's sarcophagus was carved out of a solid block of red granite and sunk partially in the floor, another pit in the floor likely contained the canopic chest.

**Giza's third pyramid.** The third Giza pyramid was built by Menkaure c2414-2396BC the son of Khafre, it was by far the smallest (right) reaching a height of only 213 feet. Although Menkaure reigned for eighteen years it seems it was not long enough to complete the mortuary temple and finish the granite casing of the lower courses. Heaps of unfinished red granite blocks can be seen today littering the

approach to the north entrance face. The casing of Menkaure's pyramid has been completely robbed; the ugly vertical gash on the north face (above) was an attempt by Saladin's son Othman to demolish the pyramid in 1196AD, after eight months of work he gave up. Resiner's excavation of the valley temple in 1908, discovered seventeen intact statues of the king. This beautiful

life size greywacke diad statue (left) with his wife Khamerernebty 2 holding him with both hands, is in the Museum of Fine Arts, Boston. The Egyptian Museum, Cairo houses this powerful triad basalt statue (right) showing the king with Hathor on his right accompanied on his left by the personification of the Cynopolis deity. Both of these are considered to be Old Kingdom masterpieces of sculpture in the round.

Vyse in 1837 came across a beautiful basalt sarcophagus, rich in detail with a projecting cornice inside the burial chamber. Unfortunately, this sarcophagus now lies at the bottom of the sea, sinking with the ship Beatrice, as she made her way to England, it was one of only a handful of extant Old Kingdom sarcophagi. The anthropoid coffin, however was successfully transported on a separate ship and is today in the British Museum, London. Menkaure's pyramid is particularly notable as it was the last of the giant stone pyramids ever to be built.

His son **Shepseskaf**, c2396BC reigned for only four years, it is believed that he fell out so badly with the Re priesthood that he chose not to incorporate Re into his name. He moved the site of his tomb south to Saqqara and reverted to building this relatively modest two tier fifty nine foot high Mastaba el Faroun (right). The causeway from the mastaba to its valley temple was poorly built and never completed. The reason for the mastaba tomb choice may have been forced upon him by pressure of time. He was left with the task of trying unsuccessfully

to complete the extensive Giza pyramid complex of his father Menkaure. The particularly labor intensive task of smoothing and polishing the sixteen granite casing courses was too much and only five courses were completed on the north face. There were other signs that time was running out for Shepsekaf to complete his father's complex. The causeway from the pyramid's mortuary temple to the valley termple was hastily built in mud brick and the pavement around the pyramid itself was never completely finished.

The three giant stone pyramids of the Giza plateau (shown south to north) are of Menkaure, Khafre and Khufu. Their southeast corners are perfectly aligned and their geodetic line points directly to the religious center of Heliopolis. They were to be the last built of this scale in stone. The three smaller step and true pyramids in the foreground are the subsidiary or so called 'Queens' pyramids of Menkaure.

**The riddle of the Great Sphinx.** One of the continuing unresolved debates in Egyptology relates to the riddle of the Sphinx; who does the face of the Great Sphinx represent and who constructed it? Because it lies roughly in line with the pyramid causeway of Khafre, (below) Hassan in the 1940s argued that the

face probably represented Khafre. Countering this is the theory that Khafre had to slant the causeway to his valley temple well south of the traditional perpendicular east-west line to avoid the pre-existing sphinx. Certainly the lion body of the Sphinx predated Khafre. It was created from the stone rump left behind from the south quarry used to build the pyramid of Khufu; so could the face be that of Khufu? In 2004 Dobrev, based on the examination of historical records, claimed that the evidence indeed suggested the face was sculpted by Djedefre in the image of his father Khufu. Stadelmann supported this Khufu theory based on the style of the headdress. He argued that the style is more indicative of Khufu than Khafre and underlined his theory by observing that the tiny ivory statuette of Khufu, like the Sphinx, does not have

a beard, whereas all the statues of Khafre, and for that matter, Menkaure, show him wearing one. Stadelmann believes the two beard fragments housed in the British Museum (right) and the Egyptian Museum are a later addition; the circular shape and plaited style are both of the New Kingdom. Domingo using his own detailed measurements taken of the Sphinx, determined through forensic drawings and computer analysis that the face of the Sphinx and the face seen on statues of Khafre could

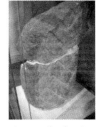

not be the same person. Peck, in 1992 proposed still another theory; the face is a generic one representing monarchs rather than one specific king. The Egyptian historian al-Maqrizi, writing in the fifteenth century AD, attributed the nose damage to the religious zeal of Muhammad Sa'im al-Dahr. He recorded that al-Dahr c1378AD discovered the practice of local farmers making offerings to the Sphinx in the hope of increasing their harvest. Outraged he destroyed the nose; he was later hanged for his vandalism.

**The 5th Dynasty 'Solar' Kings.** The death of the last king of the 4th dynasty Shepseskaf, led to dynastic and religious chaos. We have seen that he had fallen out with the influential Re priesthood of Heliopolis, furthermore, he died without an heir apparent. The lack of an obvious heir presented a golden opportunity for the Re priesthood to become king maker and establish

a sympathetic pro-Re ruler. They supported the ascent of one of their own high priests who was also of royal blood. **Userkaf** c2392-2385BC, here unusually shown wearing the red crown of the south (Egyptian Museum, Cairo) was the great grandson of the now God Khufu and held the post of high priest of Heliopolis. With the support of the religious establishment he was able to ascend to the throne. To consolidate his legitimacy to rule he married Khentawes the sister of late King Shepseskaf.

Manetho credits him as the founder of a new 5th Dynasty mainly because it marked the final departure from the construction of giant stone pyramids. Instead these 'solar' kings built smaller pyramids of inferior construction at the new site of Abusir south of Giza. Most of these pyramids, like that of Userkaf, were constructed of an inner core of rough hewn blocks in a step structure held together with a mortar of mud, they are now all hopelessly ruined. These rulers additionally constructed a new concept, a separate 'sun' temple, each with a squat stone block obelisk, a symbol of the Re temple at Heliopolis. Userkaf left an inscription at the first Nile cataract and after a short seven year reign may have been succeeded by his wife Khentawes for a year and then by his son **Sahure** c2385BC- 2373BC. His twelve year reign was notable for an inscription in Sinai, trade with Byblos and the first recorded Punt (Somalia) trade expeditions as well as possible campaigns in Libya and Nubia. His small pyramid is mostly ruined, but inside it and on the causeway to the valley temple, excavated in the early 1900s, are extensive fine reliefs superior to those from the 4th Dynasty. Some of the low-relief cuttings are masterpieces of their kind and still in place at the site. They are the first to record Bedouin figures suffering from famine, a harbinger of events to come.

Five little known kings with short reigns followed until we reach king Djedkare Isesi c2340BC who built a new palace and capital south of White Wall and a pyramid, now ruined, near that of Djoser. His royal inscription in the Sinai is the first there to mention a vizier by name; Ptah Hotep. This is a powerful sign which along with others suggest that the king is no longer all powerful and the kingdom is under internal stress.

**Unas and the first pyramid texts.** He was succeeded by a king of unknown origin Unas, c2312-2282BC who built his pyramid right beside the south wall of Djoser's complex in an attempt to associate his reign with the legendary innovator. King Unas made a breakthrough in Egyptian art; the interior of his burial chamber is decorated with a number of reliefs detailing events during his reign as well as a number of inscriptions. However, the main innovation and one that was

to be characteristic of the remaining pyramids of the Old Kingdom was the first appearance of the Pyramid Texts. These texts (left page) included verses and spells intended to help the king in overcoming hostile influences in the underworld and helping him pass to the afterlife. The king would then spend his days in eternity sailing with Re across the sky in a solar boat. However, there are ominous warnings during his long thirty year reign of the growth in strength of the local Nomarchs, one of which audaciously takes the name 'great lord', it also appears that the south is beginning to break away.

This once magnificent, and now partly restored, causeway (right) of Unas stretches for a mile down to his valley temple. Vistors can observe portions of the restored causeway roof with painted yellow stars and blue night sky as well as beautiful colored wall reliefs of exotic animals, men hunting lions, leopards and giraffes, boats transporting granite columns from Aswan, battles with Asian

enemies and the transport of prisoners; he claimed to have conducted five campaigns in Canaan and Syria. However, there is a repeat of the disturbing Sahure scene of emaciated people with their ribs clearly showing, suffering from the effects of famine (left). It was originally believed that the scenes record the economic decline of this period, but new theories counter this assumption and it is believed that the reliefs refer to starving Bedouins migrating to Egypt to avoid famine at home.

**The 6h Dynasty kings.** When Unas died there was again dynastic turmoil and the background to the new king **Teti** c2282-2270BC is unknown, we do know that he married Iuput, the daughter of Unas, to legitimize his reign. During Teti's twelve year reign high officials were beginning to build funerary monuments that rivaled that of the Pharaoh. For example, his powerful chancellor and scribe, Meruruka, married his daughter and built a

magnificent mastaba tomb for himself (right) wife and son, directly beside the king's pyramid. The huge mastaba tomb consisted of thirty two rooms, all covered with beautifully created, richly colored reliefs. It is considered to be perhaps the finest ever built. Kagemni, another high official, built a second fine mastaba tomb close by which was decorated by the same artist. These are considered as potent signs that wealth was being transferred from the king to senior government officials and local Nomarchs. This was the beginning of a slow process that would two

hundred years later culminate in the end of the Old Kingdom. In a power struggle between the royal family and senior members of the court, Teti was murdered by Hezi, the vizier for the Delta region, who then became king changing his name to **Userkare**. He ruled for only five years before the son of Teti, called Pepi, managed to recover the throne and dispose of Userkare.

The forty six year reign of **Pepi I** c2265-2219BC at last ushered in a period of stability and economic prosperity along with major military expansion. His father's minor court official Uni (Wny) quickly gained favor and power. His tomb at Abydos contained a limestone wall block (Egyptian Museum, Cairo) which gives the longest narrative inscription and the most important historical record from the Old Kingdom. Uni was promoted and called on to raise an army. He commanded an expedition, using Nubian troops, into north Sinai; his tomb inscription recorded five victories over the Bedouin there. General Uni then took an expeditionary force by sea to Gaza, in south Canaan, and marched north east towards Gezer between the coast and the Dead Sea. This was the first known campaign by Egypt into Canaan. Uni recorded it in his tomb and proudly described his victory over the army of the 'sand-dwellers'. General Uni employed innovative military tactics, he levied troops from the Nomes prior to the war and established a core household unit to provide training and cohesion to the disparate Nome militia; he was also the first to incorporate Nubian troops into the Egyptian army.

The expansionist campaigns during the reign of Pepi I marked the largest extent of the Old Kingdom. The wealth from these wars was used for a country wide expansion of temple building at Bubastis, Aswan, Abydos, and Dendera. Pepi I built what was considered to be a particularly impressive pyramid complex, which in time gave its name to the whole of the surrounding area including the nation's capital. Originally called the mansion of the soul of Ptah, hikan ptah, the capital became commonly known as men-nefer short for 'established and beautiful (pyramid complex)'. This was abbreviated to Menfi and led to the Greeks, two thousand years later, naming the Egyptian capital Memphis. Art also blossomed with exceptional sculpture. Two copper statues of Pepi I and his son Merenre I (Egyptian Museum, Cairo) were found at Hierakonpolis; the stautes depict the two royals symbolically 'trampling underfoot' the enemies of Egypt.

**Merenre I** suceeded his father c2219BC for a short seven year reign. He continued the military activity of Egypt. Merenre (right) promoted his father's general Uni to Vizier of Nubia where he was instructed by the king to dig 'five canals' to facilitate trade and army movements. Uni also records that the king ordered him to escort the royal sarcophagus and pyramidion from the black granite quarry at Aswan to the site of Merenre's Saqqara pyramid. Harkhuf, an Aswan noble, was

the successor to Uni when he died. His important Aswan tomb inscriptions describe four (three under Merenre and one under Pepi 2) land based trading expeditions as far south as Yam, modern Khartoum, and beyond. He returned with incense, ebony, panthers and ivory. The king himself was recorded as visiting the second Nile cataract twice.

After the premature death of Merenre I, **Pepi 2** c2212-2118BC came to the throne at six or ten years of age. He has been generally credited with having the longest reign of any monarch in history at 94 years, though this figure has been heavily disputed in favor of a more reasonable, shorter, reign of 64 years. He was once thought to be the son of Pepi I and Queen Ankhesenpepi 2, but based on a recently discovered inscription from her mortuary temple, it is now

believed that Pepi 2 was in fact the son of Merenre I, who married Ankhesenpepi 2 after Pepi I's death. Pepi 2 is therefore the grandson, rather than the son, of Pepi I. Because of his youth, his mother (left) and vizier Zau acted as regents. In regnal year two, vizier of the south and *'caravan conductor'* Harkhuf made a fourth trading expedition south to Yam and delighted the young boy king by bringing him a gift of a dancing pygmy or dwarf. Pepi 2 was so grateful he sent a letter of thanks to Harkhuf, which was copied on his Aswan tomb wall. The letter instructs

Harkhuf to *'Come northward to the court immediately... inspect (the dwarf) ten times a night...'* The Elephantine nobleman and general Pepi Nakht 2 undertook two military campaigns in north Nubia (Wawat). However, there was a military set back when admiral Enenkhet and a troop of soldiers were killed on the Red Sea coast by 'sand dwellers' (Bedouin) whilst building ships for an expedition to Punt. Pepi Nakht 2 was sent to recover his body. The governor of Aswan was Sabni, he reported another set back in his Aswan tomb inscription. He recorded that his father, Mekhu, was killed during a Nubian campaign and Sabni had to lead an expedition to retrieve his body for embalment. Sabni's Aswan inscription also hints at the construction of barges to transport two granite obelisks north to celebrate the jubilee of the king.

Although from the royal inscriptions it would appear that all was well in the kingdom, in reality the closing years of the reign of Pepi 2 marked a sharp decline in the Old Kingdom. There were many distressing early warning signs, ten viziers and senior advisors were punished for corruption and there were reports of drought and of Nomarchs abusing their power. It is thought that the extraordinarily long reign of Pepi 2 itself may have been a significant contributing factor to the general breakdown of centralized royal rule.

His son and successor **Merenre 2** c2118BC appears only to have reigned for one year. He may himself have been very old when he ascended the throne of Egypt. There were constant reports of famine, severe tax increases and even canal maintenance failures; central authority was demonstrably collapsing. This situation almost certainly produced a succession crisis and also led to a stagnation of the administration. Here can be seen the weakness of a regime centered on an absolute ruler. Pepi 2 survived into extreme old age, and was probably physically and mentally extremely frail, but he could not be replaced because of his 'divine' status.

**The end of the Old Kingdom.** While the power of the Nomarchs grew and their positions became hereditary, the power of the king faded and in the absence of strong central government local nobles began raiding each other's territories. The Old Kingdom lost momentum and ground to a close within sixty years of the end of the reign of Merenre 2. In that period thirty named kings occupied the throne, each of a hopelessly short duration. So ended a glorious five hundred year period, the days of a supreme divine ruler were permanently over as was the era of building giant stone pyramids. The future kings of the Middle Kingdom were never to have the same privileged position of absolute god-like power that the rulers of the Old Kingdom had created and enjoyed.

# Chapter Four

# The Invention of Writing

By definition history begins with written records. Evidence of human culture without writing is categorized as the realm of pre-history. The writing process evolved from economic necessity. In the ancient Middle East the earliest civilizations to develop writing were Egypt and Mesopotamia, with both jockeying for position as to which came first. The Egyptian writing system is of particular interest to us as it was the one copied and developed through the ages by different subsequent civilizations into the alphabet we use today.

As we have seen in Chapter 1, sometime around 4500BC the Egyptian farmers, needing to make simple records of stocks and commercial transactions, developed what was to later become the hieroglyphic system of writing. Some of the precursors for hieroglyphics can be seen as decorations on early pottery, which later developed into the Naqada 2 (Gerzean) style pottery in the Fayum. The name hieroglyph comes from the Greek word meaning 'sacred carving'. The Greek visitors correctly observed that most of the early hieroglyphic writing was in tombs or on temple walls and was associated with religious texts honoring the gods.

Dreyer excavating at Abydos (modern Umm el Qa'ab) in the late 1980s excavated tomb U-j of a pre-dynastic noble, and recovered many clay labels inscribed with very early crude hieroglyphs (right) dated to the late Naqada period c3300BC.

Hieroglyphs were cut originally on cylinder seals and rolled onto fresh clay jar stoppers, examples of these cylinder seals have been found in 1st Dynasty tombs. Granite cylinder seals were still in use during the time of Pepi I c1200

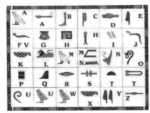

years later but were replaced by scarab seals by the Middle Kingdom. By c3200 BC we see the use of more refined yet simple hieroglyphs (left) to denote names used by the royal family on the Scorpion and Narmer ceremonial mace heads at Hierakonpolis. From around the same time, we have already described the Narmer pallet which uses a series of hieroglyphs and scenes to describe possible historical events, thus it is considered to be the world's first document.

The first full sentence written in hieroglyphs, so far discovered, was found on a seal impression in the tomb of King Seth Peribsen of the 2nd Dynasty at Abydos, which dates from c2700BC. From the Old Kingdom to the New Kingdom about 800 hieroglyphs were in use, however, by the Ptolemaic/ Roman period, they exceeded 5,000. Hieroglyphs consist of three kinds, phonetic glyphs, which functioned like the letters of an alphabet, others which indicate pronunciation while still others narrow down the context

and therefore the sense of a word. The original hieroglyphics were extremely labor intensive and both costly and slow to write. As writing developed and became more widespread in Egypt, from the 1st Dynasty onwards, the need for a simplified version grew. We refer to this shorthand version as hieratic, meaning 'priestly'. The New Kingdom papyrus of Ani's Book of the Dead was written in hieratic (left) and it can be seen that there are many characters which still clearly resemble the original hieroglyphs. However, the written form became even more abbreviated, and much later, by around 650BC, a final shorthand version was in common use. This is referred to as demotic

meaning 'popular'; an example can be seen in this extract from the Rosetta stone (right) c196BC. Apart from the advantage of the speed of writing, these shorthand versions were also more suited than hieroglyphs for use on papyrus. A shorthand script was essential to efficiently handle the growing administration demands of

managing the complex government as a result of the territorial expansion from the Middle Kingdom onwards. Hieroglyphic writing was not, however, completely replaced by these shorthand successors but existed alongside them especially in religious, royal and other formal texts.

Hieroglyphs continued to be used under Persian rule and after Alexander's conquest. During the ensuing Ptolomeic and then Roman periods the 'sacred carving' began to gain a reputation by non Egyptian authors as a magical system transmitting secret, mystical knowledge, consequently it began its decline into oblivion. The Rosetta Stone contains parallel texts in hieroglyphic, demotic and Greek which by this time had become the language of government in the eastern Mediteranean. By c300AD apart from the priests, few Egyptians were now capable of reading hieroglyphs. The 'writing was on the wall' for hieroglyphics when Constantine prohibited persecution of Christianity across the Roman Empire in 313AD, paganism was now on the retreat. The last nails in the coffin followed swiftly. Hieroglyphic pagan writing became outlawed after Christianity became the official religion of the Roman Empire as decreed by Emperor Theodosius the Great in 380AD. Pagan temples and worship were subsequently banned in 391AD and the process of closing the temples commenced. Finally Emperor Justinian 527-565AD introduced his sweeping legal and religious reforms and commenced the *'zealous destruction of paganism'* in 529AD. The remnants of the Isis temple at Philae, being so far from the Roman capital in Alexandria, survived the longest. However it too was eventually closed in 545AD and was converted into a Coptic Christian church. Ironically it was not the last Isis temple to close, one in Roman Britain outlasted Philae by a few more years.

**A message to the future.** The last known inscription in hieroglyphics is from the temple of Isis at Philae. It is referred to as the Graffito of Esmet-Akhom, dated precisely to August 24th 394AD three years after the language

was outlawed in the decree of Theodosius. The text is located by the western gate of Hadrian and was written by Esmet-Akhom, one of the last documented priests at the temple. He wrote in poorly formed hand scatched hieroglyphics (left) on the birthday of Osiris, 'year 110' after the Roman Emperor Diocletion 284-305AD. *'Before Merul son of Horus, by the hand ...of ...*

*Esmet-Akhom....son of Esmet, second prophet of Isis, forever and ever....'* Under this, the last hierogphic inscription, he ends his message to the future using the more common, at that time, demotic script writing. *'I performed work on this figure of (the god) Mandulis for everlasting, because he is kindly of face... unto me'.*

**The early attempts at decipherment.** There is circumstantial evidence that living in Egypt around 450BC was a linguistic scholar who called himself Horapollo. His was a curiously contrived name, made up of a combination of the Egyptian god Horus and the Greek god Apollo. To him is ascribed the 'Hieroglyphica' originally said to have been written in Egyptian but translated into Greek by a later writer Phillippus. The work is in two volumes and suspiciously they first turned up only in 1422AD and are now in the Laurenziana Library, Florence. At best, volume one was a genuine attempt to record the meaning of parts of the lost language but in fact was a completely false explanation of 189 true hieroglyphs. However it possessed such an aura of authenticity and attracted such popular interest, that a printed version was produced in 1505AD. Unfortunately, it became a long term constraint to the true decipherment of Egyptian writing. It also heavily influenced Renaissance symbolism and thinking, and to some it strengthened the belief in Egyptian occultism which grew in the late seventeen hundreds and is still in existence today. The first known attempts at the proper deciphering of Egyptian hieroglyphs were made by medieval ninth and tenth century Arab historians dwelling in the two main centers of learning at that time, Baghdad and Alexandria. By then, hieroglyphs had long been forgotten in Egypt, and were replaced by the Arabic and Coptic alphabets. These medieval historians were able to decipher hieroglyphic writing partly by making use of the related contemporary language still being used by the Coptic priests. The word Copt is a derivation via Latin and Arabic, of the Greek Aigyptos for Egypt (kmt). The Egyptian Coptic Christian faith was reputed to have been established by St Mark in Alexandria in 42AD and continues to thrive in Egypt and to a lesser extent elsewhere in the world today. Copts make up a sizeable, approximately ten to fifteen percent, minority of the eighty three million population of Egypt today. The modern town of Aswan not far from the Temple of Philae, boasts a particularly fine Orthodox Coptic church.

With the Turkish conquest of Egypt in 1517AD, the country became more accessible to 'Franks', the Crusader era name given to any European. This travel relaxation made it less dangerous for monks and priests to visit their brothers in the Coptic community and this then opened the door to allow various western scholars to visit Egypt. In his book 'Hieroglyphica' published in the 1560sAD, the Dutch physician and linguist Becanus made a poor attempt at hieroglyphic decipherment. However, more and more texts were being discovered in Egypt by collectors of Coptic manuscripts, in 1636AD Della Valle brought back many Coptic texts which Kircher used in 1644AD to prove correctly that Coptic and Hieroglyphic writing were very strongly related. However, progress from there was exceedingly slow for the next hundred years. The next significant advances were made first by Batholomey, who in 1761AD correctly proposed that the letters inside a cartouche (Egyptian shenu) was a royal name, followed by Zoega, in 1795, who accurately deduced that hieroglyphics had a phonetic component. The word cartouche is a relatively modern term it comes from the French word for a gun cartridge, which it resembles. However, the real breakthrough which was to provide the key to decipherment was to come four years later, in July 1799, when, by accident some French soldiers building fortifications near the Delta town of al Rashid (Rosetta) unearthed the lower half of a broken stone stele containing a trilingual text.

**The Rosetta Stone** erected in 196 BC, is a Ptolemaic period stele with a carved text comprised of three translations of a single passage, one in hieroglyphic, one in the later shorthand demotic and one in ancient Greek. It is one of only three trilingual royal decrees that have survived from the Ptolemaic period. The earliest is the Decree of Canopus by Ptolemy 3 in 239BC, which includes the inauguraton of a festival in honor of the deceased princess Berenice and it is particularly important as it contains the most number of different hieroglyphs. This was followed by the Decree of Memphis by Ptolemy 4, in 216BC, and finally the Rosetta Stone, dated 27 March 196BC which is also a Memphis decree, from the ninth regnal year of Ptolemy 5. It was common practice for copies of these decrees to be erected in the top ranked temple courtyards however only a few have survived, fortunately two versions of each of these three important ones have done so.

Following Britain's victory over Napoleon in Egypt in 1801, Hamilton was sent out to recover the Rosetta stone and other antiquities. It was dispatched

to London in 1802, however French
scholars were permitted to keep
imprints and plaster casts; its secrets
were to emerge stepwise over the next
thirty years. On March 11, it was
presented to the Society of Antiquaries
of London. Later it was taken to
the British Museum (right) where it

remains. In 1808, Hamilton published a translation of the Greek text. In
1814 the British scientist, Young, finished translating the demotic text, and
began work on the hieroglyphic script. He made the next breakthrough by
realizing that hieroglyphics were both letters and phonetic. The penultimate
step came in 1815 when the British Egyptologist and outstandingly accurate
copyist Bankes, discovered a fallen obelisk at Philae, containing a bilingual
text, the hieroglyphic portion was inscribed on the obelisk itself and the Greek
text was written on the pedestal. The Greek translation demonstrated that it
was erected at the request of Ptolemy 9 and his wife Cleopatra 4, in 112BC;
the text is a petition from the Isis priests at Philae.

The next year Bankes sent copies of the Philae obelisk texts to Young
hoping it would help him with the hieroglyphic portion of the Rosetta stone
decipherment. Young made progress and in 1819 he published an early but
only partly accurate demotic vocabulary. Although he still could not complete
the full decipherment of hieroglyphics, he continued to share his thoughts
with other researchers including Champollion. Finally, in 1823, he drew
together all of his work and published what he knew of the decipherment of
hieroglyphics. He then moved on to pastures new. He was a brilliant scientist
and is best remembered in scientific circles for his pioneering work on the wave
theory of light, elasticity and surface tension. He died in 1829, three years
before rival Champollion.

Meanwhile, from 1821 to 1824, the gifted French
scholar and Orientalist, Champollion, greatly
expanded on Young's work. Champollion could
read both Greek and Coptic (left) and he worked
backwards from the Coptic to trace the demotic
signs and then further back to the hieroglyphic signs
themselves. He was able to decipher accurately some
hieroglyphs but had to make guesses at others. He
made his famous quote: *'It is a complex system, writing figurative, symbolic, and phonetic
all at once, in the same text, the same phrase, I would almost say in the same word.'*

By the end of 1821 the Rosetta Stone had provided him with 1,419 hieroglyphics
from 486 Greek words. The next year the Bankes obelisk texts sent by Young,
gave him the Cleopatra and Ptolemy translation. First, he identified the
cartouche for Cleopatra in Greek (Kleopatra) and from its position in the text

found the equivalent cartouche, containing Cleopatra's name in hieroglyphs.

Then by comparing these with the Greek and hieroglyphic cartouches for Ptolemy (Ptolmys), he was able to identify the common hieroglyphs for the letters p, l and o, then by process of elimination the others. One of the pages from his manuscript (left) shows a famous example of this deductive work from an Abydos papyrus. This gave him the confidence to publish in 1822 this milestone letter (below) to Dacier of the French Academy of Inscriptions setting the framework for the future. Sadly Champollion was unwilling to share the credit with either Young or Bankes even though initially he had not recognized that hieroglyphics were phonetic. It took hard work by many experts over the next thirty years before enough hieroglyphs were known and an accurate translation of the Egyptian texts could be made. In 1858, the Philomathean Society of the University of Pennsylvania published the first complete English translation of the Rosetta Stone. The final footnote came from Lepsius in 1866. During his second expedition to Egypt, he had discovered the 'Canopus Stone' stele at Tanis in the east Delta and was able to use its decree text to double check and confirm the Rosetta Stone decipherment using Champollion's system.

The **Rosetta Stone** text is a typically verbose Ptolemaic Decree. It first lists the king's numerous titles and extensive pedigree; the body of the text then lists his specific decrees. He reminds his subjects that he has remitted (cancelled) personal and temple debts owed to the crown, he has provided an amnesty for long term prisoners, he has allowed temples to continue to receive income from their estates, he has reduced the tax on becoming a priest, he has cancelled the need for priests to travel to Alexandria annually and he has prohibited the unpopular naval practice of impressment. This is followed by a list of his past good works for the kingdom including securing the borders, providing an army and navy and making gifts to the temples. Finally the king decrees a new national five day temple festival and concludes with the instruction: *'This decree shall be inscribed on hard stone in sacred (hieroglyphic) and native (demotic) and Greek characters and set up in each of the first, second and third ranked temples beside the image of the ever living king.'*

**How hieroglyphs formed our language today.** Hieroglyphs survive today indirectly, as the inspiration for the original alphabet that was the foundation of the Indo European family of languages, of which English is a member. The Indo-European languages comprise a family of several hundred related languages and dialects, including most of the major languages of Europe, the Iranian plateau, much of North Asia and the Indian subcontinent. Geographically the language group extends from the extreme north west of Europe to Bangladesh in the east. The Indo part of Indo-European refers to the Indian subcontinent. The Indo-European language group has the largest numbers of speakers in the world today. It is spoken by approximately three billion people, shown in the world map in black below. Because of the importance and influence of the Egyptian Empire, hieroglyphic writing was known to many of the civilizations in the ancient Middle East, particularly from the New Kingdom onwards. Examples of stele texts written by Thutmosis I c1500BC have been found as far north as Carchemish (Edessa) on the Turkey-Syrian border at the head of the Euphrates River. However, the area most continually influenced was the coastal strip from Gaza north up to Byblos over which Egypt had established sovereignty from Thutmosis I onwards.

Around 1300BC a new wave of Indo-European migrations swept south into Greece and east into Turkey. Mycenae and Troy were overwhelmed around 1260BC by this seemingly unstoppable huge migration of peoples and by around 1210BC they had brought the superpower of the Hittite Empire to the edge of famine and subsequent military collapse. These 'northerners' then began spreading further south down the Mediterranean coast and via the Greek islands into North Africa. The two mass movements led them into direct conflict with Egypt for the first time.

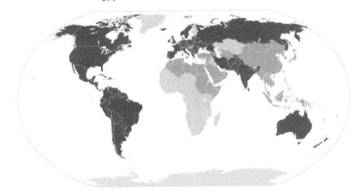

The Libyans, supported by the 'people of the north' invaded the western delta but a major victory in 1207BC over the invaders was recorded by the Egyptian king Merenptah, the son of Ramesses 2. The annals of Merenptah record emergency shipments of relief grain to support the remnants of Egypt's old enemy the Hittites in their losing battle against the migrant tidal wave. It was not to be enough and the Hittite Empire already on its knees, fell to the weight of migrating peoples and then disappeared after five hundred years of dominance in Anatolia. It was to remain lost until 1880AD, when Sayce was able to translate a bi-lingual silver disc seal in Istanbul, written in Akkadian cuneiform and in Hittite. Twenty-six years later, Winkler discovered the Hittite Royal Library containing ten thousand tablets which were eventually translated by 1915.

The eastern Mediterranean was in turmoil; however, Egypt had a respite for fifteen years before trouble again broke out. This time it threatened the very existence of Egypt, as the migrant wave approached its borders from both the northeast and the west. The last major Egyptian king, Ramesses 3, won successive victories on land and at sea in 1180BC which were duly recorded in his surviving fortified temple complex, Medinet Habu opposite Thebes. The magnificent scenes on the inside of the temple walls show gruesome details of the king counting the hands of the dead, as well as unique historically significant battle scenes which allow us to identify some of the main tribal components of this wave of new comers. One large group of well established tribes called themselves the Peleset (Palusata). They are easily identified by their tall feathered war caps. The dominant victory by Rameses 3 forced the Peleset to look elsewhere in the south eastern Mediterranean for a homeland. Ramesses 3 later claimed, in the Harris papyrus, that he allowed them to settle north of the eastern frontier with Egypt. They subsequently occupied, or were settled by Egypt, in the 'five cities' of Gaza, Ashkélon, Ashdod, Ekron, and Gath, along the coastal strip of southwestern Canaan, which had been vassals of Egypt in the past. The Peleset in time became known as the Philistines and absorbed the Canaanite culture. The land was later to be named after them. It was to be called Philstia and was to become ultimately known as Palestine.

The Old Testament stories of Samson, Samuel, Saul and David describe extensive accounts of Philistine conflicts. The Philistines long held a monopoly on iron working, a skill they probably acquired during their conquests in Anatolia, and the biblical description of Goliath's armor is consistent with this iron technology. A branch of the Philistines migrated north along the coast and integrated with the inhabitants of Tyre and Sidon bringing with them their sea faring skills. These two ports in time became the core of the great sea trading civilization of Phoenicia. Based out of their fortress ports, the Phoenicians set up maritime trading colonies throughout the Mediterranean most notably Carthage in modern Tunisia and others on the East coast of Spain.

The Peleset/Philistines did not posses a writing system of their own and borrowed very heavily from Egyptian hieroglyphics. The Phoenician writing system was adapted from this Philistine/Caananite script around 1100BC. Their writing system comprised an alphabet which like hieroglyphics consisted only of consonants. Discovered in Malta in 1694AD was a text inscribed in two languages, Ancient Greek and Carthaginian/Phoenician. This made it possible for French scholar Abbe Barthelemy, in 1760AD, to decipher and reconstruct the Carthaginian alphabet, which was found to contain twenty four letters, very close to our own twenty six letters but lacking any vowels. The earliest known inscription in Phoenician comes from Byblos (Lebanon) c1000BC, many Phoenician inscriptions have been found in Lebanon, Syria, Israel, Cyprus, Sardinia, Sicily, Tunisia, Morocco, Algeria, and Malta.

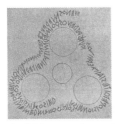

From c800BC the expanding ancient Greek city states began to trade and interact with the ubiquitous sea faring Phoenicians and lacking an alphabet themselves, yet needing writing, adapted the Phoenician alphabet using certain consonants to represent their vowels. Descendants from the Greek alphabet include the Russian Cyrillic alphabet. Greek was also adapted into the Aramaic script, from which the Hebrew script and also that of Arabic are descended. An early Cumae Greek alphabet, named after the influential Greek colony Cumae in southern Italy, gave rise to the Etruscan alphabet of central Italy.

In turn this was adopted by the early Italian peoples, the Latins, around 650BC which was later to be adopted by the Romans as the Latin language. The earliest recorded Latin text is the Duenos Inscription dated to around 525BC and found in Rome by Dressel in 1880AD. It starts with: *'The person who sends you to me prays to the gods…..'* and was written on three joined pots (above), it is now in the Berlin Museum.

So now the story of writing is almost complete, we have seen how Egyptian hieroglyphics led to Philistine then Phoenician then Greek then Latin, The Latin alphabet, also called the Roman alphabet, is the most widely used alphabetic writing system in the world today. During the Middle Ages, it was adapted to the Romance languages Italian, French and Spanish, which became the direct descendants of Latin. Latin also evolved into Celtic, German, English, Baltic, and some Slavic languages, and so to most of the languages of Europe. With the age of exploration and later colonialism, the Latin alphabet was spread overseas, and was adopted by the indigenous peoples of the Americas, Australia, East Asia, and Africa. To illustrate the transition process, below are a few examples of the development from Hieroglyphics to Phoenician to Greek to Latin/English.

| Hieroglyph | Egyptian | Phoenician | Greek | Latin/English |
|---|---|---|---|---|
| Ox | 'ALP( IH) | ALEPH | ALPHA | A |
| House | BAYT (PR) | BETH | BETA | B |
| Water | MU (NT) | MEM | MU | M |
| Eye | 'AYN(IR) | AYIN | OU | O |
| Mouth | PU (R,R') | PE | PI | P |
| Sun | RE | SIN | SIGMA | S |

To conclude, it can be said that Egyptian hieroglyphics survive today in two forms. One is through a hand full of demotic glyphs which have been incorporated into the living Coptic alphabet. The other is as the precursor for the Phoenician alphabet which evolved into our present Indo-European English writing.

# Chapter Five

# The Inventors of Medicine and Cosmetics

In very ancient times, anatomical knowledge was extremely limited and there were few surgical or other cures. Physicians relied on developing good relationships with patients and dealt with minor ailments. They could only sooth chronic conditions and could do little about epidemic diseases such as the bubonic plague, which grew out of urbanization and the domestication of animals. Until the middle of the nineteenth century AD it was commonly believed that medical information was first created by the ancient Greeks, but the discovery of four remarkable Egyptian medical papyri began to change that thinking.

 The Greek physician Hippocrates of Kos, lived between 460BC and 370BC and used to be regarded as the father of modern medicine. He and his followers were considered to be the first to describe many diseases and medical conditions. His 'Corpus' (left) is a collection of around seventy early medical works from ancient Greece. He is given credit for the first description of lung disease, lung cancer and heart disease. Hippocrates began to categorize illnesses as acute, chronic, endemic and epidemic, and use terms such as, exacerbation, relapse, resolution, crisis, and convalescence. His teachings remain relevant to present day students of medicine and surgery. Hippocrates was the first documented chest surgeon and his findings are still valid. However, Herodotus had visited Egypt c450BC around the time that Hippocrates was born. As we have seen in his 'Histories', Herodotus extensively recorded Egyptian medical practice particularly mummification. In Book 2.84 he remarked at the number of Egyptian physicians '...each physician is a physician of one disease.....the whole country is full of physicians...' So we know that the Greeks had already been aware of and most probably were influenced by, the medical expertise of the Egyptian physicians. Even earlier, the Greek poet Homer writing c750 BC remarked in Book 17 of the Odyssey '..in Egypt, the men are more skilled in medicine than any of human kind....the Egyptians were skilled in medicine more than any other art"

Earlier still were the Amarna Letters which were written between 1350 and 1330BC nine hundred years before Hippocrates. They are the royal correspondence written to the Egyptian kings Amenhotep 3, Akhenaten and Tutankamen by their neighbours the kings of the regional superpowers Assyria, Babylon, the Hittites and the Mittani. The subjects of these royal letters are, as would be expected, mostly concerned with military and political matters, but two other themes emerge. The regional superpowers desired above all two scarce Egyptian resources, gold and medical knowledge. Egypt was held in particular high medical esteem by the whole of the Middle East at this time specifically in the field of childbirth.

**The first known physicians and hospitals.** Records of healing by physicians were becoming common in Ancient Egypt from around 3300BC onwards. Egyptian medicine was relatively highly advanced and included, simple non-invasive surgery, setting of bones and an extensive array of medicines. While ancient Egyptian remedies are quite often wrongly characterized in modern culture by dubious ingredients, research shows they were often very effective. Two thirds of all the known ingredients used in medical formulae complied with the 1973 British Pharmaceutical Codex. Seventy percent are in use today, according to a 2007 report from the University of Manchester, England. Ancient Egyptian medical texts describe the specific steps of examination, diagnosis, prognosis and treatments that were more often rational and appropriate. From the mid 1800s onwards, the translation of the Rosetta stone texts finally allowed the accurate translation of ancient Egyptian hieroglyphic

inscriptions and papyri, including many related to medical matters. The earliest known physician is credited to ancient Egypt. Hesyre (left) was the 'Chief of Dentists and Physicians' for king Djoser c2570BC. Sekhet nankh was recorded as the 'nose doctor' to king Sahure c2380BC. The earliest known woman physician, Peseshet, practiced in ancient Egypt c2450BC in the time of the 4th dynasty. Her title was 'Lady Overseer of the Lady Physicians'. Peseshet graduated midwives at an ancient Egyptian medical school at Sais in the Delta. 'The House of Life', (Egyptian per ankh) was ostensibily an institution that served as a center of knowledge and learning. It's heart was a scriptorium, a depository for texts akin to a library. Within the House of Life were medical hospital institutions, an example of which has been discovered at Abydos, it was established there as early as the 1st Dynasty. There are four notable ancient Egyptian medical papyri which have enlightened the world; they are the Edwin Smith Papyrus the Ebers Papyrus, the Hearst Papyrus, and the Kahun Gynaecological Papyrus some of their contents originate as far back as 3000 BC.

**I. The Edwin Smith Surgical Papyrus** c1600BC. Edwin Smith was an American lawyer who moved to Luxor in 1859 to study hieratic papyrus texts. He bought two ancient papyri, later to be named the Edwin Smith Papyrus and the Ebers Papyrus, from a Luxor dealer named Mustapha Aga in 1862. The exact source of the two manuscripts is not precisely known but they originated in the immense Theban necropolis on the west bank of the Nile opposite Luxor. Although he recognized the importance of the Edwin Smith Papyrus manuscript and attempted to translate it, he never published it. He

died in 1906, leaving the papyrus to his daughter who donated it to the New York Historical Society. Pages six and seven are shown on the left. In 1920, the Society asked Breasted to translate it, a task he completed after ten years of work. It was to completely change the understanding of the history of medicine, demonstrating that the Egyptian medical care of injuries was based on observable anatomy and experience; in stark contrast with the often magical way of healing described in some other Egyptian medical sources, such as parts of the Ebers Papyrus below. In 1938 the Smith Papyrus was sent to the Brooklyn Museum, and in 1948 it was transferred to the New York Academy of Medicine where it remains.

The Edwin Smith Surgical Papyrus is the only surviving copy of part of an Ancient Egyptian textbook on trauma surgery. It is among the world's earliest surviving examples of medical literature. It was written in hieratic c1600BC but is based on material from a thousand years earlier. This brief document consists of a list of forty-eight trauma injury cases, with a description of the physical examination, treatment and prognosis of each. The surgical procedures in the papyrus were scientifically based although it does describe magical incantations against the plague for which there were no known treatments at the time. The text begins by addressing injuries to the head, and continues with treatments for injuries to the neck, arms and torso. Among the treatments are closing wounds with sutures for wounds of the lip, throat, and shoulder, preventing and curing infection with honey (see below) and moldy bread, and stopping bleeding with raw meat.

Immobilization was often advised for head and spinal cord injuries, which is still in practice today for the short-term treatment of these injuries. The papyrus also describes anatomical observations in minute detail. It contains the first known descriptions of the skull and brain.It specifically describes the meninges, the external surface of the brain and its fluid, and the intracranial pulsations. The papyrus shows that the heart, vessels, liver, spleen, kidneys, and bladder were recognized, and that the blood vessels were known to be connected to the heart. Physicians understood that the pulse was the 'speaker of the heart' and they were able to interpret the condition we know as angina. However, the actual functions of organs and vessels remained a complete mystery to them.

**Imhotep,** King Djoser's chief architect c2550BC and medical adviser in the 3rd Dynasty, is credited with being the founder of Egyptian medical knowledge and was also thought to be the original author of the Edwin Smith Paprus text but more recent evidence suggests that the papyrus was a compilation which had been written and edited by at least three different authors. The earliest known surgery was performed in Egypt around 2750BC during the 2nd Dynasty; this information comes from the images that often adorn the walls of Ancient Egyptian tombs and the translation of the accompanying inscriptions. The Saqqara tomb door jamb of Ankh mahor of the 6th Dynasty c2300BC has, for instance, the world's first documented rendering in art form of a ceremonial circumcision. It was carried out by priests using a flint tool.

**2. The Ebers medical papyrus** c1550BC (right) is among the two most important medical papyri of ancient Egypt, it is dated to just before the start of the New Kingdom. It, along with the Edwin Smith Papyrus, is one of the two oldest preserved medical documents. George Ebers was a German Egyptologist and writer of romantic fiction. He purchased the Ebers Papyrus from Edwin Smith in 1872 and published a copy along with an introduction in 1875 but it was not translated until 1890. Ebers retired from his chair of Egyptology at the University of Leipzig where the papyrus can be found today in the University library. The

Ebers Papyrus is written in hieratic and provides the largest record of ancient Egyptian medicines. The one hundred and ten page scroll contains some seven hundred medical formulas and remedies. Admittedly it also contains many spells meant to cure illness and protect the patient from disease-causing spirits. Despite this, there is evidence of a long tradition of empirical practice and observation. The papyrus contains a 'Treatise on the heart' and observes that the heart is the center of the blood supply with vessels attached to every part of the body. The author seems to have known little about the kidneys and erroneously believed the heart was the common link to a number of vessels which carried all the fluids, blood, tears, urine and sperm. Because the ancient Egyptians believed the heart acted as the brain, mental disorders are therefore listed under the 'Treatise on the heart' which describes disorders such as depression and dementia. There are also chapters on contraception, diagnosis of pregnancy, intestinal illness, parasites, eye and skin problems and dental matters. It goes on to describe surgical treatment of abscesses and tumors, bone-setting and burns. The treatment for asthma prescribes *'a mixture of herbs to be heated on a brick so that the patient could inhale their fumes'*. Regarding the treatment of cancerous tumors or as the physicians called it 'a tumor against the god Xenus' it recommends 'do thou nothing there against' implying there was no known cure.

**Honey.** The Ebers Papyrus proposal for the treatment of burns is truly remarkable, it recommends *'to apply much honey to the burn and then to wrap it soundly'*. Modern science has discovered that honey is acidic and these acids prevent the growth of bacteria. When honey is applied as a wound dressing it combines with a natural enzyme to form hydrogen peroxide, a commonly used antiseptic today. The naturally occurring hydrogen peroxide won't harm the tissue and no scarring occurs. A recent comparison between a modern artificial antiseptic and honey to treat the same burn gave outstandingly good results for honey.

**Willow bark.** The use of willow bark dates back to the time of ancient Egypt when patients were advised to chew on willow bark to reduce headaches, fever and inflammation. Willow bark continues to be used today for the treatment of pain, particularly low back pain, osteoarthritis, headaches, and inflammatory conditions such as tendinitis. The bark of white willow contains salicin, which is a chemical similar to aspirin (acetylsalicylic acid) and is thought to be responsible for the pain-relieving and anti-inflammatory effects. In the late 1800s, salicin was used to develop aspirin; white willow appears to be slower than aspirin to achieve pain relief but its effects last longer.

**3. The Hearst medical papyrus** was named after the mother of press magnate William Randolph Hearst, who sponsored Resiner and the University of California's work in Egypt in the early 1900s. According to Reisner, the Papyrus was a gift from a local farmer in 1901 to the Hearst Expedition camp which was working in the Theban necropolis. The papyrus was published in 1905 and has been dated to the 18th Dynasty during the reign of king Tuthmosis 3 c1450BC. The text however is thought to be much older and dates back to the Middle Kingdom, c2000 BC. It is kept in the University of California, Berkeley. The Hearst Papyrus records treatment for headaches, digestive problems, tooth decay, urinary problems, lung ailments and even bites from a hippopotamus. However like the Ebers Papyrus the Hearst Papyrus included a section on magic spells that should be performed on the patient throughout the treatment. It comprises two hundred and sixty paragraphs in eighteen columns of medical prescriptions written in hieratic. However some practices were ineffective or even harmful, it is estimated that three quarters of the medical prescriptions in the Hearst Papyrus had no known curative effect. Some even contained animal waste, products of fermentation, moulds and bacteria posing a potential threat to the patient. It is considered an important medical manuscript, but some doubts still exist about its authenticity.

**4. The Kahun Gynaecological Papyrus** c1825BC was found by Petrie in 1889 at the Middle Kingdom pyramid town of Kahun in the Fayum. It is only three pages long and is a fragment of a bigger work. The text is divided into thirty four sections, each dealing with a specific medical problem. It contains diagnoses and treatment, however, no prognosis is suggested. On the first page were instructions beginning with the words *'Remedy for a woman who suffers from. . .'* Treatments were non surgical, focusing on medicine applications. The womb was considered to be the source of many complaints which manifest themselves in other body parts. The Papyrus specifically treats women's complaints, including problems with conception and is the oldest surviving medical text of any kind ever discovered. Egyptian physicians commonly described hemorrhages, menstrual irregularities, tumors, inflammation of abdominal organs and the breasts and displacement of the womb *'it must be made to go back to it's place'*. In this branch of medicine there were no lack of spells, superstitions and ineffective prescriptions. There were also major anatomical misconceptions such as the belief that the womb was open at the top. A popular prescription *'to prevent conception'* was to take *'Acacia spikes (shown on the wall of the Middle Kingdom tomb of Khnum hotep at Beni Hassan) ground fine with dates and honey, rubbed on a wad of fibers and inserted deeply'*. It has been discovered that acacia spikes contain a gum which forms lactic acid when in contact with fluids. Stone in 1936 demonstrated that lactic acid preparations do have some spermicidal effect, and commercial lactic acid-based contraceptive jellies are available today. The Kahun papyrus describes a pregnancy test *'you must put wheat and barley in a cloth bag. The woman is to urinate on it daily...if both germinate, she will bear. If the wheat germinates ., she will bear a boy. If the barley germinates, she will bear a girl'*. It was only in 1926 that Aschheim and Zondek announced their ground breaking research that female urine can be used to determine the onset of pregnancy based on the secretion of hormones from the pituitary gland. The world was astounded in 1933 when Manger demonstrated that the urine of pregnant women, who later gave birth to boys, actually accelerated the growth of wheat while that of women who later bore girls accelerated the growth of barley.

**Hygiene.** Today it is recognized that many of the medical practices and surgical procedures described in the various ancient Egyptian medical papyri were actually very effective. Interestingly most of the physician's advice for staying healthy was to wash and shave the body, including under the arms, to prevent infections. They also advised patients to look after their diet and avoid foods such as raw fish or other animals considered to be 'unclean'.

**Surgical skills and instruments.** It is ironic that surgical skills in ancient Egypt were perfected primarily for the benefit of the dead. Embalming necessitated the careful removal of organs to ensure preservation of the corpse for the afterlife. Trepanning procedures into the skull to remove pressure were known and were occasionally successful based on skulls which have been discovered showing healing having taken place after the operation. Surgeons had available to them a remarkable array of instruments, evidenced by the fine

relief at the rear of the Ptolemaic temple of Kom Ombo, (right). We have clear evidence that Egyptian physicians used knives, scalpels, retractors, lances, bone saws, suction cups, forceps, tweezers and clamps as they do today. Although they did not have the technology to produce the surgical steel scalpels of modern times, knives with obsidian blades have been found with exceptionally sharp cutting

edges. Unlike surgical steel, obsidian has the advantage of a non corrugated microscopic surface and is still used today to reduce tearing in delicate skin surgery.

We have even discovered delicately crafted prosthetics, such as this leather and
wood toe fitted after an amputation to aid  normal walking. It was found in a nobles tomb dated to the time of Amenhotep 2 c1400BC. The amputation wound of the female owner had completely healed implying that the prosthesis had been in use for some time and was intended to join the owner in the afterlife.

**Tooth decay.** The diet of the Ancient Egyptians included much abrasive material such as windblown sand and small stone particles from grinding flour. The teeth of relatively young Egyptian adults were often in a very poor state. The upper jaw of Seqenenre Taa 2 c1558BC showed his teeth were heavily worn, but otherwise healthy and tartar free. Caries and the wearing away of the enamel caused the loss of teeth at an early age and abscesses were known to have resulted in the premature death of even kings. Mutnodjmed c1328BC, king Horemheb's second wife and sister of Nefertiti, had lost all her teeth by the time that she died in her forties. Djedmaatesankh, a Theban musician who lived c850 BC suffered from thirteen abscesses, extensive dental disease and a huge infected cyst, which probably killed her aged about thirty five. On the other hand farmers appeared to have minimal incidence of caries and often a healthy set of teeth, thanks to the absence of sugar in their diet. The wealthier, whose food was more refined, seem to have suffered more from caries than the poor.

**Medical insurance and sick leave.** By the time of the 19th Dynasty some employees enjoyed such benefits as medical insurance, pensions and even sick leave. Much earlier, in the time of the construction of the Giza pyramids injured workers were offered light duties or even in severe cases a disability pension. The Turin Papyrus stated that *'neither sick nor broken were commanded to lift stones'*. There is even reference to a temple worker who suffered an industrial injury and was able to make a claim against the temple priests for medical treatment costs.

**Antiseptics.** The conditions of life for most ancient Egyptian peasants were unsanitary. They often lived in crowded villages and towns lacking sewer systems and fresh running water; usually their animals lived close by. They burned dried dung in open fires and were plagued by flies and vermin. Not so in the houses of the nobles and royalty. One particular advantage possessed by this wealthier segment of Egyptian society was the import and burning of rare and expensive incense. It was often used for religious purposes, but for those who could afford it, incense was the favored means for fending off foul odors and disease. The burning of incense did have medical justification. One of the main products of combustion was phenol, more commonly called carbolic acid, which is a well known powerful germ killer and one of the most common antiseptics.

## Cosmetics.

When the ancient Greeks visited Egypt they remarked that both women and men wore, what seemed to them, extravagant, amounts of facial cosmetics. This is confirmed in numerous intact colored tomb reliefs and paintings. In fact cosmetics are as old as vanity. In Egypt their use can be traced back almost to the earliest period. The Narmer ceremonial palette c3100BC was used for grinding and mixing cosmetics for application to the cult statues of the temple gods. Cleanliness and personal appearance were highly regarded by the ancient Egyptians. For the priests, cleanliness was strictly prescribed, they had to wash several times a day and had to be clean shaven all over to control parasites such as lice, the eggs of which have been found in the hair of mummies. Water was convenient and plentiful and they had access to simple natural soaps. Deodorants were also popular for both men and women. They were advised to rub pellets of the ground up pods of the carob tree into the skin, or to place little balls of incense where limbs met.

Three ladies of the court of Thutmosis 3 c1450BC were buried with costly cosmetics contained in purpose-made decorated containers; two of these jars still contained a cleansing cream made of oil and lime. There are prescriptions for a type of body scrub mentioned in the medical papyri. A remedy to treat wrinkles consisted of gum of frankincense and wax, fresh moringa oil, and cyprus grass all ground finely and mixed with fermented plant juice. The instructions were to *apply daily*. A simple remedy of gum applied to the face after cleansing had a similar effect. To cover up scars, an ointment was used made from red ochre and kohl, ground and mixed with sycamore juice. An alternative treatment was a bandage of ground carob pods and honey, or an ointment made of frankincense and honey.

Egyptians used a brush doubling as toothpaste, from the salvadora persica tree native to southern Egypt and Nubia. The root has been used for dental care in Egypt since then. To improve their breath the Egyptians chewed herbs, gargled with milk, and chewed frankincense.

**Eye and face make up.** The almond shape of the Egyptian eyes was emphasized by the application of two types of facial make up. Black kohl was extensively used as an eye liner and mascara, and green malachite was used as an eye shadow. Lipstick and blusher were made from ochre. The eye make up Udju was made from the green copper ore malachite, which was extensively mined at Wadi Maghera in the Sinai. Its mines were considered under the spiritual dominion of Hathor, ancient goddess of beauty, joy, love and women. She was known as the 'Lady of Malachite' and nebet mefkat meaning 'Mistress of Turquoise', a Middle Kingdom temple dedicated to her was built nearby and expanded in the New Kingdom. Mesdemet eye make up was made from a dark gray ore of lead (or antimony) called galena (lead sulphide) supplemented by lamp soot. Galena was found at Aswan and on the Red Sea Coast and was mentioned as being among the goods brought back by Hatshepsut's c1470BC expedition to Punt.

Eye make up was kept in lumps and was ground on a palette to a fine powder. The powder was poured into vases from which it was extracted with a moist application stick. The gilt statue of the goddess Selket (right) shows a typical example of its application. Men and children also wore eye make up in this style. Eye make up was also beneficial in curing or preventing eye diseases caused by the ever present wind-blown organisms prevalent in the  dry dusty climate and was useful in repelling flies. The heavy metals, copper and lead used in the eye make up killed bacteria. Over many decades their application would have resulted in negative medical side effects, but since the average lifespan was only thirty to thirty five years, this was not a factor. To cool the eyes a finely ground green mineral, jasper or serpentine, mixed with water was applied to the lids. Alternative preparations were ground carob and fermented honey, or emmer grains steeped in water overnight. An eye wash was prepared from ground celery and hemp.

Red lip gloss made from fat with red ochre or red antimony was applied with a brush or spatula. Surviving tomb paintings illustrate that the application of lip gloss has not fundamentally changed in over three thousand years. Facial rouge consisting of red ochre with resin has been discovered in a tomb c2000BC having survived satisfactorily for four thousand years. Chalk and white lead pigment were used to provide the sought after traditional white skin appearance for women, some Egyptians appear to have dyed their fingernails using henna.

**Cosmetic manufacturing.** An analysis of Egyptian cosmetic powders dating back to as early as 2000BC has revealed a very high level of sophistication in the way they were prepared. It is well known that they were using fire based technology to produce blue pigments for faience before 2500BC. Chemists have recently been able to identify all the main organic and mineral ingredients used in ancient Egyptian makeup powders. The two main mineral ingredients were the naturally occurring ores galena and malachite. However researchers have found laurionite and phosgenite, both of which occur only rarely in nature. Because of their relatively common occurance in cosmetics it has been concluded that Egyptians were capable of artificially synthesizing the compounds as indicated by later Greek historians. The entire process took several weeks of continual purification to complete. The manufacturing of these compounds has revealed a previously unknown level of sophistication of ancient Egyptian chemistry.

**Hair.** The appearance and style of the hair was of supreme importance for visual effect and erotic symbolism. Men and women both wore wigs made of human hair for special occasions, but they also tried to keep their natural hair in good condition. Jars of setting lotion have been found to contain a mixture of beeswax and resin. These were remedies for problems such as baldness and graying hair. For baldness, juniper was said to stimulate the scalp and in order to promote hair growth chopped lettuce was placed on a bald patch if the baldness occurred after an illness. The number of treatments for graying hair was extensive. A common remedy was black ox blood boiled in oil. The black horn of a gazelle made into an oil was said to prevent grey hairs from appearing. Also suggested was an ointment made of juniper berries and certain plants kneaded into a paste with oil and then heated. One of the unpleasant alternatives was putrid donkey's liver steeped in oil. A simpler remedy was the use of natural coloring matter from plants.

The ancient Egyptian equivalent to a wash bag for both men and women would often contain a bronze razor for removing body hair. Alternatively, hair removal creams were used. One particularly strange cream consisted of boiled crushed bird bones mixed with fly dung, oil, sycamore juice, gum, and cucumber. The mixture was heated and applied, then pulled off when cold with the hair adhering to it, similar to today's hot wax method of hair removal.

Cosmetics have been used for as long as there have been people to use them. They were an inherent part of Egyptian vanity, hygiene and health and were as important to the ancient Egyptians as they are to women in today's society.

— Chapter Six —

# The Middle Kingdom – Expansion into Nubia

We have seen in Chapter 3 that at the end of the Old Kingdom c2000BC, central government had collapsed and Egypt entered into a period of approximately one-hundred years where a number of separate kingdoms ruled in parallel, known as the **First Intermediate Period.** A new north kingdom, centered on Herakleopolis, had been the first to separate from Memphis although it was located only sixty miles to the south. There are few official records covering this period, just a list of scarcely known kings all called Akh Toy, making up Manetho's 9th and 10th Dynasties. Fictional texts known as the Lamentations from the early period of the subsequent Middle Kingdom shed some light on what was occurring during the First Intermediate period. One notable source is the 'Ipuwer Papyrus' or Papyrus Leiden 344. This text reflects on the breakdown of strong central rule and the incursions of an Asiatic tribe which has *'overun the Delta'*. Society and order in general seems to have degenerated *'trade with abroad is at a standstill'*. There is a reference to unpopular and unfair high taxation even in times of distress when the inundation failed and the waters of the Nile were low. *'Dry is the river of Egypt, and one can cross it by foot'*. It is believed that during these lawless years all of the Old Kingdom pyramids and tombs were thoroughly robbed if they had not already been robbed during the Old Kingdom itself. The texts recount *'those who were entombed are cast on high ground'*. The people despaired thet Re has deserted them, *'where is he today...behold his might is not seen'*.

Around 2160BC, the Herakleopolis kings gained control of Memphis and managed to consolidate the north. At the same time a southern kingdom based at Thebes and nearby Herment emerged known as the 11th Dynasty. The border oscillated between Akhmin and Abydos. Over the next thirty years the war between the two sides raged back and forward. The north managed to bring in Asyut and their notable general Kheti on their side, whereas all the southern nomes supported Mentuhotep, king of Thebes. Particularly important was the strong link between the royal families of Thebes and Koptos which was strategically placed mid-way between Thebes and Abydos. Famine at one time affected both sides so badly that the war had to be suspended.

The Theban king Intef 2 ruled for forty nine years and managed to extend the border north when he succeeded in taking and holding both Abydos, and Thinis, aided by his military commander Djari. The next Theban king, Intef 3, brokered a peace partly because of a second major period of famine in the Abydos war zone.

**The Rise of the Middle Kingdom.** The next Theban ruler was the great king **Mentuhotep 2** (montu is content) c2066-2014BC. He ruled for fifty-two years and finally united the country. For the first part of his reign, the peace of Intef 3 continued, then the north made a tactical blunder and, in his regnal year fourteen, attacked southern controlled Thinis, which provoked the start of an all out war at the end of which Mentuhotep 2 was the undisputed ruler of a united Egypt with it's new royal capital at Thebes. He then took the name Sema tawy, 'the uniter of two lands', although his predecessor, Intef 2, had prematurely claimed this on an earlier inscription. Mentuhotep 2 was held in great respect by subsequent rulers as the second founder of the Egyptian state, after Menes had first united the two lands 1000 years earlier.

Nubia had gained independence at the end of Pepi 2's reign when the Old Kingdom was decaying. An inscription at the Silsila quarry, north of Aswan, confirms that Mentuhotep 2 intended to recover north Nubia, and personally commanded military campaigns there reaching as far as the second Nile cataract. Winlock, in 1920, was excavating near his mortuary temple at Deir el Bahri (above) and excavated a mass grave containing the bodies of sixty soldiers who had reportedly died during a frontal assault on a heavily defended Nubian held fort. All their wounds were from the front and downward. In year thirty he celebrated his

Heb Sed jubilee, this notable statue (right) shows him in his jubilee robes wearing the unified crown, (Egyptian Museum, Cairo). It was found at his mortuary temple just south of that of the later female king Hatshepsut. On the walls of his temple are reliefs which descibe his successful military campaigns leading to the recovery of north Nubia. In year forty-one, an Aswan inscription records that chancellor Khety took the new Nubian fleet north from the 2nd cataract to Aswan, on a show of strength in the region; there may also be evidence for a military

action in Canaan. The king reorganized the country and placed a vizier at the head of a new central civil service. Mentuhotep 2 was succeeded by the third of that name, 2014-2001BC, about whom we know very little apart from the fact that during his thirteen year reign his treasurer, Henu, led a trading expedition to Punt. Mentuhotep 4 c2001-1994BC was the final king of the 11th Dynasty. Although he is omitted from some king lists being a suspected usurper, his reign is confirmed from inscriptions in Wadi Hamamat in the eastern desert that record his expedition to the Red Sea coast and to quarry stone for the royal monuments. The leader of this expedition was his vizier Amenemhet, who is believed to be the future king Amenemhet I. He is assumed to have either usurped the throne or assumed power after Mentuhotep 4 died childless in 1994BC.

**Amenemhet I** (Amen is at the head) 1994-1964BC was the first king (left) of the magnificent 12th Dynasty which provided a succession of seven powerful kings spanning a glorious two hundred year period. This Golden Age saw the flourishing of art, literature, medicine and major territorial expansion in the south. At the start of his thirty year reign he chose not to continue to use Thebes as the capital. Instead, he built a new capital in the north known after the founder as Itj tawy (seizer of two lands), to be able to maintain control of the delta and prevent incursions from the Asiatics, thus keeping the country united and secure. Amenemhet I may have had to put down a revolt in the north when he first came to the throne. There is a surviving relief and inscription which tantalizingly refers to a twenty ship Delta battle having been won. The precise location of the new capital has never been discovered and, as it was built using mud brick, is presumed to have been destroyed. However, from much circumstantial evidence, it is strongly suspected to be El Lisht, twenty miles

south of Memphis. Here he built his pyramid (right) tomb, it was the source of his relief, above. The pyramid core was constructed in brick but given a Giza limestone casing; its height reached 180 feet but when the casing was later robbed the brick core collapsed into the rounded ruin shown. The burial chamber is now submerged under the water table.

Amenemhet I successfully cemented the country together and exerted his authority over the potentially divisive Nome princes (Nomarchs). Since the collape of central power at the end of the Old Kingdom, the Nomarchs had established great power and accumulated huge wealth One of the major Nomes was the Oryx, with it's capital at Beni Hassan where the Nomarch Khnum hotep later built a magnificently decorated rock carved tomb. Concerned over the danger of invasion from the Asiatics, the king commenced the construction of 'The walls of the Prince' (inebw heka), a string of fortresses on the eastern border of the Delta. In regnal year nineteen the king survived an assassination attempt, which led him to make a significant move to underpin his dynasty. In 1974BC Amenemhat I established his son, crown prince Senusret I, as his junior co-regent who ruled with his father for ten more years. This was the first time a co-regency had been created, and it was to start a pattern for the rest of Egypt's history. The co-regency provided enormous stability for the 12th Dynasty, confirmed by its almost two- hundred year unbroken family line of kings.

**Assasination.** The crown prince was given specific responsibility for military campaigns. He raided to Kerma, south of the third cataract deep into south Nubia, the region known as Kush, as well as into the Sinai and into south Canaan. By regnal year twenty nine, Egypt had established firm control of all of north Nubia (Wawat), up to the second Nile cataract. The next year 1964BC, crown prince Senusret was campaigning in Libya when a second assassination attempt on king Amenemhet I was successful, this time at the royal palace. It is most likely to have been orchestrated by a noble and perpetrated by a member of the royal bodyguard. Crown prince Senusret left the Libyan campaign and raced home to Itjtawy to establish his regal authority and prevent a takeover of the government by an opportunistic Nomarch. The strategic value of the co-regency was demonstrated, the new king had acquired useful military and government experience by the time he would start his sole reign and he could ascend to the throne as the clear heir apparent. The assassination, however, came as a severe shock to the country and became the subject of Egypt's finest work of literature, the 'Tale of Sinuhe', discussed later.

**Senusret I** (Man of the godess wosret) 1974–1929BC ruled for forty five years and successfully continued the policy of his father to extend territorial advances into Nubia. To secure the military resources needed to campaign continually, he established the first, albeit small, national militia, the forerunner for the later great standing armies of the New Kingdom. He also seems to have reached an early compromise with the Nomarchs. He allowed the influential Oryx Nomarchy to become hereditary in gratitude for Nomarch Ameni's loyalty and military support in Nubia. In year three, the king began the construction of the Re Atum temple at Heliopolis, also that year he undertook a campaign in Canaan. The major expansion into Nubia only began in year nine. He commenced the construction of a series of what would ultimately become seventeen giant mud brick forts spread along both sides of a one

 hundred miles stretch of the Nile, between the first and second cataracts. The southern boundary was now established at the giant Buhen fort (left) the only one to have been fully excavated. It had brick walls fifteen feet thick and thirty five feet high. This series of seemingly impregnable defensive forts built over the next twenty years was to become the greatest military barrier of the ancient world. It would lay the foundation for permanent control of north Nubia throughout the Middle Kingdom. General Ment Hotep erected a victory stele opposite Buhen at Wadi Halfa to celebrate this territorial expansion. The chain of forts not only allowed the area of north Nubia to be pacified it also established control over the vital trade route from the deep south into Egypt and impaired any attempt by the south Nubian tribes to gain influence in the region. Emery was able to partially excavate the forts before the waters of Lake Nasser submerged them in 1964; he demonstrated that they were

indeed the precursors to the great European medieval castles. Senusret I celebrated his thirty year jubilee in 1944BC with two remarkable pieces of construction. He erected a pair of red granite obelisks, outside his temple at Heliopolis, this one (left) still remains and is the oldest continuously standing obelisk in Egypt. It rises to sixty seven feet and weighs one hundred and twenty tons.

The second construction was a beautiful work of art probably never surpassed in ancient Egypt. It is a white alabaster open bark shrine known as the White Chapel (ipt swwt) decorated with superbly crafted reliefs. All along the base of the outer walls runs a series of reliefs depicting the various Nomes (sepat) with their emblems and individual local deities. On the western side are the ones for south Egypt, on the eastern side the ones for north Egypt. The White Chapel columns (right) show the king being crowned and embraced by the major gods Amen, Horus, Min and Ptah. It was a continuation of his work extending the Amen temple at Karnak and is now on display after being successfully reconstructed from its individual stone blocks discovered by Chevrier in 1926. They had been used as filler for the giant third Karnak pylon of Amenhotep 3 during the New Kingdom. Senusret 1 also remodeled

the Temple of Osiris at Abydos, amongst his other major building projects. In year 35 he appointed his son Amenemhet 2 as co-regent and later led a gold expedition with Nomarch Ameni into Nubia. He built his pyramid just south of his father's at El Lisht, the construction of the core was unique, it consisted of eight radial stone retaining walls each segment was rubble filled. It was then cased but is a ruin today; the burial chamber is below the water table.

**Amenemhet 2** (1932–1896BC) ruled for a substantial, and successful, thirty six year period but strangely few records have survived and consequently little is known of his reign. It appears that he continued to allow the position of some of the Nomarchs to remain hereditary thus weakening the centralized government. He recorded trading expeditions to Lebanon and Punt, and even sent troops on a long range raid into Syria. He is notable for the sixteen colossal statues of himself made for his mortuary temple which was located north of the capital Itjtawy at Dashur just east of Snefru's Old Kingdom red pyramid. His 'White' pyramid was so called because of the immense field of white limestone fragments surrounding it. The pyramid was quite modest in size for the Middle Kingdom; it had a brick core with stone casing but is now totally ruined. Succession seems to have passed smoothly to his son crown prince Senusret.

**Senusret 2** (1900–1880BC) chose to
locate his mortuary temple and black mud
brick pyramid (right) at a new location
south of Dashur called El Lahun. Here he
built a granite funerary temple and complex
of buildings. A marvelous gold and inlaid
royal uraeus was found in 1920. It was part

of Senusret 2's looted burial treasure and was discovered in a flooded chamber
of the king's pyramid tomb and is in the Egyptian Museum, Cairo.

Senusret 2 was the first to start to develop the Faiyum oasis region which
was to greatly expand the agricultural potential of Egypt, with it came an
explosion in population growth. He began work on an extensive irrigation
system; he constructed a massive dike at El Lahun and a network of drainage
canals to conduct and then store the Nile inundation water. The intent was
to significantly increase the amount of farming land. The importance of this
project is emphasized by his decision to build his pyramid and royal necropolis
nearby. El Lahun remained the administrative and political capital for the rest
of the 12th and 13th Dynasties, a period of three hundred years. The first
known worker's town was established in the nearby town of Kahun, where
Petrie discovered the famous Gynaecological Papyrus.

Senusret 2 maintained good relations with the wealthy and extremely influential
Nomarchs His regnal year six is recorded in a wall painting from the tomb
of local Nomarch Khnum hotep 2 at the Oryx Nome capital Beni Hassan.
This rock cut tomb (tomb number three) is of supreme interest to historians
as painted on the wall is the frieze above depicting colorfully robed Asiatic
traders entering Egypt with their entire families, goods and animals. Some
Old Testament scholars believe this is strong evidence supporting the story of
the Hebrew Joseph's descent into Egypt. In any case, this important migration
of Asiatics was a powerful omen that two hundred years later was to tear the
kingdom apart.

**Senusret 3** (1881-1840BC) was the son of Senusret 2 but oddly there was
no co-regency with his father. He was a great leader and reformer and was to
become one of the most notable of all Middle Kingdom monarchs, ruling for
forty one years. He strengthened central power and reformed the government
by dividing the country into three administrative divisions (or warets), Egypt
North, Egypt South and north Nubia (Wawat). Each was administered by
a council (djadjat) who in turn reported to a vizier. This calculated move
achieved its objective; it sufficiently weakened the power of the Nomarchs who

had again begun to challenge the central government. Most of the Middle Kingdom rulers were acutely aware of the threat that strong independent Nomarchs could bring. During his reign concern was growing over Canaan and a campaign there led by Sobekhu was recorded on his tomb stele at Abydos.

However, Senusret 3's main focus was undoubtedly Nubia (right). In year eight, he prepared for his southern military campaigns by improving navigation through the first Nile cataract at Aswan. His ambition was to continue the territorial expansion of his great grandfather, Senusret I, to expand trade and secure gold supply. He was a warrior king, often personally leading his troops deep into Nubia. In year eight he penetrated as far as the second cataract and set up a boundary stele at Semna. He went on to build four new forts at Semna and Kumma to establish Egypt's formal

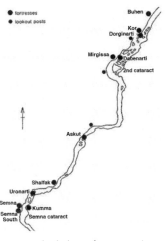

new southern border at this latitiude. In year ten he led another campaign to the second Nile cataract in Nubia building a fort at Wadi Halfa. He marked his third campaign in year sixteen by erecting a border stele (right) at Semna, now in the Berlin museum. The text also makes mention of a second campaign in Canaan that year. By the end of his southern campaign in year nineteen, he had pacified all of northern Nubia as far south as Semna and incorporated the territory into the kingdom. In the second half of his reign he conducted more Asiatic campaigns in Canaan and even into Syria. To protect the

border with Canaan, he strengthened the series of forts along the east of the Delta as well as building temples there. In year twenty, half way through his reign, he appointed crown prince Amenemhet as his co-regent he may even have allowed him to become the senior partner.

His reign is also noted for achieving a peak in naturalist art. His facial expression (left) is meant to demonstrate his concern for his country; he is shown thoughtful with care worn heavy eye lids. This may have been propaganda employed to help implement unpopular reforms, in particular, the suppressing of the autonomy of the Nomes. He built a fine religious temple at Abydos, although now destroyed, the surviving reliefs show the high quality of the decoration. His brick pyramid was erected at Dashur close to that of his grandfather

Amenemhet 2 and the Red Pyramid of the Old Kingdom monarch Snefru. The pyramid temple complex was enormous and was surrounded by a paneled temenos wall similar to that of Djoser. Unusually, its entrance was from the west, in place of the traditional northern entrance, perhaps chosen with a view to making robbery more difficult. Senusret's fame and reputation for bravery, reform and national leadership was so great that he was deified at the end of the Middle Kingdom. Like some of the kings of the 3rd and 4th Dynasties he was later worshipped by the rulers of the New Kingdom.

**Amenemhet 3** (1840–1794BC) had almost a fifty year reign and was the last great king of the Middle Kingdom. Combined with his father's reign, this ninety year period was to be the apex of the Middle Kingdom's Golden Age. He expanded greatly the Fayum irrigation projects of his grandfather, possibly because food shortages were occurring as the population grew. He built a twenty-seven mile wall to retain inundation water for later distribution, and constructed a new 'office' complex just east of the Fayum, to house the expanded centralized government administration now required for efficient management of his expanded kingdom. The new complex was located at Hawara and covered an area 1,000 feet by 800 feet; it was made of mud brick and consequently has now completely disappeared. However, Greeks visiting over a thousand years later, were in awe at its size then. Herodotus c460BC reported that it contained 1,000 rooms and it was given the name the 'Labyrinth', after the legendary Minoan Labyrinth at Knossos. The organizational reforms of his father were consolidated; the three powerful viziers were responsible for their regions and answerable only to the king. He was strong enough to discontinue the hereditary practice where the son succeeded the ruling Nomarch, all Nomarchs were now selected and appointed only by the king. Nubia was at peace and there were no major military campaigns recorded. On the southern border at Semna he built a Nileometer to help gauge the annual inundation and tax. Late in his reign it would appear that the economy began to falter, the annual floods may have begun to weaken, and there was a report of taxes reaching the abnormally high level of twenty percent, six percent was more trypical.

Amenemhet 3 was one of the few kings to build more than a single pyramid.

 He chose Dashur (left) as the site for his first; it was located south of that of his father and due east of Snefru's Bent pyramid. However he made the same mistake as Snefru in choosing a location with unstable subsoil, in this case it was clay, and the structure began to sink as it rose higher. The extensive underground corridors and numerous rooms, along with water seepage into the foundations, caused cracking in the roof of the burial chamber. He persevered, and after fifteen years the 246 feet high pyramid was complete, however he chose to abandon the imperfect tomb as Snefru had done before. Today its cladding is

missing and the 180 feet mud brick core rises dramatically out of the desert escarpment in the form of a lonely 'Black' stump.

For his second pyramid (left) he chose the site of Hawara, this was closer to  home at the entrance to the Fayun and beside his new Labyrinth administrative town. Like all the Middle Kingdom pyramids, this was built relatively cheaply out of mud brick. The Romans later completely quarried away the casing for their nearby construction; consequently the pyramid is a ruin today.

However, the burial chamber itself is truly notable. Petrie in 1889 was the first to investigate it although it was partly under water. The lower chamber (right) was cut out of a single block of quartzite stone, at one hundred and thirty tons it is the heaviest Egyptian funerary object. The roof of the tomb is also made out of one slab weighing forty six tons. So that this slab could be easily lowered in a controlled fashion, the builders constructed the first known sand lowering device. The blocks that supported 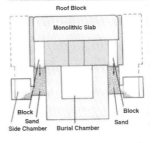 the roof slab rested on sand filled shafts on either side of the vault. After the king's coffin was laid to rest, the sand was removed through side galleries and the supporting blocks gently descended along with the monolithic roof slab.

The last recorded event of his long reign was in regnal year forty-four when the great builder constructed a massive perimeter wall around the expanded vulture goddess temple complex at El Kab (Nekheb) opposite Hierakonpolis.

**Amenemhet 4** was the adopted son of Amenemhet 3 and ruled for thirteen years (1798–1785BC) or less before dying prematurely, without an heir. No records or monuments remain apart from a suspected ruined pyramid south of that of his father. Following his death, Amenemhet 4's daughter briefly reigned as Sobek neferu (1785-1781BC) and was included in the Saqqara Tablet king list. This was still a moderately prosperous period and Nubia remained quiet for now, however, with no male heirs the glorious 12th Dynasty came to a close, as did the Golden Age of the Middle Kingdom.

## Middle Kingdom Literature

The 12th to 16th Dynasties have provided us with some of the most remarkable historical writings which rank at the summit of all of Ancient Egyptian literature. In particular the c1950BC Akhmim (Mathmatical) Wooden Tablet, the c1950BC Heqanakht (Monetary) papyri, the c1825BC Kahun

Gynaecological Papyrus, the c1800BC Berlin (Mathmatical and Medical) papyrus, the c1800BC Moscow (Mathematical) Papyrus, the c1535BC Rhind (Mathematical) Papyrus, the c1600BC Edwin Smith (Medical) papyrus and the c1550BC Ebers (Surgical) papyrus. The three medical papyri are discussed specifically in Chapter 5. In addition the Middle Kingdom has given us six of the finest pieces of fictional literature. Ancient Egyptian Literature is in modern terms not pastoral or lyrical, but mostly didactic (Greek meaning teaching) and rather unromantic, although not lacking in personal feelings. Most deal with personal themes, concerned with the heart and conscience. Mankind's ethical life is their central concern not personal emotions such as romantic love. Probably the most famous and popular classic of all of Egyptian literature is the 'Tale of Sinuhe' written shortly after the reign of Senusret I. The earliest surviving manuscripts date from the reign of Amenemhet 3 one hundred years afterwards. Later copies show that it was read for at least seven hundred and fifty years, twice as long as we have read the Shakespeare plays. It is the story of a court official Sinuhe, who flees Egypt on the assasination of Amenemhet I and travels to Retjenu (Canaan), where he endures various adventures before returning to the protection of the court and a welcome from the new king. Other notable popular tales are that of the 'The eloquent Peasant', the 'Shipwrecked sailor', the 'Court of king Cheops' (Westcar papyrus), the 'Dialogue of a man and his soul' and 'The teachings of king Amenemhet I to his son'

**The Middle Kingdom decline.** There then followed a period of around one hundred and fifty years with more than seventy kings. During the 13th Dynasty the kingdom was mostly stable but there was no consistently strong central control, bureaucracy was growing and the period was one of general decline with two notable exceptions. **Neferhotep I** 1720-1709BC was a usurper, who built at Karnak and Abydos. He established a sufficiently stable regime to be able to campaign in Byblos (Lebanon) and left an inscription at Buhen in Nubia below the second Nile cataract. **Sobekhotep 4** 1709-1700BC was the last significant ruler campaigning in the south, but he was only able to delay Nubia from ultimately gaining its independence ten years later.

From then on Egypt's central control fatally declined, there were reports of flooding, less tax revenue and growing Nome independence. The once impregnable Nubian fortresses were taken back one by one, even the great fort at Buhen was attacked, taken and burned. Most of north and south Nubia became independent by c1690BC. A new kingdom was created with its capital at Kerma just above the third cataract of the Nile. This Kushite kingdom extended as far north as Aswan which became the new diminished southern border of Egypt.

The Middle Kingdom capital, Itjtawy, was abandoned and Canaan c1675BC was lost as a buffer zone, thus allowing Asiatics to flood into the east Delta. Famine was widely reported and the Karnak stele of Sobek hotep 8 c1650BC recorded that even 'Karnak is flooded. . . . the irrigation system is failed'.

The next dynasty was Manetho's ephemeral 14th. The Egyptian rulers had lost their grasp over the whole country but seem to have been able to hold on to the Delta region. Around 1650BC a ruler of Canaanite origin in Avaris (the 15th Dynasty) emerged, for now he still acknowledged the sovereignty of the Delta king. Egypt had now entered the Second Intermediate Period, in which some of the Asiatic settlers in the eastern Delta grasped power over northern Egypt. They were to be referred to as the despised Hyksos rulers.

The Middle Kingdom government was feudal in nature. The king, unlike the rulers of the Old Kingdom, was no longer all powerful and was forced constantly to balance his authority against that of the powerful Nomarchs, This period was more similar to the Middle Ages in England c1100-1400AD where the king also had to accommodate the landed Barons, than the Old Kingdom with it's absolute god-like kings. The Middle Kingdom was a period of tremendous Nubian territorial expansion, government reform, important literature and art of an unsurpassed level. Overall, however, our knowledge of this important period is still inadequate because its forts, palaces, government buildings, and pyramids were mostly constructed from mud brick and these along with much of their vitally important reliefs and inscriptions were not to stand the test of time. In contrast, the magnificent stone structures and durable inscriptions of the next ancient Egyptian era, the New Kingdom, have survived much better and with them more detailed records of their ruler's achievements.

# CHAPTER SEVEN

# The Hyksos and Early New Kingdom

The Hyksos c1665-1557BC monarchs were called hkw hswt or 'foreign rulers' by the Ancient Egyptians, Manetho later called them the 'Shepherd Kings'. They were an Asiatic Semitic people from Canaan (later Palestine) who gradually migrated into the eastern Nile Delta towards the end of the Middle Kingdom. They came either through the caravan trade or simply as immigrants looking for work and a new life. Over time the migrants prospered and were so influential that they rose to become the rulers initially of the East Delta and then, extending their influence south, they controlled middle Egypt. According to Manetho and the Turin Royal Canon papyrus, they ruled for one hundred and eight years, Manetho calls this period of six Hyksos kings the 15th Dynasty. The Hyksos were often characterized by their Canaanite names which incorporated their Semitic deities such as Anath or Baal. The modern evidence supports the above migration model and disputes Manetho's version that the Hyksos aggressors conducted a specific military invasion, sacked the east Delta and Memphite region and imposed their military authority there.

**New military technology.** The Hyksos introduced many new superior tools of warfare into Egypt, most notably the powerful composite recurve bow, improved bronze weapons, the horse-drawn, two-wheeled lightweight attack chariot, mailed shirts, metal helmets and improved arrow heads. With them came a new, to the Egyptians, more dynamic method of conducting warfare.

The heavy four-wheeled battle chariot (above) had been in common use by the Sumerians since c2400BC and its use had progressively spread into northern Mesopotamia (Iraq). However, the two-wheeled light weight attack chariot was a new technology spreading from central Asia in the period c1700–1300 BC. It was introduced most notably by the Hurrians based in north east Syria and north Iraq, who were to come into contact with Egypt later as the Mittani during the New Kingdom. It typically carried a driver and one lightly armoured archer. A division of these lightweight, manouvrable, fast moving, two-wheeled attack chariots became the ultimate super weapon for the next two thousand years.

The Egyptian Hyksos kingdom was based in the eastern Nile Delta, it spread as far as Memphis but never permanently extended into the south which was under the control of the Theban princes of the 17th Dynasty. Initially the relationship between the Hyksos and the rulers of Thebes was business like. They traded with each other, Thebes gained transit rights through Hyksos controlled middle and north Egypt and even secured grazing rights in the Delta. The Hyksos even had limited transit rights up the Nile to conduct trade with Nubia. Thebes recognized the Hyksos rulers and may even have been forced to pay tribute.

The Hyksos took over the Middle Kingdom city of Rowarty and established there a new capital. It was highly fortified and was protected by a wall twenty five feet wide. The Greeks gave it the name Avaris (modern Tell el D'aba, left) located at what was then the eastern arm of the Nile. They also maintained a satellite government center at the traditional administrative Egyptian capital of Memphis. The important four Hyksos rulers were Sak ir har, (Manetho's Salitis), Khayan, Apepi I (Greek=Apophis) and finally Khamudi Apepi 2. Avaris today is a complete ruin, excavations have been underway since the mid 1990s and although huge stables have been unearthed, so far no evidence of chariots has ben recovered.

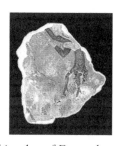

The Hyksos were a sophisticated people who traded throughout the Eastern Mediterranean, their Avaris palace walls were decorated with the Minoan style bull leaping frescoes (right) and a vase bearing the name of Apepi has been found in Knossos, Crete. There is even a minority view that the Minoan art form was influenced by Hyksos/Egyptian art, supported by the observation that Minoan figures represented men with brown/red skin and women with light or white skin in the Egyptian style. Progressively, like all invaders of Egypt, they

adopted the Egyptian culture, for example these inscribed scarabs (left) were found in Canaan. They also adopted Egyptian relief styles, used Egyptian royal titles and even built a temple dedicated to the worship of the Egyptian god Seth.

Both the weak Egyptian 16th Dynasty, controlling only the west of the Delta, and the 17th Dynasty Theban princes, notionally recognized the Hyksos kings. However, the deeply rooted Ancient Egyptian Xenophobia showed through in their oft repeated hatred of these foreign invaders, despite the prosperity and stability they provided. Most of the history of the impending war to expel them has been written by the Thebans and is thus rather one-sided; nearly all traces of the Hyksos occupation which would have provided a balanced picture have been erased. *'History is written by the victors'*, wrote Winston Churchill.

As in the beginning of the Middle Kingdom, it was the royal family of Thebes that initiated the movement to re-unite the country, this time by expelling the Hyksos. There is clear evidence that in the early 17th Dynasty the Hyksos made a strategic alliance with the Nubians and began raiding up to Thebes itself. Theban king Rahotep c1585BC repulsed them and there was no further military activity until thirty years later when Taa I emerged as an energetic leader at Thebes. He built a new palace there and at Abydos left a stele dedicated to his Great Wife Tetisheri, the first to a female. He was succeeded either by a son of the same name, Taa 2, or he changed his name, following a battle with the Hyksos, from Senakhtenre to Seqenenre Taa, qen meaning brave.

**The war against the Hyksos** began in earnest in the closing years of the 17th Dynasty at Thebes. The Theban king **Seqenenre Taa 2** 1558-1553BC was a contemporary of the great Hyksos ruler Apepi I (Greek=Apophis). The accuracy, and impartiality, of the later Theban written records for the events of the next episode is rather questionable. 18th Dynasty Theban tradition claimed that Apepi I sent a complaint to Seqenenre Taa 2 demanding that his sport of harpooning of hippopotami be discontinued *'as the noise of these beasts is such that in Avaris I am unable to sleep'.* Their displeasure was more likely that their adopted principal god Seth was represented as part hippopotamus and was a rival to the Theban chief god Amen. Seqenenre Taa 2 seems to have been the first to escalate matters militarily; he allied himself with the prince of El Kab (fifty miles to the south) and led a seemingly unsuccessful combined

military campaign against the Hyksos. Judging by the multiple head wounds found on his mummy (right) in the Egyptian Museum, Cairo, he may have died during one of these battles. The wounds were delivered by an axe, the preferred weapon of the Hyksos, presumably while the victim was lying on the ground, as the wounds were delivered in a downwards direction. There is evidence that his Great Wife Ahotep I played a role in government and even the military after the death of her husband. Their two year old son was too young to rule and his uncle Kamose became king, he was to be the last ruler of the 17th Dynasty at Thebes.

**Kamose** (soul is born) 1553-1549BC. One main source for the early part of his short four-year reign is an inscribed stuccoed wooden board found in a Theban tomb in 1908 known as the Carnarvon Tablet I. Kamose claimed his reason for launching his attack on the Hyksos was nationalistic pride. He complained that he was *'..surrounded by the Asiatics in the north and the Nubians in the south, each holding his slice of Egypt, dividing up the land with me... my wish is to save Egypt and to smite the Asiatics!'* In year three he called a council of war. He allegedly chastised his advisors when they cautioned him against moving against the Hyksos, the councilors stated '. . . we are at ease in our Egypt. Elephantine (Aswan) is strong, and the middle is with us as far as Cusae (north of Asyut). The sleekest of their fields are plowed for us, and our cattle are pastured in the Delta. Emmer is sent for our pigs. Our cattle have not been taken away. . . He (the Hyksos) holds the land of the Asiatics; we hold Egypt.' Kamose ignored the advice to be cautious and planned a two pronged attack. He first had to prevent the Nubians from joining forces with their Hyksos allies so the king initially moved south with Admiral Ahmose son of Ebama, and delivered a tactical defeat to the Nubians, which kept them out of the impending war with the Hyksos. Admiral Ahmose son of Ebama recorded, in his historically important El Kab tomb texts, that king Kamose actually killed a Nubian chieftain in hand to hand combat. Later in regnal year three, having secured his southern border from a Nubian/Hyksos pincer movement, Kamose sailed north and commenced to take the Hyksos cities down the Nile. He first captured the southernmost garrison of the Hyksos just north of Cusae and pressed on down river with apparent great success. He moved past Memphis and invaded the east Delta even managing to threaten the outskirts of Avaris itself. However his supply line was by now too stretched and he was not strong enough to besiege the strongly fortified city, instead he razed the surrounding territory and withdrew.

Kamose was also distracted by a new threat in the south at this time. The texts of Admiral Ahmose son of Ebama mentioned the capture of a messenger from the Hyksos king to his ally the ruler of Kush (south Nubia) encouraging him urgently to revenge the defeat Kamose had inflicted earlier. Kamose moved swiftly to occupy the strategic Bahariya Oasis in the Western Desert thereby ensuring control of the desert route to the south and Nubia. He then sailed back to Thebes to celebrate his success. It is likely that the text on the Carnarvon Tablet I overstates his penetration to Avaris; his was more likely to have been a glorified raid on the unsuspecting Hyksos-controlled towns in Middle Egypt. In fact, he may only have reached the southern edge of the Fayum region and may even have died in battle there. In regnal year three Kamose had appointed Ahmose I the six year old son of his brother Seqenenre Taa 2 as co-regent. One year later king Kamose passed away. The mummy of Kamose is mentioned in the Abbott Papyrus, which records an investigation into ten royal tomb robberies during the reign of Ramesses 9, about four hundred years after Ahmose's death. The Abbott Papyrus includes the description of the condition of five of the 17th Dynasty Theban royal tombs. While the Kamose tomb was mentioned as being 'in a good state', it seems that his mummy was moved afterwards, as it was discovered in 1857 in the Theban necropolis, deliberately hidden in a pile of debris; and in very poor shape. Buried with the mummy were a gold and silver dagger, amulets, a scarab, a bronze mirror, and a pectoral in the shape of a cartouche bearing the name of his successor king Ahmose I. The great Hyksos king Apepi I had reigned for forty years and had outlived Seqenere Taa 2 and much of the reign of Kamose. The last Hyksos ruler Khamudi Apepi 2, had a relatively short reign of ten years which fell within the first half of the reign of young king Ahmose I.

**Ahmose I** (the moon is born) 1549-1524BC came to the throne at seven years of age and his mother, Ahhotep I, initially acted as regent. Manetho regards him as the first king of the Empire building 18th Dynasty. The main source for his reign ,like that of Kamose, are the reliefs in the El Kab tomb of his namesake, Admiral Ahmose son of Ebama, a military noble from El Kab still the main ally of Thebes. In regnal year ten, at the age of seventeen Ahmose was at last ready to re-start the campaign to drive the hated Hyksos from Egypt. He assembled a southern coalition army and moved north. After two years of campaigning he and his El Kab allies had succeeded in taking first, the capital Memphis and then the religious center of Heliopolis. The axe head below, shows Ahmose striking down a Hyksos soldier, it was found in the tomb of his mother.

Later in regnal year ten, he commenced the final phase of the war. He besieged Avaris and conducted numerous naval attacks on the city and its surrounding allies. Almost everthing we know of this particular campaign comes from a brief but invaluable contemporary commentary on the back of the Rhind Mathematical Papyrus c1535BC which illustrates some of the military strategy used by king Ahmose I when attacking the Delta. After entering Heliopolis in July, he moved down the eastern Delta and deliberately by-passed Avaris to invest Tjaru (Sile) which fell three months later. This was the key border fortification on the 'Horus Road' from Egypt to Canaan. In taking Tjaru he was carefully planning a tactical blockade of Avaris, thus isolating the Hyksos from help or supplies from their homeland in the east. After three years Avaris fell and the Hyksos were finally dislodged from the east Delta and then driven out of Egypt entirely. Admiral Ahmose of Ebama fought with his king throughout and left tomb inscriptions describing the campaigns. One narrative describes his pride, following on foot, as his King went into battle in his Hyksos designed war chariot. This is the first mention of a chariot being used by the Egyptian army. For his services Admiral Ahmose son of Ebama was awarded the highest military honor the *'Gold of Valor'* on three occasions. He describes the fall of the Hyksos capital *'Then Avaris was despoiled. Then I*

*carried off spoil from there: one man, three women, a total of four persons. Then his majesty gave them to me to be slaves.'* The dagger on the left bears the name of Ahmose I, it belonged to Admiral Ahmose son of Ebama, and is now in the Ontario Museum, Toronto.

**The Exodus** After the fall of Avaris, the defeated Hyksos were systematically pursued by the Egyptian army across the top of the Sinai and into southern Canaan. Now determined to destroy the power of the Hyksos in their homeland, the Egyptians attacked their last stronghold the fortified desert town of Sharuhen, south of Gaza. According to the tomb texts of Admiral Ahmose, the siege was to last six years. The Hyksos immigration into the Delta has been interpreted by some Biblical scholars as the time in the Old Testament of the sojourn in Egypt of Joseph and his brothers. This has led to the hypothesis that the expulsion of the Hyksos coincided with the Exodus. One major flaw is the anachronistic reference in Exodus I.11 *'And they (the children of Israel) built for the Pharaoh treasure cities, Pithom and Raamses'*. These cities were in fact not constructed until three hundred years later by Ramesses 2. There is also no record of the Exodus mass expulsion in Egyptian texts. The Hyksos expulsion in the Theban records refers only to the Asiatic royal family itself along with their military and government leaders, it definitely does not indicate a mass expulsion of the ordinary people i.e. peasants and farmers, who remained in Egypt and integrated with the other Delta inhabitants.

**The lasting impact of the Hyksos.** There is no doubt that the Hyksos period was a strategic turning point for Egypt in a number of ways. The kingdom could no longer ignore the new Asiatic superpowers gathering in the region north of its eastern border. Ironically there is evidence that the later king Ramesses 2 had Hyksos connections. His family had hereditary estates in the region of Avaris, his father was named Seti after the Hyksos adopted chief god Seth (Baal), he gave a Semitic name to one of his favorite daughters Bintanath, and moved his capital city to Avaris naming it after himself Pi Ramesses. Fragments of the so called Tempest or 'Storm Stele' were found in 1947 by Chevalier in the giant 3rd pylon of Amenhotep 3 at the Karnak Amen temple, it had been used during later construction as fill. The stele was originally erected by king Ahmose I at Karnak between regnal years seventeen and twenty two. The text describes a great storm which strikes Egypt destroying tombs, temples and 'pyramids' in the Theban region and lists the extensive work of restoration ordered by king Ahmose I. The storm is probably a religious euphemism and most likely a piece of royal propaganda. It refers to the hardship of officials and priests of the war torn Theban capital when the crown had to draw on the financial resources of the Karnak temple treasury to fund the escalating conflict with the Hyksos.

Egyptian attitudes to women were also changing. King Ahmose erected a stele at Abydos to mark a 'Donation to god's wife of Amun' meaning his wife, this was only the second time a woman had received such recognition and the first mention of the important title 'gods wife'. The importance of the two roles of wife to the king and mother to the next king in relation to succession was growing.

There were a number of later post-Hyksos military campaigns in south Syria and Nubia. These were recorded in the tomb of another Ahmose I namesake, Ahmose Pen Nekhbet also from El Kab. The focus had now switched to recovering Nubia which had been lost during the Middle Kingdom decline one hundred and seventy years before. In year sixteen the navy moved south via the canal built by Senusret 3 at Aswan, and retook the ruined lost Buhen fortress downstream of the second Nile cataract. Thuwre was named the first Commander of Buhen and campaigned as far south as Sai island in Kush, half way between the second and third cataracts. Egypt had now regained full control to the second cataract and a new Nubian regional capital was established at Buhen.

While Ahmose was in Nubia there was a revolt, possibly led by a Nomarch called Teti. It was put down with the direct assistance of either, the Queen mother Ahhotep I or his wife Ahmose Nefertari, who was awarded the supreme military honor of the 'gold flies' (left). Admiral Ahmose son of Ebama recorded the naval battles which won the day. This revolt led Ahmose I to revamp the government of his growing southern dominions. Because of its remoteness from Thebes, Ahmose I now needed a trusted senior figure to manage Nubian affairs on his behalf and to continue with the expansion into Kush. He founded the office of Viceroy and appointed Si tayit to the position; he was the father of Thuwre the Commander of Buhen, who later inherited the Viceroy position.

Personal tragedy struck the royal family around year seventeen, when the two, young, eldest sons of the king died. In regnal year twenty two, Ahmose opened new limestone quarries at Tura for the Memphis temple he had commenced. In the same year, Egypt made its first major long range penetration into Asiatic territory, Ahmose campaigned deep into north Syria passing beyond Byblos and perhaps even reaching the Euphrates with Admiral Ahmose. On the domestic front he introduced a sweeping reform; to avoid the constant tension with the Nomarchs, experienced during the Middle Kingdom, he dramatically strengthened central control by replacing every Nomarch except his loyal supporter at El Kab who was his closest ally during the wars with the Hyksos.

At the remarkably young age of only thirty two, after a momentous twenty five year reign, he went to his destiny remembered by subsequent generations as the savior of the country from the evil Hyksos occupation and the founder of the New Egypt. He constructed a small stone pyramid at Abydos, the last in Egyptian history; it contains some of the earliest reliefs showing the horses, that the Hyksos introduced into the country. By building the stone pyramid he wanted to associate his New Egypt with the glorious Old Kingdom. His mummy (right) is in the Egyptian Museum, Cairo. His third son, Amenhotep I, at nine years of age was too young to reign, so his mother, Ahmose Nefertari, became regent of what had now become a military powerhouse.

The final and perhaps the most important of all the changes that the ascendant Theban royal dynasty brought was a religious one. Thebes became the religious and political center of the country, its chief local god Amen was credited with inspiring Ahmose I in his victories over the Hyksos. The importance of the temple complex at Karnak grew and that of the previous dominant cult of Re, based in Heliopolis, diminished.

**Amenhotep I** (Amen is pleased) 1524-1503BC (Throne name: Djeser ka re) was the second king of the 18th Dynasty of Egypt. His reign of twenty one years was relatively peaceful although poorly documented. He consolidated his father's newly united New Kingdom, maintaining firm control of Nubia and the Nile Delta. In the early part of his reign, while his mother was regent, both opened the new valley of the kings tomb-worker village at Deir el Medina on the west bank opposite Thebes; this was to remain in business for four hundred years.

Amenhotep I took for his Great Royal Wife, Meryetamen, she was also his sister. They had a son but he died very young which was later to present a succession challenge. He remained extremely close to his mother all of his life. Although many statues of Amenhotep I have survived, most were made for his funerary cult and crafted much later; there are only a few surviving contemporary images of him in the round. The features of this rare head (right) of Amenhotep I, now in the Museum of  Fine Arts in Boston, show that he copied the Middle Kingdom style of kings Mentuhotep 2 and Senusret I.

At the age of sixteen, regnal year seven, he was now old enough to lead his fist military campaign. The objective was to consolidate north Nubia by completing his father's process of recovering all of the Middle Kingdom Nubian forts and expand south into Kush. He advanced past the second Nile cataract and in regnal year eight left an inscription at Semna relating to a victory over the Nubians. He then progressed further south as far as Sai island, just short of the third cataract, where he built a new temple, Sai then became the new southern boundary of the kingdom. Now came the major decision to colonize Nubia. He upgraded the Viceroy position adding the impressive titles of 'King's Son of Kush' and 'Overseer of the gold lands for the lord of the two lands'. His father's trusted veteran military commander, Thuwre (Turo), was the first appointed to this vital role. He was based at Buhen. This government office was critical to the prosperity of the country and it was to continue to the end of Ancient Egypt, the role was often passed from father to son.

The tomb of noble Ahmose Pen Nekhbet refers to a campaign in year eight in Lamu Kehek, believed to be in Libya, Amenhotep I was accompanied by both of his father's trusted veteran military commanders the two Ahmoses. It is possible that Amenhotep I also retook the western desert and their oases at this time. There is also a possibility, but no records, that he may have repeated his father's raid deep into north Syria, perhaps even all the way to the Euphrates; two references to the Mediterranean coast support this idea. However there are dark warnings made to the rising threat of a warlike nation originally based in northwest Iraq, which by c1550BC had already become well established on the Euphrates. This civilisation was a branch of the Hurrian peoples, called the Mittani, who were to play a significant role in the history of Ancient Egypt from now onward.

There were two particularly important written achievements during the reign of Amenhotep I. The first was the oldest funerary tomb text called the Amduat or 'The book of the secret Chamber' also called 'That which is in the Underworld'. Based on the Old Kingdom Pyramid Texts, it was a precursor to the later Book of the Dead. The second is the Ebers Medical Papyrus described in Chapter 5. During his reign there is the first mention of the water clock, implying that an accurate measurement of the hours in a day was now being made. His architect and vizier Ineni expanded the Amen temple at Karnak, Inenis tomb also mentions the construction of a new colossal gateway at the southern entrance. We know that this gateway was later demolished by Thutmosis 3. This relief (right) of Amenhotep I is from the Karnak temple and is now in the Brooklyn Museum, NY. Other Karnak building projects of his were unfortunately later dismantled by Amennhotep 3 to fill his giant third pylon. In south Egypt Amenhotep I also built temples at Elephantine, Kom Ombo, Abydos, and the Temple of Nekhbet at El Kab, his important ally.

**Tomb and mortuary temple.** Amenhotep I constructed a mortuary temple to the north of Deir el Bahri but Hatshepsut later removed the stonework to make way for the lower terrace of her own stunning tiered monumental mortuary temple; only a few bricks inscribed with Amenhotep I remain. The location of the tomb of Amenhotep I is lost. There are two competing alternatives, one just south of the Valley of the Kings, KV39, and the other further southeast at Dra Abu el Naga. The latter is considered the more likely as it contains objects with his name. On his death, at the young age of thirty,

he was deified and made the patron god of Deir el Medina along with his mother Ahmose Nefertari. They are both shown (left) in a stele in the Brooklyn Museum, New York. Amenhotep I was acutely aware that to die without an undisputed successor could spell doom for the fledgling New Kingdom. He made a truly gifted choice by selecting as his heir his trusted general Thutmosis I, a relation, possibly a cousin, who was a little older than himself. He married Thutmosis I to his sister Mutneferet to secure complete legitimacy. Amenhotep I may even have appointed Thutmosis I as his co-regent some years before he died. This is based on the evidence that the son of Thutmosis I was shown and mentioned on Amenhotep I's Karnak bark shrine.

**Thutmosis I** (Thoth is born) 1503-1491BC (Throne name: A kheper ka re). Although his reign of twelve years, as recorded by Manetho, seemed modest in length, he was able to implement his strategic vision to create a true empire by extending the boundaries of Egypt both south and north east, further than ever before. This head (right) from his royal statue is in the British Museum, London. He was married to Mutneferet the daughter of king Ahmose I. They had a son, Amenmose who became the 'great army commander of his father' but he died just before his father did. With Mutneferet, Thutmosis I also had a second son, who immediately succeeded him as Thutmosis 2. However Thutmosis I had a second wife Ahmose. With her he had an important daughter, Hatshepsut, who eventually became the greatest Egyptian female king.

**Kush year two.** Thutmosis I, shortly after coming to the throne in his early forties, created the first national standing army twenty-thousand strong, the largest the world had yet known; it incorporated the first Egyptian chariot divisions. The first campaign was focused on territorial expansion deep into south Nubia, the land of Kush, south of the second Nile cataract. In year two the army moved south into Kush and with them went the veteran Admiral Ahmose son of Ebana who by now had campaigned with three Egyptian kings. His El Kab tomb records that the army sailed up the Nile,

led by the king himself, to the region of third Nile cataract where he cut this rock inscription at Tombos (left), recording the construction of a fortress there and another at Sai island. Moving further south, he passed through the third cataract and ordered a fort at Kerma to be built. This was particularly significant, as Kerma had been the Kushite kingdom capital when it broke free of Egypt c1675BC, during the Middle Kingdom decline, and had remained independent for one hundered and seventy years since then. In this campaign, Admiral Ahmose, in charge of the war fleet, claims that the king took part in the fighting and personally killed a Nubian chief, whose body was then draped over the bow of his ship when he returned to Thebes. The army raided even further into Kush, well beyond the fourth Nile cataract to reach Kurgis for the first time in Egypt's history. The king left an inscription there to commemorate the event. Kurgis was strategically important as it commanded the south end of the desert short-cut for the major trading route from the deep south to Quban and Aswan. Viceroy Thuwre recorded, at the first cataract, that before the king could return with the Nubian built fleet to Thebes, he cleared the partially blocked Aswan canal built by Senusret 3 of the 12th Dynasty. By pacifying the territory between the second and third cataract Egypt had for the first time permanently extended the Egyptian border from Buhen to Tombos and Kerma, two hundred miles further south.

**Syria year three.** He wasted no time after returning from Nubia and Kush and turned his attention north to Canaan and then Syria in regnal year three. Both of the seasoned Ahmoses joined him for this long distance journey into new territory. His army advanced north through Canaan (Retjenu) into Lebanon then north past Byblos and into Syria as far as Tunip. He engaged and defeated the Naharin, the Mittani branch of the Hurrians, who by this time had gained control of the region west of the northern Euphrates as far as the Orontes river. This was the first time the Mittani had been mentioned by name, their western capital was the strategically important ford city of Carchemish (Edessa).

Thutmosis I had now reached farther north that any Egyptian king has been proven to have campaigned. To celebrate this huge expansion northwards, he crossed the Euphrates below Cachemish, still held by the Mittani, where he set up a commemorative stele which has since been lost. On his return south, he celebrated his victories by conducting an elephant hunt at Niy where the Euphrates bends east. He accepted the Syrian and Lebonese cities' allegiance and collected immense tribute from them on his homeward journey. This annual tribute income grew to become a major source of revenue for the Empire. However, once he and the army had returned to Egypt, the Syrian princes no longer paid their annual tribute and instead prepared to defend themselves for when the Egyptian army would inevitably return. The Egyptians, knowing only the Nile, which flowed from south to north, assumed all major rivers did so and remarked about the Euphrates '. . .*that inverted water which flows upstream..*' At the end of his Nubian and Syrian campaigns, Thutmosis I had created an Egyptian Empire, the dark shaded area on the above map, which had reached its greatest extent; it was never to be matched. Although not wishing to belittle the success of his Syrian campaign it must be placed in context. He had surpise on his side, the Mittani and the Syrian princes had not been prepared for such a strong Egyptian military force so far from home. His succesors were never to enjoy such an advantage. The term 'Empire' here must also be qualified. Nubia was an Egyptian province governed by a Viceroy who possesd an army and fleet and taxed the region as part of Egypt. This

was never so for Syria, probably because Egypt had a highly superior attitude towards Asiatics; the region was visted annually to collect tribute but it was never managed as an integrated province of Egypt.

Thutmosis 1 recognized the talents of his predecessor's chief adviser and architect, Ineni and reappointed him. His Theban tomb (TT81) texts describe the king's great building program at Karnak. He was the first king to significantly develop the Middle Kingdom central court temple area at Karnak. He greatly extended the temple axis westwards by adding the fourth and fifth pylons, he also built the first wall to run around all of the inner sanctuary. To the east of his pylon four, he had the first hypostyle hall constructed. Hypostyle is a word first coined in 1831 from the Greek, meaning 'under pillars', referring to a hall which has a roof supported by a row of columns. This narrow hall employed cedar columns which were replaced in stone by his grandson Thutmosis 3, fifty years later. In regnal year nine he celebrated his Heb Sed Jubilee to mark thirty years since his predecessor and mentor Amenhotep 1 came to the throne. To mark this event he ordered Karnak's first two obelisks (right), they were made of red Aswan granite and stood sixty-four feet tall outside the fourth pylon. One was not inscribed or erected until Thutmosis 3 did so in honor of his respected forbear. Pococke visiting in 1737AD reported that both were then standing; one has since fallen and become broken. As part of his Nubian building projects, he enlarged the Khnum temple at Semna.

**Valley of the Kings.** Thutmosis 1 was the first to develop, and be buried in, the Valley of the Kings (below). He chose the valley on the basis that it was close to the existing Middle Kingdom necropolis on the west bank, yet remote

from the general population. The valley had only one narrow entrance and therefore could be effectively guarded by the royal necropolis police. He conjectured that if the location of his underground tomb could only be kept from the robbers, then his sarcophagus and mummy may yet lie undisturbed, remaining intact for eternity. Unlike the pyramid tombs, which because of their enormous size, almost seemed to invite robbers. Although his modest two room tomb, KV38, contained a yellow quartzite sarcophagus bearing his name, his original tomb was most probably KV20, which also contains a sarcophagus with his name. It is likely that KV20 was the tomb that architect and vizier Ineni supervised, 'no one seeing, no one knowing', and where the king was originally laid to rest. His loving daughter Hatshepsut later added an extra chamber to KV20, she then moved her fathers sarcophagus to the new larger chamber and placed her own sarcophagus beside his. However, the mummy of Thutmosis I was later removed by his grandson Thutmosis 3, who created the new tomb KV38 for his grandfather away from the influence of Hatshepsut.

Ineni, in his tomb (TT81) reliefs, records building the kings mortuary temple but the evidence of its location has not yet been found. It may well have been incorporated into Hatshepsut's later mortuary temple at Deir el Bahri. Thutmosis I's mummy was discovered amongst the 1881 Deir el Bahri Royal Mummy Cache hidden, two hundred feet up in the cliffs above the Mortuary Temple of Hatshepsut.

Thutmosis I was in his mid fifties, a very good age for those times, when he went to his destiny. He had wisely secured the succession by marrying Hatshepsut, his twelve year old daughter by his wife Ahmose, to his eighteen year old son Thutmosis 2 by his wife Mutneferet.

**Thutmosis 2.** 1491-1479BC (Throne name: A kheper en re). No sooner had the eighteen-year-old, physically frail, Thutmosis 2 gained the throne than there was a revolt by Kush, hoping to take advantage during a period of national uncertainty. Too young and weak to lead the army himself, he re-appointed his fathers adviser, Ineni, now at the peak of his power, as vizier. In regnal year one, a force led by his father's veteran generals, was dispatched to Kush to help the Viceroy's army crush the revolt. Kush, as far south as the third Nile cataract, had been completely pacified by Thutmosis I but rebels from Khenthennofer near Kerma, had besieged one of the Nubian forts, possibly Buhen itself. The revolt and the subsequent resounding rapid victory are recorded in great detail on a rock cut inscription upstream of Aswan.

There is some uncertainty as to whether Thutmosis 2 actually fought a campaign against the Shasu (Bedouin) in the Sinai; it is only mentioned by the veteran officer Ahmose Pen Nekhbet in his tomb reliefs. A fragment of a Thutmosis 2's Deir el Bahri inscription hints that this campaign may then have progressed into Syria, even as far as Niy. However, it is likely that this actually was a reference to his father's earlier campaign there. North Syria was indeed becoming a concern to Egypt, as the Mittani continued to extend their influence southwards.

In regnal year two or three, his daughter Neferure was born to fifteen year old 'Gods Wife', Hatshepsut. But two years later the seed of a potentially devastating dynastic crisis was sown. His lesser wife, Iset, produced a son and heir Thutmosis 3. He was later to become Ancient Egypt's greatest warrior king. It has been speculated that Hatshepsut was the real power during the reign of Thutmosis 2 but there is little evidence. This speculation stems from the Theban tomb autobiography of Ineni which tersely states '...*Hatshepsut settled the affairs of the two lands according to her own plans...*'. Contrarily she is shown in reliefs during this period as following dutifully behind Thutmosis 2 and even behind the king's mother. As Great Royal Wife she built an appropriately modest tomb high in the Theban cliffs well outside the Valley of the Kings.

Thutmosis 2's only known Karnak monument is his gateway originaly erected in front of pylon four, it was later dismantled and used in the foundation of Amenhotep 3's giant pylon three where it was recovered in the twentieth century AD. He commenced to build his mortuary temple at Deir el Bahri and had only decorated part of it when he went to his destiny after a twelve year rule. Hatshpesut was to adopt it as her own and turn it into one of the most magnificent of all the Egyptian temples. It was extensively restored by Winlock between 1914 and 1931. Its beautiful setting against the Theban cliffs is breathtaking.

Thutmosis 2's mummy (left), was part of the Deir el Bahri cache of 1881. Maspero in 1886, observed that he had died around the age of thirty from some form of disease. On describing the mummy he wrote '....the skin had many scabs and was covered with scars...his body was thin shrunken and lacked muscular power'.

After a rather short and uneventful reign, in comparison to the achievements of his father, Thutmosis 2 left behind his heir, the eight year old Thutmosis 3 and his twenty four year old wife, Hatshepsut, along with her eight-year old daughter Neferure, to inherit the country.

# CHAPTER EIGHT

# Hatshepsut, the Great Female King and Thutmosis 3

Hatshepsut (Foremost of noble ladies) 1479-1458BC (Throne name: Maat ka re) reigned for twenty-one years, longer and more successfully than any other female king. She was only the third known female king to have ruled, the first being Meryetneith of the 1st Dynasty and the second was Sobekneferu's short reign at the close of the 12th Dynasty. On his father's death the eight-year old Thutmose 3 was too young to perform the role of king, so instead, his step-mother and aunt Hatshepsut became regent.

In year two of her regency, she built a temple in Semna at the second Nile cataract, the reliefs there show a conventional picture with the regent standing correctly behind the king Thutmosis 3, now ten years old. Between years two and five she, as regent, supervised the construction of pylon seven at Karnak the first expansion of the southern axis. The reliefs and texts appropriately refer to it being dedicated to the young king Thutmosis 3. This abruptly changed in year seven, when no longer content to be just the regent she ascended to the throne itself with the throne name maat ka re, and became a female king; there was no word for a ruling queen in ancient Egyptian. Her statue above (Metropolitan Museum, NY) is from the time she first became ruler, it shows her wearing the rulers headdress and the uraeus but not yet the false beard. Although she had taken the title of king there is strangely no indication of friction with the now fifteen-year old Thutmosis 3. In fact, there were no challenges to her authority during her entire reign. Her co-ruler appears to have remained content in a secondary role. He spent more and more time with the military eventually becoming Commander in Chief, which would have given him every opportunity to replace her as usurper if he so wished.For the remaining fourteen years of her sole reign, she was never seen portrayed simply as a woman in feminine clothing, she was always shown in royal attire, with full regalia (right). The Osiride statues at her mortuary temple, conveniently show her breasts obscured in the traditional Osiris pose of crossed arms holding the crook and flail of kings, and shows her wearing the false beard. She never actually wore this in person,it is also unlikely that any male pharaohs ever did so.

**Senenmut.** Ineni, the veteran vizier, had died before Hatshepsut had made the transition to female king. His tomb importantly makes no mention of her throne name maat ka re. He was succeeded by a group of influential advisors, the foremost being Neshi the Chancellor and State Treasurer, Djehuty the Royal Treasurer and mortuary temple architect and Hapusneb her tomb architect. Senior to them all was the veteran royal adviser and military leader Ahmose Pen Nekhbet who became vizier; his El Kab tomb inscriptions refer to the ruler as maat ka re and not Hatshpsut. Later in the reign an Amenhotep became vizier (TT73) and Inebni became Viceroy for Nubia. However, it was Senenmut who eventually became the most prominent and contoversial member of her inner circle. He was a commoner who rose to become her chief adviser, temple builder, intimate personal friend as well as replacing Ahmose Pen Nekhbet as tutor to her daughter Neferure. Uniquely this commoner is shown in statues (above) physically protecting the young royal daughter, this example is in the British Museum,London. Although in year seven Senenmut started his tomb in the Theban necropolis (TT71) it was never to be used.

**Punt trading expedition.** In year nine chancellor Neshi left on a trading mission to the Land of Punt in modern Somalia, the first since the Middle Kingdom. The details are extensively recorded in her mortuary temple reliefs. Hatshepsut oversaw the preparations and funding for the expedition which set out from the Egyptian Red Sea port of Mersa Gawais, east of Dendera. The fleet comprised of five ships, each seventy feet long, bearing one large sail, and accommodating forty marines and thirty oarsmen. Many goods were brought back from Punt, particulalry myrrh, which is said to have been Hatshepsut's favorite fragrance. Most notably the expedition brought thirty one live frankincense trees (right), the roots of which were carefully kept wet in baskets on board. Frankincense was valued for incense and as a deodorant. This is the first recorded transplantation of foreign trees. She had them planted in holes cut into the stone pavement of the courtyard of her Deir el Bahri mortuary temple; these holes can still be seen. The temple reliefs record an image of King Parahu and a rather unflattering representraion of Queen Iti (Ati) of Punt. The temple inscriptions also refer to a trading expedition to Byblos for cedar in year eight, and the erection of a stele in the Sinai, where she had expanded the copper and turquoise mines in both year eight and sixteen.

The Deir el Bahri texts refer to two minor policing campaigns in Nubia which were also also mentioned by Nubian treasurer Ti in an inscription at

Aswan, A stele erected by the royal treasurer Djehuty hints of an unidentified action where Hatshepsut herself accompanied the army. However, there is no mention of the growing Mittani menace, unchecked by either Thutmosis 2 or peace loving Hatshepsut, as they extended their influence southward further into Syria.

**Building projects** During her reign the country was largely at peace and had become immensely wealthy, having now incorporated the extended gold mines in Nubia. Her building projects were of a grand scale and numerous. She restored the Karnak Temples of Mut and Montu damaged by the Hyksos, and built the extensive underground rock cut Pakhet temple at Beni Hasan on the

eastern side of the Nile; the Greeks called it the Speos Artemidos. Her dedication text there condemns the ravages of the Hyksos. She celebrated her eleventh year in power with a relief showing herself with Thutmosis 3 and her daughter Neferure, however this time she was deliberately shown as the dominant figure. Hatshepsut celebrated her fifteen year jubilee, to mark roughly thirty years since the death of her father, with an extravagant monumental building program. She supervised the erection of pylon eight at Karnak, which cleverly surrounded pylon seven, dedicated to Thutmosis 3. Her Deir el Bahri temple masterpiece (above) was well underway. Its implementation, led by Senenmut, raised architecture to a

level only rivaled by Hellenic classical temples a thousand years later. It was known as Djeser Djeseru the 'Sublime of Sublimes' and was constructed at the top of a series of terraces and gardens built into the Theban cliff face that rises dramatically above it. It is still considered to be among the finest buildings in the world. The approach to the first ramp was through an avenue of two hundred and fifty sphinxes, (left) each with the face of Hatshepsut with rounded ears and with five toes.

A propaganda relief on her mortuary temple wall decalared that she was the daughter of Amen, thus legitimizing her right to the throne. This inscription was copied by Amenhotep 3 at Luxor to justify his divine status too. Also in jubilee year fifteen at Karnak, she erected her elegantly proportioned shrine, (right) known as the Red Chapel because of the pink sandstone used. The

Chapel reliefs record the details of her jubilee celebrations. Hatshepsut and her junior co-regent Thutmosis 3 are shown of equal size which is probably why he later claimed it for himself but he then had the Chapel demolished. The jubilee highlight was the erection of two giant red granite obelisks each ninety seven

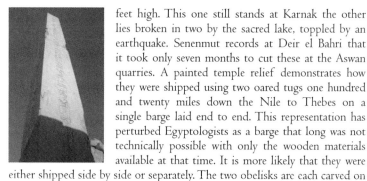 feet high. This one still stands at Karnak the other lies broken in two by the sacred lake, toppled by an earthquake. Senenmut records at Deir el Bahri that it took only seven months to cut these at the Aswan quarries. A painted temple relief demonstrates how they were shipped using two oared tugs one hundred and twenty miles down the Nile to Thebes on a single barge laid end to end. This representation has perturbed Egyptologists as a barge that long was not technically possible with only the wooden materials available at that time. It is more likely that they were either shipped side by side or separately. The two obelisks are each carved on all four sides and were dedicated by maat ka re to the gods Horus and Amun (right) and to her father on the occasion of her first Heb Sed festival. She later ordered the construction of two more even larger obelisks. On the walls of the tomb (TT73) of Vizier Amenhotep are records of this second pair being cut, one of the obelisks developed a crack in situ and remains uncompleted in the Aswan quarry to this day.

Between regnal year eleven and sixteen Hatshepsut's daughter Neferure died and perhaps, as a consequence, her guardian and tutor Senenmut began to lose his influence. There is speculation that he may have been preparing Neferure to be the successor to Hatshepsut in place of Thutmosis 3 and her death therefore marked a critical turning point in Hatshepsut's life. Senenmut had secretly built a second tomb (TT353) with the first astronomical star ceiling. Its entrance was just east of the Deir el Bahri temple but the unfinished burial chamber was directly below it. Two pieces of evidence strongly suggest that the commoner Senenmut was personally very close to Hatshepsut and may have even been her lover. Firstly, she allowed Senenmut to place his name and image in the sanctuary of the Hathor chapel in Djeser Djeseru, almost unheard of for a commoner. Second is the presence of intimate grafitti of the two of them in his unfinished tomb. From year sixteen Senenmut, once the kingdom's most senior adviser and close confident of Hatshepsut faded from view and by year nineteen he had disappeared entirely presumed dead; yet curiously he was not buried in either of his two tombs. Hatshepsut went to her destiny two years later after twenty one years of prosperous and peaceful rule, seven as regent, and fourteen as female king. Recent CT scans of her mummy suggest she was about fifty years old when she died, probably from a ruptured abscess after removal of a tooth. In any case, she would not have lived much longer as she was suffering from bone cancer, possible liver cancer and diabetes.

As mentioned above, she had begun a modest tomb as the Great Royal Wife of Thutmose 2, however, once she became king, she desired something grander. She adopted the tomb of her father Thutmosis I (KV20), the first tomb to be built in the Valley of the Kings. It appears that the original intention was to extend the tomb through the cliffs to meet the tomb of Senenmut underneath her mortuary temple, but the quality of the limestone was too poor. Instead she added a new larger burial chamber to accommodate the sarcophagus of both herself and her beloved father where they could rest together for eternity.

**Hatshepsut's mummy** was missing along with that of Thutmosis I from KV20 when Carter cleared it in 1903. Her mummy was believed to have been lost. Carter in 1902 had already found an unidentified female mummy along with Hatshepsut's royal nurse named Sit re, in nearby KV60, intriguingly the left arm of the unidentified mummy was laid across her chest in traditional regal fashion. In 1906 Ayrton re-entered KV60 and removed the coffin and mummy of the royal nurse to Cairo. Since neither Carter nor Ayrton had left drawings of its location KV60 was forgotten until it was re-discoverd in 1990, when the remaining mummy was inspected and the tomb resealed but with no firm conclusions. However, in early 2007 the tomb was opened yet again and the mummy KV60A was removed for testing. A molar tooth had been found in 1881 inside a small box bearing Hatshepsut's name among the Deir el Bahri cache of royal mummies. The tooth fitted exactly the empty socket in the KV60A unidentified mummy's jaw, furthermore her DNA matched that of the mummy of Ahmose Nefertari the grandmother of Hatshepsut. At last Hatshepsut had been identified. This very recent discovery is second only in importance to Carter discovering KV62 and finding the intact mummy of Tutankhamen in 1922.

**Hatshepsut is removed from history.** Towards the end of the reign of her successor Thutmosis 3, a crude, selective and incomplete attempt was made to remove Hatshepsut from the historical record a type of damnatio memoriae. The term originates from the later Roman practice, meaning damnation of memory. The cartouches, reliefs and statues showing her as a female king were selected and crudely hacked away, and her reign as a female king was written out of history by the royal scribes. At Deir el Bahri her statues bearing her ceremonial beard of office were torn down, broken up or disfigured. The comparison on the right shows similar statues before and after. At Karnak the lower visible portion of her obelisk showing her throne name maat ka re was walled up, the sun faded 'tide' mark can still be seen two thirds of the way up the  obelisk. Early archeologists believed that the culprit Thutmosis 3, so hated his aunt and stepmother for preventing him coming to the throne sooner, that on her death his anger exploded in a wave of destruction of her name. The motivation of hatred has now been disproven. It is most unlikely that such a successful king, general, athlete, historian, and architect would have waited untill the end of his great reign to seek revenge, leaving her significant building accomplishments and many bearded images on show to all during the bulk of his period on the throne.

Amenhotep 2, son and later co-regent of Thutmose 3 is considered to be a likely alternative suspect, although he was the son of the king it was not by his Great Wife, hence succession was uncertain. Amenhotep 2 also claimed many of Hatshepsut's monuments during his own reign. However, Thutmosis 3 still remains the prime suspect for the damnatio memoriae. At the end of his reign he may have tried to ensure, his son and chosen successor, Amenhotep 2, reached the throne by removing any record of a precedent whereby a female could become a successful king. He could then claim that legitimate royal succession only ran directly through the male line from Thutmose I to Thutmose 3 to Amenhotep 2. Finally, there is the possibility that Hatshepsut's removal was military propaganda directed at Egypt's enemies. The supreme military strategist Thutmosis 3 may not have wanted to allow his adversaries to believe Egypt's royal line was so weak it had to stoop to relying on a female to rule the country.

**Thutmosis 3** 1479-1424BC (men kheper re) came to the throne at the age of twenty nine. He was Ancient Egypt's greatest military ruler defending and consolidating Egypt's largest Empire; he was also one of it's chief temple builders completing a total of fifty. He shared the dream of his grandfather, Thutmosis I, to conquer and subdue the Asiatics; his mission was to control the critical Mediterranean costal trading route, the Via Maris, and to expand the rich annual tribute from the Asian city state vassals. He is considered to this day to be a military genius and ranks alongside history's greatest warriors.

We are remarkably fortunate to know the details of almost all of his seventeen campaigns over twenty-one years, thanks to Thanuny (Thaneni), his royal scribe and commander. Perhaps the fine reputation of Tuthmosis 3 is partly due to the fact that his battles were each recorded in such great detail on the inside walls of his jubilee hall at Karnak, and inscribed on Thanuny's Theban tomb on the west bank. There Thanuny boasts *'I recorded the victories he won in every land, putting them into writing according to the facts'*. Known as the 'Annals', (right) the inscriptions are believed to have been written towards the end of his long reign.

Egypt had by his time now matched the weapons and tactics of its Asiatic neighbors in the north east. Thutmosis 3 strengthened the standing army and reorganized it into four divisions, each of five thousand. His mastery of chariot divisions, employment of innovative tactics (e.g hauling his boats across the Syrian hills to the Orontes river) sheer military professionalism and diligence were superior to any of his enemies His annals list the capture of three hundred and fifty towns and cities. During his twenty one years as junior co-regent and understudy to his aunt Hatshepsut, he had been trained in religious affairs but as heir apparent had spent most of his time with the army. He was twenty nine years of age when Hatshepsut passed away and he began his thirty-four year solo reign. His annals commence at year twenty-one, having incorporated Hatshepsut's co-regency into his combined reign of fifty five years. His main enemy was the Hurrian Mittani empire, which had progressively expanded its influence south west across the Euphrates down into Syria and even into Lebanon while Egypt's last two kings had turned a blind eye.

**First campaign- Megiddo.** On the death of Hatshepsut, the Mittani seized the opportunity to extend their influence at Egypt's expense. They sponsored a coalition of Syrian city states led by the King of Kadesh and encouraged him to move south to take the strategically important city of Megiddo in Retjenu (Canaan) while Egypt was distracted by the royal succession. However in year twenty one, Thutmosis 3 wasted no time. In April he assembled the whole army at the fortress of Sile (Tjaru) and, reaching Gaza in nine days, then drove north arriving at Yehem below Megiddo. The Battle of Megiddo was to be the first and largest of his career. Despite advice for caution he made the brilliant move to take the unexpected narrow mountain-pass route to Megiddo. He emerged at the rear of the enemy and defeated its inferior numbers. After a siege of seven months, the city fell and he gained north Canaan whose cities were now to send annual tribute. This victory sent warning signs throughout the region, the rising superpowers the Assyrians, Babylonians, and even the Hittites sent gifts, The Mittani had lost the first round. Years twenty-four to twenty-six saw annual campaigns to collect tribute in Retjenu (Canaan), and again Assyria sent him gifts. He occupied strategic ports in Canaan and sent troops to garrison them ready for the next offensive. He started his Karnak Jubilee temple at this time.

**Campaigns five and six – Syria.** From year twenty six the king of Tunip in north Syria attempted to subvert the Egyptian coastal ports; only Tyre remained loyal. Three years later Thutmosis 3 was ready to invade Syria.

First he sent Admiral Nibamun with the fleet and army to the far northern Syrian coast near Ugarit. After taking a nearby unnamed inland city the King of Tunip attacked but was defeated and Tunip was taken. The next year, thirty, Thutmosis 3 sent his navy to Sumur to commence campaign six. The army crossed the inland range of hills but failed to take Kadesh, he then returned to the coast and captured Arvad in retaliation for it's support of Kadesh.

First Jubilee. In year thirty he also celebrated his first jubilee by completing a huge building program. The south side of his seventh pylon at Karnak (right) is decorated with reliefs showing his Asiatic victories and listing the cities taken.His Festival Hall called the

akh menu 'the most glorious of monuments' with its
unique tent pole columns (right) was completed in the
same year. The column design was meant to remind
him of his many years training and campaigning with
the army when he lived rough in tents.

A room at the rear contains the so called 'Botanical'
reliefs (below) showing the plants and animals collected

on his many Syrian
campaigns. This is the first recorded reference to a
zoological garden in ancient history. The tomb of
court official Puyemre (TT39) records that the
king instructed him to cut and erect two granite
obelisks at Karnak for this first jubilee.

Thutmosis 3 implemented a process to keep conquered cities loyal which was
to be successfully copied by both the later Assyrian and Babylonian empires.
He took hostages of key family members from the conquered ruling nobles to
live and be educated in Egypt.

**Campaigns seven and eight – The Mittani.** In year thirty-one Thutmosis
3's fleet consolidated the territory around Sumur and requisitioned local grain
to build a stockpile of supplies for the forthcoming war, this continued in
the next year. All was now ready, and in year thirty three the fleet and army
sailed to Sumur. The army crossed the coastal mountains this time hauling
their boats, and successfully took Qatna on the Orontes river. The army then
followed the river downstream all the way north to the Naharin (Mittani)
regional capital of Aleppo, which was taken. He was now deep in Mittani
territory but undaunted he pushed north east to plunder the Euphrates valley.
The army engaged and defeated a Mittani force outside the gates of their
western capital city of Carchermish on the upper Euphrates. To celebrate,
Thutmosis 3 repeated the action of his grandfather fifty years before by
crossing the river and leaving a stele record beside that of Thutmosis I; both
are now lost. Thutmose 3 then proceeded to conduct a royal hunt of one
hundred and twenty elephants at Niy, like that of his grandfather. Receiving
tribute on the way home, he returned victorious to Thebes. This time the
gifts from the Assyrians, Babylonians and Hittites were grander, eight solid
silver giant rings were recorded. Silver was twice as valuable as gold during
this period. In October of year thirty three he had returned to Thebes in
time to greet a returning Punt trading expedition, with its usual rich cargo of
exotic materials. On the domestic front he extended the Libyan border to the
Siwa oasis which was settled under Governor Intef, and continued his colossal
building program with a new city and temple in the Fayum and new temples
at Denderah, Coptos, El Kab, Kom Ombo and Edfu.

**Campaigns nine and ten** were conducted in years thirty four and five. The king captured three new towns in lower Retjenu and strengthened and resupplied the local coastal cities in that region. Cyprus gave its first tribute of copper and Nubia was recorded as supplying one hundred and thirty four pounds of gold. In year thirty four he celebrated his second jubilee by erecting two new obelisks inscribed with his victory on the Euphrates The Karnak relief (right) shows their dedication.

The area of Nuhasse, in western Naharin, revolted in year thirty-five, but the Mittani rebels were defeated at Araina near Tunip. This ushered in seven years of peace with the Mittani. In year thirty seven he celebrated his third jubilee by erecting three more pairs of obelisks at Karnak. A pair was placed south of the seventh pylon, one of which now stands in the Hippodrome at Istanbul, (left). Two more obelisks were erected at Heliopolis and now stand in London and New York.

The annals relating to the next two campaigns, eleven and twelve, have been lost. The following four campaigns, in years thirty-eight to forty-one, were relatively minor affairs at Nuges in south Lebanon, against the Bedouin at Negeb, and two years on tours of inspection, collecting Syrian tribute. In year forty, Thutmosis 3 celebrated his fourth jubilee; particularly generous were the gifts frrom Assyria. The next year treasurer Menkheper reported Nubian gold had now reached eight hundred pounds a year. With this fabulous wealth the king in year forty, planned an enormous mortuary temple called djeser akhet (sacred horizon). The temple dedicated to Amen was built at Deir el Bahri, directly to the south of Hatshepsut's temple Djeser Djeseru. Djeser Akhet was built on a raised terrace and was approached by a broad causeway and ramp. It was originally similar in design and size to the temple of Hatshepsut and because it was built on higher ground it overshadowed hers; as its architects had intended. In the time of Ramesses 4, four hundred years later, it was reported to be falling into neglect, sadly nothing now remains. It is not a coincidence that at around the same time, year forty-one or forty-two, the program to remove Hatshepsut's name from history began. Her name was removed and replaced by those of either Thutmosis 1, or 2 or 3.

His seventeenth and final campaign, took place in year forty two. After seven years of peace with the Mittani they began to promote a revolt of the key cities of Tunip and Kadesh on the Orontes river. General Amenemheb's tomb(TT85) provides the narrative here. Thutmosis 3 moved his troops by sea to Sumur then he marched north to take Erkatu on the coast and proceeded to move east to take the rebelious Tunip. He besieged Kadesh and destroyed three local towns, before returning to Thebes to celebrate his final Asiatic victory.

However it appears that he had not been successful in taking Kadesh and Tunip would continue to agitate but not until after his reign had ended.

Year forty three marked his fifth jubilee. This time a 'unique' obelisk was erected; it was called tekhen waty and was designed to stand alone. It is the tallest ever made at 106 feet, but was only erected by Thutmose 4 thirty five years later. It stands today (right) in Rome, known as the Lateran Obelisk. At this time he completed his historically important 'Hall of Records' king list also known as the 'Chamber of Ancestors' on a wall in a side room off his festival hall the akh menu. Here Thutmosis 3 is shown making offerings to sixty one of this ancestors.

 The originals (left, drawn by Lepsius) of these were removed and are now in the Louvre Museum, Paris. Nehi had been Viceroy of Nubia for twenty years; in regnal year forty-seven Nehi erected a stele at Gebel Barkel (Napata) at the fourth cataract of the Nile where he proclaimed his king's magnificent reign, Nubia and Kush had been at peace throughout. In year fifty the king ordered the clearing of the Aswan canal and felt sufficiently confident to establish a new capital of Kush at Napata two hundred miles further south than the previous capital at Kerma. He continued his north Nubia building program with new temples at Kalabsha, Amada, Wadi Halfa and Semna.

**First cathedral style** At the Karrnak ipet-sut court, between pylons four and five, he rebuilt the hypostyle hall of his grandfather Thutmosis I replacing the cedar wood columns with stone. This hall was the first in a 'basilica style' with rows of pillars supporting a ceiling on each side of an aisle. The central two rows, each of seven columns, were higher than those at the side to allow for light to flood in through lattice stone windows into the otherwise dark hall. This was to become the style for future Egyptian kings most notably Amenhotep 3 at Luxor and Seti I at Karnak. It was also to be the model for Roman basilicas and ultimately for Christian cathedrals and churches from the European Middle Ages onwards.

At the age of fifty-five, the momentous reign of Thutmosis 3 ended and he went to his destiny. He was buried in the Valley of the Kings in tomb KV34. Its entrance is positioned brilliantly, sixty feet above the floor of the valley, and set far back in the cliff face and well out of sight. It is a very impressive tomb and quite challenging to enter. It was first discovered by Loret in 1898 but it had been robbed in antiquity. The burial chamber contains two columns and has a star-decorated roof. In the middle of the chamber is the large

beautifully decorated red quartzite sarcophagus in the shape of a cartouche. The walls are decorated with simplistic figures (left-bottom) of scenes from the New Kingdom religious book the Amduat. On a central pillar in the burial chamber is this unique 'stick man' image (right) depicting Thutmosis 3 being suckled by the goddess Isis in the form of a tree.

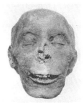

The mummy (left) of Thutmose 3 was discovered in the Deir el Bahri royal mummy cache of 1881. Maspero in 1886 reported that '... *his forehead is abnormally low, the eyes deeply sunk, the jaw heavy, the lips thick, and the cheek bones extremely prominent.'* In stark contrast, his bust (right) shows refined intelligent features, almond eyes, high eye brows an aquiline nose and a gently curved mouth.

In the early 1900's Grafton Elliot Smith originally reported that the mummy had a height of only five feet and four inches, initiating the fallacy that he was a short man. He failed to mention that the feet of the mummy were missing; we now know that one of Egypt's greatest military kings was of normal height for his time.

Thutmosis 3 bequeathed to his royal successor a consolidated largely peaceful Empire. Its boundaries had been greatly extended in the south and east, the Asian vassals and the Mittani were for now dormant. It may have been around this time or a little later, that the so called Kurustama Treaty was agreed between Egypt and the Hittites. The undated treaty, only known from later Hittite sources, allowed the residents of the north Anatolian town of Kurustama to resettle in the Egyptian controlled Asiatic lands. At this juncture, the Mittani were seen by Egypt as by far the most dangerous threat in the region; the Hittites at this time were not the dominant force they were to become sixty years later under king Suppiluliuma I.

The flow of wealth into Egypt was now unprecedented, gold from Nubia and tribute from the Asiatics filled the treasury, heralding in a new golden and peaceful era.

# Chapter Nine

# The Sun Kings, Amenhotep 3, Akhenaten + Tutankhamen

Thanks to the enterprise of Thutmiosis 3 the Egyptian Empire was now at its peak. The transition was initially slow but the focus of the kingdom was starting to move away from military conflict with its north-eastern neighbors to one of reconciliation, peace treaties and compromise. Initially this was a successful strategy when dealing with the Mittani but later the kings of Egypt become distracted by internal religious friction which brought the Empire to the brink of disaster when the more powerful aggressor, the Hittites emerged.

**Amenhotep 2** 1424-1398BC (a kheperu re) cartouche right, inherited the empire from his father when he was eighteen years old, he was to rule for twenty-six years. Amenhotep 2 was the son of Thutmose 3 by the commoner minor wife Meryetre-Hatshepsut, there was no competition from the children of his father and his Great Royal Wife, as they had all died whilst young. He grew up in Memphis, not Thebes which gave him a weaker link to  the dominant Theban Amen cult. He is principally known from the Karnak and Giza inscriptions relating to his athletic skills with the bow, as an oarsman and as an army commander. It was said *'no man could draw his bow'*. One relief shows him putting an arrow through a three inch thick copper target and it was reported he could row his ship faster than anyone in the navy. After becoming ruler, he married a non royal called Tiaa from the Re cult center of Heliopolis, her son was to become Thutmosis 4. She is deliberately hardly mentioned, to minimise the potential of her in a dynastic role as Great Royal Wife seen in the Hatshepsut interlude.

As was customary in the ancient world, when a new Egyptian king ascended to the throne it was marked by an uprising in the Asiatic cities and ports. According to his Karnak stele, in the middle of regnal year two, Amenhotep 2 led the army overland and defeated the rebellious Canaanite coalition of princes at the unknown city of Shemesh. He then proceeded north and crossed the Orontes at Senzar into Tikhsi (south Naharin) where he defeated a coalition of Tikhsi princes, capturing seven of them. With the rebellion now broken, he set out for home, calling at Niy on the Euphrates which *'opened their gate to him'*. However, here he heard of a revolt at Ikathi (unknown) which he put down and only then returned to Memphis. On his way back, he collected the astounding amount 1,660 pounds of gold in Asiatic tribute, equivalent to two whole years production of the entire Nubain gold mines. His undeserved reputation for cruelty stems from the next documented incident mentioned in the Theban tomb of General Amenemheb (TT85). He is reported to have personally killed the seven Tikhsi princes and hung their bodies on the prow of his ships as he celebrated his success during visits to Thebes and Napata (Kush). Their bodies were then hung on their walls '*...in order to cause to be seen the victorious might of His Majesty for ever and ever...*' This was apparently meant as an example of the consequence of rebellion. Nubia and Kush interestingly both remained quiet throughout his reign.

The next campaign took place in year, seven in response to another Mittani-sponsored revolt by their vassals in Nuhasse east of Ugarit. Amenhotep 2 sailed to Byblos, then crossed to the Orontes and proceeded downriver to raid into Nuhasse. He returned south and punished the Orontes towns of Niya, Qatna, and Laish (east of Tyre) for their support of the rebels. The campaign seems more of a policing action than one of conquest. His last campaign took place in year nine, the army raided into Retjenu (Canaan), took the city of Gath, defeated a rebel prince at Megiddo and returned with the hugely exaggerated total of ninety thousand captives.

The Mittani were now at their peak but becoming concerned about the new rising superpower of the Hittites on their western border, as well as Babylon, growing to their south. In year nine instead of making peace with the more powerful and dangerously expansionist Hittites, Amenhotep 2 responded to the Mittani and concluded an informal non aggression pact, in an attempt to jointly hold off the Hittites. The border was set around Kadesh, his pact was to become a fully fledged peace treaty in the reign of his son.

In year twenty-two his jubilee was celebrated with the construction of a rather modest temple pavilion at Karnak south of pylon eight. This kneeling statue (Egizio Museum, Turin) shows him making an offering to Amen there, it is one one of two extant in this pose. The temple comprised a court of square pillars with reliefs and decorated walls. Most importantly, this temple and its gardens, although dedicated to Amen, contained decorations featuring royal regalia which showed strong Re connections, such as sun discs on  top of crowns, a portent of the future religious upheaval. The temple was destroyed either during the Amen purges of Akhenaten or during Horemheb's building projects; the stones were later used in a Seti 1 building. The temple has now been rebuilt by van Siclen.

Amenhotep 2 also erected a victory column between the fourth and fifth pylons describing the above campaigns and Mittani tribute. His most notable Nubian temple construction was at Amada north of Buhen. He built his small mortuary temple just east of the later Ramesseum on the west bank;, like his father's it was quarried in ancient times. His building work at Giza is notable. He built a temple dedicated to Horemakhet,a sun-god associated with the Great Sphinx. The Sphinx and its adjoining temple complex became the site of a cult of royalty, including Amenhotep 2 himself, and his son Thutmosis 4, who later set up the great Dream Stele between its paws. The Sphinx's Horemakhet cult lasted well into Roman times.

The following year, twenty-three, he wrote a personal letter to his Nubain Viceroy Usersatet reminding him of their successful Asiatic campaigns together. He emphasized Egyptian racial superiority and warned him to be on his guard when dealing with foreigners *'..do not trust the Nubians, but beware of their people and their witchcraft. ..... do not listen to their words and do not heed their messages!'* The text, which curiously mildly admonished his old colleague the Viceroy, was copied and engraved by him on a stele at the second cataract, it is now in the Boston Museum.

A schism had been building between the king, who seems to have favoured the cult of the sun god Re, and the powerful Amen priesthood. Towards the end of his reign Amenhotep 2 acted, he enforced his will by selecting and appointing the high priest of Amen himself. Interestingly a stele at Giza shows the first image of the sun disc the Aten, with rays ending in the ankh of life. This religious conflict will tear the country apart forty years later.

**Royal mummy cache.** Amenhotep 2 was buried in tomb KV35(right) which was well located, hidden at the end of a western gully in the south west segment of the Valley of the Kings.His mummy was discovered in 1898 by Loret, inside his large red quartzite sarcophagus. He was one of only two kings to have been found intact, apparently ignored by the ancient tomb robbers. KV35 is a large well decorated tomb which is an architectural delight. The tomb walls contain the full text of the Book of Amduat and painted scenes from it laid out as if the walls were a papyrus roll. On the ceiling is the familiar  pattern of gold stars on a dark blue background.Within the western walled up annex, Loret found a true treasure, the second great royal mummy cache. It contained the sarcophagi and mummies of nine other royal mummies as well as Amenhotep 2's son, prince Webensenu, and probably his mother, Hatshepsut-Meryetre. These kings included Tuthmosis 4, Amenohotep 3, Merneptah, Seti 2, Siptah, Setnakhte, Ramesses 4, 5 and 6. In all, he found the remains of seventeen royal burials in this unviolated cache. Its discovery ranks very highly indeed in Egyptology. The cache was placed there for safe-keeping three hundred and fifty years after the death of Amenhotep 2, by the 21st Dynasty High Priest of Amen, Pinedjem 2, to protect them from tomb robbers during a period of financial chaos and lawlessness c1035BC after the collapse of the New Kingdom

His reign ended in a confused dynastic succession. The crown prince, also called Amenhotep, was the eldest son and heir to Amenhotep 2. The evidence suggests that he was usurped by his younger brother Thutmosis 4. In the ensuing power struggle, his grandmother Meryetre seems to have backed her eldest grandson, the crown prince. and was disgraced as a consequence. The treausurer, Amenken, may also have backed the wrong prince as his name has been removed from his tomb.

### Thutmosis 4 1398-1388BC (men kheper u re).

Little is known about the short ten-year reign of Thutmose 4 (right, Louvre, Paris) who came to the throne at nineteen. He is most famous for his 'Dream Stele', erected at the Sphinx and still present today. It is a marvelous piece of propaganda to legitimize his right to the throne. He claims that as a young prince he was hunting in the desert at Giza and stopped to rest in the shadow of the Sphinx, at that time mostly buried in sand. Falling asleep he dreamt the Sphinx told

him that if the prince restored the Sphinx he would become the next ruler. In regnal year one to mark the restoration Thutmosis 4 placed this inscribed tall stone tablet (left) between the paws of the Sphinx. The stele was a reused door lintel from Khafre's nearby Old Kingdom mortuary temple.

Like his father he chose to live at Memphis not Thebes, his Great Royal Wives were Nefertari and his sister Laret, he also married a little known commoner called Mutemwiya, 'Mut is in her barque', who bore him a son and successor, the great Sun King Amenhotep 3. Later, for diplomatic reasons, he also married a Mittani princess, the daughter of king Aratama I. Some believe that she changed her name and may have been Mutemwiya;, there is no evidence for this. However, it is the first recorded time that an Egyptian king married a foreign wife.

After almost twenty years of peace, Mittani unrest broke out in Naharin (Syria). In his first campaign, in year six, Thutmosis 4 'defeated' the rebel Naharin princes; their tribute was recorded in Karnak. His second campaign was a policing operation in Retjenu (Canaan) and the collection of tribute and cedar from Sidon (in Lebanon). Personal tragedy struck in year seven, when his son by Nefertari died, so he appointed his seven-year old son by Mutemwiya as crown prince. In year eight his Konosso (near Philae) stele records that he put down a gold mine camp unrest in the Eastern desert and conducted a policing action to protect the gold mine routes out of Nubia. In the inscriptions he is referred to as 'Conqueror of Syria'. In year eight a formal *peace treaty of one hundred years* with the Mittani was concluded. Apart from letters of cooperation and the marriage to the Mittani princess, we know little about the detail other than Alakah (Antioch) remained under the Mittani. There was never to be another conflict with them. Thutmosis 4 also also concluded a friendly alliance with Babylon.

For thirty-five years the last obelisk planned by Thutmosis 3 had lain unfinished in the Karnak temple. Thutmosis 4 now had it engraved in his grandfather's name and recorded also his own work in having it erected. It was placed alone at the extreme east end of the temple complex. The so called 'single' obelisk of red granite was at one hundred and six feet the tallest obelisk ever erected in Egypt, and is now in Rome at Laterano. The erection of the obelisk is thought to have commemorated a little known jubilee. The most

notable work of art from his reign is this exquisite black diad granite statue of the king and his mother Tiaa. (Egyptian Museum, Cairo)

Thutmose 4 died at the young age of twenty- nine and was buried in the remote tomb KV43 which was found by Carter in 1903. The robbed tomb contained his war chariot, decorated with victories over Asian and Nubian tribes. His mummy was found seaparately as part of the royal mummy cache in KV35 of 1898. The red sarcophagus still remains in the tomb; it is breathtaking. Hieratic text on the south wall of the antechamber comes from the reign of Horemheb and refers to the robbery and Horemheb's restoration of the tomb. His mummified body shows signs of extreme illness, it appears he was wasting away for the final months of his life. It is belived that in the end he died quite suddenly, as the decoration of his tomb was not completed in time. His reign is seen as a prelude for the religious sea change which was to come in the next thirty years. There are clear hints that royal patronage was shifting away from the cult of Amen towards the 5th Dynasty solar cult. There are images of and reference to the sun disc, the 'Aten' and the king showed favor towards the Helipolis priests versus the dominant Amen priests of Thebes, which he tried to control. Royal art was also changing; Thutmosis 4, towards the end of his reign, is shown in one statue (see JEA 436) with pronounced feline eyes. There was no co-regency with his son Amenhotep 3, who came to the throne at around eleven years of age to become the great Sun King

## Amenhotep 3 (1388-1349BC) (neb maat re)

Amenhotep 3, like his father, lived in Memphis, he spent the first twenty five years there with visits to Thebes the religious capital. The length of his solo reign is of much debate and hinges on the length of the co- regency if any, with his son Amenthotep 4 (later Akhenaten). However, it is generally accepted that Amenhotep 3 reigned in total for thirty nine almost entirely peaceful, years. He was the master diplomat; he allied Egypt to most of the kings of the superpowers through diplomatic marriages with their daughters or sisters, coupled with regular generous gifts of gold, as attested in the royal correspondence consisting of three hundred and eighty two 'Amarna letters'.

He inherited the most powerful and wealthy Empire the world had yet seen. For over one hundred years gold had been flowing north from Nubia and huge tribute was being paid annually by the Syrian provinces. The Amen cult religious centers of Karnak and Luxor alone had grown to a population of ninety thousand souls. He was to make good use of this wealth in the largest construction program yet seen and he left a record one thousand statues. Since he was only eleven when he came to the throne, his mother Mutemwiya may have acted as regent but there is no record of this. He started early, in his first and second regnal years the Tura limestone quarries were expanded  and construction commenced. He produced over two hundred and fifty statues of himself during his lifetime, many of colossal proportions often including his wife and daughters. He was the first to produce a series of over two hundred large commemorative scarab seals, akin to the earlier Assyrian and Babylonian type cylinder seals,which have been found all over his empire. In year two,at fourteen years of age, he produced a scarab boasting of his hunting and killing of ninety six bulls at Wadi Natron in the Delta. Another scarab, in year two announced his marriage to ten year old commoner Tiy (above, Berlin Museum), in many of her statues she is shown as being rather plain. She became his Great Royal Wife and lifelong companion eventually outliving him by twelve years. This magnificent colossal diad statue (right)  of the king and Tiy from his mortuary temple, is around thirty feet high and is the tallest ever made. (Egyptian Museum,Cairo) The parents of Tiy were Yuya and Tuya, commoners from Akhmim (near Girga). Because of his relationship to the king, Yuya rose at court ultimately becoming General of Chariots. As commoners, they were given the singular honor of being allowed to have a tomb (KV46) in the Valley of the Kings. Along with Tutankhamen they are the only almost intact 'royal' tombs yet discovered.

In October of regnal year four came a Nubian tax revolt, he travelled to the first cataract with the southern army and fleet to suppress it. The next year his Viceroy Merimose, perhaps accompanied by the king,crushed a minor harvest tax revolt near Sai island, his stelae at both Aswan and Semna record this modest victory, seven hundred and forty prisoners were captured. Merimose also raided further south past Kurgus on the 4th Nile cataract. His Aswan inscription records that he reached the fifth cataract, the deepest south ever reached. The gold brought back was used to fund the start of his massive Karnak (ipt sut) third pylon, now mostly quarried. At that time it was the main entrance to the temple complex. Silver had become more plentiful and gold by this time was valued at one and a half times silver, a reversal from earlier times as the silver mines in Anatolia were expanded by the Hittites.

In year ten a commemorative scarab boasted that he had killed a total of one hundred and two lions so far in his reign. Over one hundred copies of this particular scarab have survived. He then started on his master work, the Luxor temple complex or ipt rsyt meaning the southern residence, of Amen.

The earlier shrine buildings erected by Thutmosis 3 and Hatshepsut were cleared and replaced with a thirty two column hypostyle hall, he then added the peristyle open solar court and finally his true masterpiece, the Great Colonnade (right) consisting of two rows each of seven columns rising to a height of fifty-two, feet decorated with attractive open papyrus capitals. The Great Colonnade hall was one hundred and sixty-four feet long, however its side walls, roof and decoration were left unfinished. It was here that he copied the Hatshepsut inscription at Deir el Bahri claiming he was the son of the god Amen.

Also in year ten, a commemorative scarab, of which only five have survived, announced his marriage to Giluk Hepa, daughter of Shuttarna 2, king of the Mittani; she arrived with a reported retinue of 'three hundred and seventeen' female servants. Amenhotep 3 took great pains to emphasize on the scarab that Tiy was still his Great Royal Wife. Clearly this was purely a diplomatic wedding in an attempt to promote the Mittani alliance in the face of the expanding Hittites.Giluk Hepa is never heard of again. In the famous Amarna letter EA4 there is a complaint by the Babylonian king that he has not been permitted to marry one of the daughters of Amenhotep 3. Egyptian kings were paranoiac on this subject, as they feared a subsequent child could be a contender for the throne of Egypt itself.

In year eleven the last of the commemorative scarabs, the 'lake' scarab, described how he built in fifteen days a boating and irrigation lake for Tiy at her home town of Akhmim to emphasize her importance. It records that '...his Majesty was rowed in the royal barge the tehen-aten...' Tehen aten means the dazzling sun disc. It was to become his favorite title.

**Religious friction.** During the reigns of the previous two kings we have seen tantalizing incidents of friction between the royal family and the powerful cult priesthood of Amen at Thebes. Since the start of the New Kingdom the Amen, priests had been the religious driving force supported by the ruling family. For over two hundred years they had grown ever more powerful and supremely wealthy. By the time of Amenhotep 3, they now controlled one third of the fertile land and thereby twenty percent of the population. From regnal year twenty onwards, the power struggle between the royal family and the Amen cult priests of Thebes began to escalate. Around year twenty-five the king appointed his son, crown prince Thutmosis, to the role of high priest of Ptah at Memphis, thus overshadowing the Amen cult. Thutmosis was responsible for the first mummification and burial at Saqqara of the bull representing the god Apis. However, he was later to pre-decease his father. In year twenty-five his son Amenhotep 4 was born, being the second son he was not groomed for the throne. It is curious that both sons were rarely shown in reliefs or statues, unlike his daughters, leading to the speculation that they may have been deformed. In fact the only reference to his son Amenhotep 4 during his father's entire rule is a single wine jar label from Malkata towards the end of the reign.

**Year twenty nine** is pivotal. Friction with the Amen priests continued when the king himself appointed Nbnfr as high priest of Amen and, rather strangely, he built a fort in Karnak equiped with a full royal military garrison. At the same time he commenced the construction of an enormous brick royal government complex, not on the east bank but at Malkata (per hay), on the west bank well away from the Karnak and Luxor temples and the Amen cult priests. Malkata contained an Amen temple along with a festival hall and a royal palace called the 'splendor of the Aten'. There is speculation as to why Amenhotep 3 chose this precise timing. It is belived that a major plague had broken out in Memphis and the king moved his palace and the government south to Thebes. Malkata today is a flat almost complete ruin.

**First jubilee and deification.** Amenhotep 3 celebrated his first Heb Sed jubilee in year thirty at the now finished Malkata palace complex, complete with a huge Nile linked harbor one mile long by a quarter of a mile wide, which was used as a boating lake for the king and Tiy on ceremonial occasions. In the dedication texts Khaemhat, the overseer of granaries, reported a bumper harvest and that tribute from the Asian vassal cities had set a record. In celebration, a magnificent new temple with two open solar courts, each three hundred feet long, decorated with two fine red granite lions, was built. The location was highly significant. It was deliberately not in Egypt proper, but far away in Kush, at Soleb, below the third Nile cataract. The temple was dedicated to the worship of himself, as the Aten, with his son Amenhotep 4 as the high priest. Being deified in his own lifetime was a shrewd political and religious strategy designed to temper the power of the Amen cult and its priesthood. However, he was careful not to provoke the Amen cult priests by promoting his worship as a god in Egypt itself.

**Mortuary Temple.** However, there were signs that his health was beginning to fail and he started to extend a tomb WV22, commnceed by his father not in the Amen dominated Valley of the Kings but in the close-by West Valley. He also started the construction of his mortuary temple (Arabic, Kom el Hetan) on the west bank opposite and south of Thebes; it became the largest mortuary temple ever built in Egypt.He deliberately chose to build at the edge of the flood plain to allow the inundation waters to lap up to the solar court walls reflecting the Ancient Egytian legend of the origins of the world. Over time the innundations destroyed the three mud brick entrance pylons; the stone constructions survivied but were tragically quarried by king Merneptah

for his own temple two-hundred years later. All that now remains are the 'Colossi of Memnon', two massive quartzite sandstone statues (right) of Amenhotep 3 looking east towards the rising sun and the river Nile. They are now sixty-five feet high having lost their five-foot crowns, and weigh seven-hundred tons each. They were each originally created from a single massive block, brought four-hundred and twenty miles from a Cairo area quarry. However an earthquake in Roman times c27BC left the north statue badly damged which caused it to 'sing' at dawn. The great builder, Libyan born Emperor Septimius Severus 193-211AD, repaired the damage. The large blocks used by his engineers c199AD came from Edfu along with the stone platforms on which they now stand. In smaller scale, on the base of each statue beside his legs are his wife Tiy and his mother Mutemwiya. He also erected 730, significantly twice the number of days in the year, smaller statues of the healing lioness god Sekhmet, some have been found across the river in the Karnak Temple of Mut. It is believed that he built this giant mortuary temple complex, which was even larger than the Karnak temple complex at the time, along with the Temple of Montu to dilute the influence of Amen.

Many of the series of twenty-six feet high statues of himself at Kom el Hetan were 'adopted' by later kings such as Ramesses 2 and 3 and Merneptah. Excavations at Kom el Hetan from 2002 onwards have uncovered and restored an important giant sandstone stele thirty feet high. It was originally gold plated and showed the 'station of the king' and recorded the policy of educating Syrian princes at the Egyptian court. Another stele, ten feet high,

was found reused by Merneptah; it recorded Amenhotep 3's gifts of bronze and cedar doors for his mortuary temple. Only in 2004, a perfectly intact twelve feet high statue of Tiye was uncovered by the Colossi of Memnon as well as several beautiful diad statues of Amenhotep 3 and Tiy. Gone however, are the two obelisks and the avenue of jackals.

In 1989 in the solar courtyard of Amenhotep 3 at Luxor, a cache of statues including this (left) eight feet high pink quartzite masterpiece were discovered. It was made in year thirty, after he was deified, yet he is shown in a youthful form.

The eyes are emphatically feline, like those of Thutmosis 4 mentioned above, a second prelude to the naturalistic Amarna art style shortly to come. It is has been perfectly preserved and is considered to be amongst the most magnificent of all Egyptian statues in the round.

Perhaps the most notable official of the king was the scribe Amenhotep, son of Hapu. He (right) was not given elevated titles but was very close to the king being a key religious adviser and the architect of his building and sculpture programs. He designed and built the Karnak south axis gateway, which was later replaced by Horemheb's pylon ten. He also constructed two sixty-seven feet high colossal statues similar to the 'Collossi of Memnon'. They were positioned outside his Karnak southern gateway but have been quarried; all that remains in situ is a lonely giant left foot. In year thirty-one, uniquely for a commoner, he was allowed to build a mortuary temple for himself on the west bank and was later even worshipped as a god. The same year Amenhotep 3 appointed his second daughter, Sitamen, as ceremonial Royal Wife. Ominously, later that year, the Mittani king Tushratta wrote Amarna letter EA17 to Amenhotep 3. In it he reported that the Hittites had launched a major invasion of his lands but he had succeeded in holding them off, for now. Records from here to the death of Amenhotep 3 are sparse. Wine-jar labels, found in his tomb, show that items were already being stored there in preparation. His mother and Tiy's parents had recently died; the latter,although commoners, were buried in the Valley of the Kings.(KV46)

He celebrated his second jubilee in year thirty-four with more building and decoration projects at Memphis and Kush. At Sedenga, near to his own divine temple at Soleb, he built a new smaller version dedicated to wife Tiy the first time a royal wife had been so honored. Around this time he married (Amarna letter EA32) the daughter of the king of Arzawa, in western Anatolia, to strengthen the coalition against the growing Hittite threat. In total he married five foreign princesses during his reign. An Aswan rock inscription from this time records the cutting of six obelisks for Karnak; none remain.He also had constructed a small square temple on Elephantine Island, which is considered to be the model the Greeks used for their temple designs around nine-hundred years later.

In year thirty-six he married a second Mittani princess, Taduk Hepa, the daughter of king Tushratta, this time the retinue of the princess was only three hundred strong. It is presumed that the previous Mittani princess Giluk Hepa had by now died. By now, his health was failing fast, his mummy shows that he was probably in constant pain during these final years from abscesses below his badly worn, pitted teeth. There is a hint that he sought medical help; Tushratta sent a statue of the healing goddess Ishtar (Sasuka) of Nineveh (Amarna letter EA23). However the arrival of the statue coincided with the marriage to

Taduk Hepa and there is no specific mention of his ailments in the letter. Year thirty-six was the last to provide an historical text from his reign; it was a stele in the Sinai. Although he celebrated his third jubille in year thirty-six or seven, there is only one record of this from the Theban tomb of Kharuf. Reliefs of Amenhotep 3 from his last three years have been found at Soleb, Theban tomb TT192, and a painted limestone shrine base from Amarna. They all show the king as a bentover infirm figure who may have also suffered from arthritis and appears quite obese, consistent with the focus in the jubilee years on produce and food offerings. He went to his destiny half way into year thirty-nine. After the traditional period of mourning he was taken from the Malkata palace to his mortuary temple to be embalmed and then laid to rest in his West Valley tomb. He left behind an empire, on the surface, seemingly at the very height of its power and influence, commanding immense respect in the international world. In the end, he died rather suddenly, and was unable to complete the decoration of his tomb and his Great Colonnade hall at Luxor.

He left two crises about to boil over. One was the religious conflict with the Amen priesthood which would crystallize soon after the ascent of his son and successor Amenhotep 4 (right). The other was the growing threat of the second most powerful superpower in the region, the Hittites. They were threatening to destroy his allies the Mittani and overwhelm the Nuhasse cities of Ugarit, Senzar and Qatna in north Syria. In the last years of his life there are indications that Amenhotep 3 was forced to send troops to bolster his Asiatic bases against Hittite-sponsored incursions. The balance of power in the region was about to change. However, it is interesting to observe that the Hittites did not use the death of Amenhotep 3 to sponsor a general uprising of the Mittani vassals in north Syria. The Hittites probably observed, what appeared to the outside world as, a stable transition of power in Egypt from the late king to his heir. In any case, the Hittite royal family had internal court problems of their own which keept them occupied for the next ten years.

## Amenhotep 4 c1360-c1343BC later to be called Akhenaten

There has been intense debate for over a hundred years concerning the co-regency issue between Amenhotep 3 and his son. The majority of Egyptologists today believe there was no co-regency or one lasting one to two years at most. However their opponents strongly support a much longer co-regency of fifteen years or more. It is an important issue as it distorts the chronology of both monarchs. The arguments from both sides are persuasive, however, until new evidence emerges it will remain unresolved. The chronology referred to here, follows his seventeen regnal years.

Amenhotep 4 was around thirteen years old when his father passed away, since his elder brother had already died the young prince came to the throne probably with his mother Tiy and other members of his father's court staff acting as advisors. A year or two before becoming king he had married the ten or eleven year old Nefertiti 'the beautiful one has come' who became his Great Royal Wife. Although not royal, she was very well connected being the daughter of Ay the brother of Amenhotep 3's wife Tiy. Her early portraits show her as being quite beautiful; this world famous painted bust (Altes Museum, Berlin) has made her the most recognized woman of the ancient world. Amenhotep 4 had, at ten years of age, already married his first wife, Kiya who is refered to as his 'greatly beloved wife;' she delivered him two sons. Smenkhare was born around the time of his father's coronation and Tutankhamen was born ten years later.

At first everything seemed normal. Amenhotep 4, lived in Thebes at his father's west bank Malkata palace and administration center, although the state government capital remained at Memphis. In year one, he added his name to his father's Karnak giant west entrance pylon three and the south axis gateway. In the following year, a relief, on a small 'talatat' building block found in pylon ten, showed the king with Nefertiti in a boat. She was in a most unusual pose striking down an enemy along side her husband, implying equality to the king. He curiously celebrated his Heb Sed jubilee in only year three, it is believed that this was an early show of strength. He wanted to demonstrate to the Amen cult priesthood that although still young he was in control. Like his father he built temples deep into Kush at Sesebi and Kawa, but both were conventionally dedicated to Amen.

**The Aten temples.** A little later Meretamen, (afterwards Meretaten) the first of six daughters by Nefertiti, now only around fourteen years old, was born. He opened the sandstone quarries at Silsila and from the inscriptions there comes the first indication of the movement away from the Amen cult. The dedication inscription at the quarry is not only to the conventional national gods Amen and Re but also to the Aten; his first reference to the Aten sun disc.

Now the pace of change accelerated. He started to refer to Thebes as *'the city of brightness of Aten'* and in year four and five commenced two huge temple projects plus two smaller shrines at Karnak, importantly he selected a site outside the

established precinct of Amen well to the east. The two temples were called gem pa aten (the sun disc is formed) and hwt bnbn (the mansion of the ben ben). To save construction time both used small standardized stone block talatats (left); they were easier to cut and transport than the traditional much larger stone blocks. All of the young kings's new temple buildings were later dismantled and the forty thousand talatat blocks were re-used as foundations and fill for later Karnak pylons. A notable relief at gem pa aten, on one of the thirty-five feet high piers, showed the Aten rays ending in tiny protective hands which touched Nefertiti and her daughter Meretaten. The texts on the smaller temple hwt bnbn only mention Nefertiti implying it was dedicated to her alone and not to the king. In year four Nefertiti had a second daughter Meketaten, she is shown on reliefs at hwt bnbn along with the third daughter, Ankhesenpaaten.

**The first monotheist.** Year five was the pivotal year, The Karnak Aten temples had been completed and his relationship with the priests of Amen-Re deteriorated. Amenhotep 4 took steps to raise the Aten to preeminence over Amen but did not proscribe Amen or other gods. To emphasize this further he changed his name to Akhenaten the 'servant of the Aten'. His split from Amen was now complete. He began the construction of a new capital, Akhetaten the 'Horizon of Aten', at Amarna a completely new site, chosen to be mid way between Thebes and Memphis. He constructed a total of three new Aten cities; the other two were at Sesebi in Kush, south of his father's Kush solar temple at Soleb, and one in Canaan, which has been lost. At Akhetaten, he constructed massive temple complexes in the style of his father's solar court at Luxor. The Aten was worshipped in the open sunlight, rather than Amen's dark gloomy temples. He composed the wonderful monotheist (one god) 'Great Hymn to the Aten' which bears uncanny resemblance to the Old Testament Psalm 104. Historians of religion regard him as the world's first monotheist and his new Aten based religion as the forerunner of the later three great world religions Judaism, Christianity and Islam. Akhenaten's monotheism appears in history at least two hundred years prior to the first archaeological and written evidence for Judaism found in the Levant. Sigmund Freud even proposed that the Old Testament figure Moses (Egyptian for son of), had been an Atenist priest, forced to leave Egypt with his followers after Akhenaten's death.

In year six the boundary stelae for the new city were completed along with the Aten temples. The temple reliefs showed Nefertiti and Akhenaten worshipping with their daughters. The royal family and the entire government had moved to Amarna, by year eight, which grew to a peak of around seventy-five thousand inhabitants. By year nine, seeking greater visibility, he developed a novel royal routine. He apppeared each day to his subjects as he rode in an open chariot with Nefertiti and his daughters from the royal palace to the Aten temples. This ready accessibility of the ruler to his people was unique. It ended at his death. Progressively he removed the name of Amen frorm public gaze including the Amen part of his father's Amenhotep titles and any reference to the plurality 'gods'. He closed most of the Amen temples at Karnak disenfranchising tens of thousands of Amen cult priests and attendents in the process. However, he did not completely prohibit the worship of Amen and other gods thoughout the kingdom.

**Amarna Art.** Along with the new religion came a new art form, the so called 'Amarna style'. The royal sculptor Bek was responsible for creating the images from the first part of Akhenaten's reign. A typical example of this 'early Amarna style' is the king's head shown at the start of this section. Bek recorded that he was taught by the king himself. The feline eyes, so remarkable in the statues of this early period of Akhenaten's rule, are a continuation of a style seen to be developing late in the reign of his father, Amenhotep 3, and even observed in the reign of his grandfather, Thutmosis 4.

The Aten itself is usually shown as a rayed solar disc (right) in which the sun's rays end in hands often touching and protecting the members of the royal family. This early Amarna art style is a radical departure from tradition; it is very humanistic and rather unflattering. Theories rage as to whether Akhenaten was actually deformed or suffered form Marfan's syndrome. It is much more likely that he simply wanted to differentiate himself from the rulers of the past and the traditional Amen art style.

However when royal sculptor, Bek, died in year twelve the art style of his successor the sculptor Thutmosis softened. The royal body shape was less exaggerated and become quite realistic as seen in the famous late period bust of Nefertiti and in this late full statue of her in middle age (right). Akhenaten too was shown in a more natural style; his exaggerated narrow face and feline eyes from the early period statues have given way to a more realistic but still quite unflattering style which shows him with rounded shoulders (left) and with a protruding belly not unlike that of his father when in old age.

**Queen Tiya.** In year nine, it appears that his wife Kiya died perhaps giving birth to Tutankamen, a relief in the Amarna royal tomb (room A wall F) shows a distressed, grieving Akhenaten.However, no reference to her has been found after regnal year six implying that she had fallen from favour. An Amarna Royal tomb stele shows Kiya's name replaced by his daughter Meretaten who became his consort and was referred to as 'wife and beloved of Akhenaten'. Around year ten and eleven daughters five and six were born to Nefertiti, still seemingly trying for a son.

**The Hittites** The great Hittite general, prince Suppiluliuma assasinated his older brother Tudhaliya 3 and ascended to the Hittite thrown c1350BC, this corresponds to around year ten of the reign of Akhenaten. That year the

Hittites made a lightening invasion deep into the Mittani lands; they defeated king Tushratta, Egypt's main ally, and destroyed his state capital. Suppiluliuma I, on his homeward march, then took the western capital of Carchemish and moved south to take Allepo and the strategically important city of Kadesh, on the border with Egypt. From the Amarna letters we learn that King Tushratta and the princes of Tyre and Sidon sent pleas for military help and gold. No military support was sent; Akhenaten was a man of peace and had treaties with both sides. In regnal year eleven, Supiluliuma I and the Hittite army consolidated north Syria then penetrated east again, into the Mittani heartland, this time Tushratta was killed. The Hittites then pressed south and with their new vassal, the prince of Kadesh, attacked and captured Damascus, but were very careful not to attack the key Egyptian vassal Byblos which could have seriously provoked Akhenaten.

With the Pax Egyptica now broken, the Syrian vassal princes were free to attack each other, thus threatening all of the Egyptian Asiatic territories. The Apiru (Amurru) expanded into the vacuum created by the defeat of the Mittani, and took the Egyptian ally Sumur on the coast; then unchecked they moved south and captured both Byblos and Beirut. Feeling free to act, the Shasu (Bedouin) under their leader Labayu now raided in succession the Canaanite cities of Gezer, Askalon and Lachish. Apart from sending some troops under general Bikhuru to protect Egypt's eastern border, and make a vain attempt to police south Canaan, Akhenaten seemingly refused to act militarily to save his Asiatic empire. He resorted to chastising Aziru the leader of the Apiru, and sending supporting messages to the Egyptian vassals under threat. The Apiru leader was called to the Egytian court, but was allowed to return home; he then allied himself to the ascendant Hittites. To illustrate the growing lawlessness in the region, previously policed by Egypt, the king of Babylon (Amarna letter EA8), wrote to Akhenaten to complain that his caravans to the Mediteranean were being pillaged.

**Year twelve - plague.** Despite these events the Egyptian texts from the tomb of court official Huta and others reported that in year twelve there was a great reception for foreign royal ambassadors and huge tribute from the Asiatics was received along with a strong flow of gold from Nubia. In that year, Viceroy Thutmosis conducted a policing action in Nubia to suppress a minor revolt and maintain the trade routes and gold supply. This was a modest event, only one hundred and forty five captives were recorded in a stele at Amada and at Buhen. In the same year there was a very serious outbreak of a bubonic plague, polio or influenza in Egypt. It spread slowly throughout the whole of the Middle East and many years later killed Suppiluliuma, the Hittite King and devastated his people. The epidemic may explain in part the speed with which Akhetaten was subsequently abandoned and why the population considered that the gods had turned against the Amarna monarch. A year later there is personal tragedy for Akhenaten, his eleven year old favorite daughter Meketaten died either from plague or in childbirth. The grieving parents are shown in the Amarna royal tomb, in room G wall A. Neferetiti is not mentioned again she may have also died from the plague or become disgraced. The last known statue of her is not flattering and shows her rather care worn.Her daughters replacd her role at court from this time onwards.

The grand old queen mother, Tiy, who had moved to Amarna with her son, died in year fifteen. To protect the succession and perhaps suffering from ill health himself Akhenaten made his sixteen year old son, by Kiya, Smenkhare, co–regent. Akhenaten married him to his step sister Meretaten. From then onwards her name replaced that of Nefertiti in the Amarna temples.

Two years later, after seventeen turbulent years, the monotheist pacifist poet went to his destiny. Breasted referred to Akhenaten as *'the first individual in history'*. He was buried in the royal tomb at Amarna, with his mother Tiy. Their coffins were later removed after the court returned to Thebes and reburied in the Valley of the Kings in a 'nobles' tomb KV55 now called the Amarna tomb. This coffin (right) was originally made for his wife Kiya but the lid was remodeled for Akhenaten; its death mask was ripped off and his cartouche was removed soon after re-burial at Thebes. In 2007, DNA tests finally confirmed that the KV55 Akhenaten mummy was very closely related to his youngest son, Tutankhamen, found intact in tomb KV62 by Carter in 1922. After a wait of almost three and a half thousand years, Akhenaten, with his name and mummy now re-established, could at last pass safely to the afterlife.

**Smenkhkare** c1343BC. Akhenaten's successor and co-regent for the last two years of his reign is one of the most mysterious of kings. The majority view is that he was the eldest son of Akhenaten and Kiya and married to his step sister Meretaten. They are seen as king and wife in an Amarna tomb relief and possibly in a stele now in the Berlin museum. He held his coronation at a specially built solar hall at Amarna containing '544' columns but ruled for only one year. It appears that the Hittite king Suppiluliuma I sent him a congratulatory letter (Amarna letter EA41) on his accession, offering peace. Smenkhare started his mortuary temple at Thebes, implying that he was making a return to the cult of Amen. His golden portrait Osiride style coffin was reused for his younger brother Tutankhamen in KV62.

**Neferneferuaten** c1343BC Is the most ephemeral of Ancient Egyptian rulers. Some have suggested that Nefertiti was in fact both Smenkhkare and Neferneferuaten, as she had earlier adopted the name Neferneferuaten and the throne name of both Smenkhare and Neferneferuaten are similar, they both contain Ankh keperu re. Research in 2004 however, has demonstrated that the form of the monarch's name is definitely female and the ruler is most likely to have been either Meretaten or Meretaten tasheret, her daughter, or even the fourth daughter of Nefertiti. Some even believe that this ruler was Smenkhkare who was obliged to change his name to an Aten epithet. Neferneferuaten ruled for only three years; in the final year, the ruler started a tomb in the Valley of the Kings and then disappeared mysteriously. The ruler was buried in Kiya's re-used coffin at Amarna. These were very dangerous times for Egypt; with four kings in three years the royal succession and government was seemingly in chaos. Her powerful enemy, the king of the Hittites, watched as events unfolded.

**Tutankhaten** (later **Tutankhamen**) 1343-1333BC Tutankhaten (right) is most likely to have been the younger brother of Smenkhkare and a son of Akhenaten and Kiya. Although there is a minority view that he was the son of Smenkhare and Meretaten, this theory has mostly been discredited, due to the relative ages of the three. He is depicted only once as a prince, on a building block found at Hermopolis, but originally from Amarna, where he is called Tutankwhaten. He was around nine years old when he came to the throne and married his twelve year old stepsister Ankhesenpaaten to secure legitimacy from both sides of the family; initially they lived in Amarna. As was customary in regnal year one he added his Aten name and images to his father's Aten temples at Karnak, the following year he commenced construction of his tomb 29, at the Amarna royal cliffside necropolis, seemingly following his father's devotion to the worship of the Aten.

In year three a revolutionary change occurred. The movement was led by the still immensely powerful yet disenfranchised Theban cult priesthood of Amen. It was supported by Chancellor/Vizier Ay, the Nubian viceroy Huy, general Horemheb and state treasurer Maya. Tutankhaten changed his name to Tutankhamen and moved the royal family to the traditional capital Memphis; the government moved there the following year. In Karnak the king was shown, in reliefs, restoring the Amen temples and erecting statues of Amen with the king's face. Later kings usurped most of these fine statues, two of the most magnificent are the striding colossal quartzite statues found in 1933 by the University of Chicago's Oriental Institute in the mortuary temple of Ay and Horemheb. Work commenced at Luxor to complete the decoration of Amenhotep 3's Great Colonnade where Tutankhamen's cartouche can be seen partly overwritten by that of Horemheb. In the Valley of the Kings his original tomb KV57, later taken by king Horemheb, was started. The name change and the restoration of the Amen temples did not mean that worship of the the Aten was prohibited at this time, although there is evidence that the king allowed talatat blocks to be used from the Aten temples for new building work at Karnak.

**The Syrian war with the Hittites.** By year nine the country was stable and it was well overdue to settle affairs in Syria. Egypt first made an alliance with the great Assyrian king Ashur Urbalit 1365-1330BC, who had already captured the rival nearby Babylonian kingdom. The alliance strategy was for Assyria to attack the Hittites from the east whilst Egypt attacked from the south. Generals Horemheb and Amenemone moved up the Levant and lead the army straight towards Kadesh. However, before they could strike, the Hittite king Suppiluliuma I defeated the Assyrians and pushed them back east of the Euphrates. He then moved south, repulsed the Egyptians and went on to consolidate all of Syria north of Kadesh. It was the first time Egyptians and Hittites had engaged directly. General Horemheb had to accept the border being set between Byblos and Kadesh. Egypt was not strong enough alone to dislodge the now well established Hittites from the old Mittani lands in north Syria. However he had managed to recover Canaan and south Syria and Viceroy Huy recorded in his tomb that tribute form this region had restarted. General Horemheb then secured the Libyan border and supported Viceroy Huy in Nubia. For these military services he was promoted to Commander in Chief and Vizier, now second only to Ay. His wealth and position in the kingdom is reflected in his grand tomb at Saqqara. It had two 21 feet undecorated pylons accompanied by two columned courts. The walls are beautifully decorated with scenes showing his Syrian campaigns and Nubian prisoners.

Ankhesenamen (previously Ankhesenpaaten) and Tutankamen had two daughters but both died before their first year. Their tiny mummies were found in Tutankhamen's hurriedly completed noble's tomb KV62, originally intended for Chancellor Ay.

The young king died suddenly and mysteriously, without an heir in regnal year ten, at the age of nineteen, leaving his twenty-two year old wife to continue to rule alone. His second inner coffin (left) belonged to his older brother Smenkhkare. According to the Hittite royal archives king Suppuliuma was campaigning near Carchemish when he received a letter from a certain 'Da kham anza' presumed to mean in Egyptian 'ta hemet nesu', or king's wife presumed to be Ankhesenamen. The widowed queen of Egypt was requesting a husband. Suspicious, Suppiluliuma I sent a messenger seeking confirmation; in reply he received a stern letter from the king's wife urgently requesting one of his sons as husband. The Hittite archives record that fourth son, young prince Zannanza, was selected to travel south but was killed at the Egyptian border, most likely on the orders of Genral Horemheb or Chancellor Ay. The Hittite king was enraged when he heard of the treachery and dispatched Crown Prince Arnuwanda to take south Syria, and then invade Egypt, in revenge. However, the army was decimated by an epidemic of the plague and limped back to Hati bringing the disease with them. The epidemic raged in Hati for more than twenty years devasting the population. The great king himself fell victim, as did his successor, Arnuwanda, two years later.

The cause of Tutankhamen's death was unclear when Carter inspected the body in 1922. In recovering the valuable items stuck in the embalming resins, the five foot eleven inch body was badly damaged and the skull became separated. The mummy has since been X-rayed three times, in 1968,1978 and in 2005. The 1968 X-rays showed a dense 'fragment of bone' at the lower back of the skull. This was seized upon by some notable Egyptologists, who for almost forty years used this 'evidence' to support their theory that the king had been murdered. Speculation ran riot as to who committed the murder, the two with the most to gain became the main suspects, Ay and Horemheb.

However in 2005 the results of a CT scan uncovered no evidence of a blow to the back of the head and no evidence of foul play, the so called 'fragment of bone' turned out to be hardened embalming resin. There was a hole in the skull, but it appeared to have been drilled by embalmers. The CT scan discovered that Tutankhamen had severely fractured his left thigh bone shortly before he died, and it had become severely infected. The 2005 medical team concluded that the bad fracture was most likely caused by a fall from some height. Tutankhamen eventually died from gangrene poisoning but lived for a period of time, some days or even weeks, after the injury. Two of his favorite chariots found in pieces in his tomb and reliefs showing him in a war chariot (right) may offer a clue that the broken leg was caused by a chariot-racing accident or even while on campaign with Horemheb in Syria, although there are no records to substantiate his participation in any military activity.

**Ay**, 1333-1328BC was sixty five years old when he succeeded Tutankhamen and oversaw his buriual in KV62. This tomb was originally intended for Ay as vizier. Records state that the burial was strangely delayed for eight months, probably to complete and decorate the tomb. Ay can be seen on the wall of the burial chamber performing the ritual opening of the moth ceremony on the young king's mummy. Vizier Ay was born a commoner but had been very well connected at court for twenty-five years. He was the son of Yuya and Tuya, brother of queen Tiy, the Great Royal Wife of Amenhotep 3, and the father of Nefertiti. However, Horemheb, also a commoner, was Commander in Chief of the Army and Tutankhamen had already designated him as crown prince 'rpat' and his deputy 'idnw' and clearly next in line to the throne.It appears that Horemheb was outmaneuvered, he could well have been with the army in Syria or Nubia at the time of the king's death and may not have been able to return in time to stop Ay. Ay immediately married Ankhesenamen, the widow of Tutankhamen, thus legitimizing his claim to the throne. The only evidence for this marriage is a ring in the Berlin museum. Ankhesenamen is never heard of again; she was disgraced after her failed attempt to put an enemy Hittite prince on the throne.

The ageing Ay ruled for only five years; supported by treasurer Maya and Viceroy Paser, he consolidated the return to Amen and constructed a mortuary temple north east of the later Medinet Habu. A stele in the Berlin Museum records that in year four he appointed a military officer Nakhtmin as successor. He may have been Ay's son based on an inscription on a funerary statue of Nakhtmin, which suggests he was crown prince and king's son. It appears that Nakhtmin died before Ay. Horemheb was therefore able to ascend to the throne with the backing of the army and the Amen priesthood.

**Horemheb** 1328-1298BC (setep en re) reigned for thirty important years; he finally brought stability to the kingdom and the permanent restoration of Amen as the predominant deity. He is shown in this superb diad statue (right, Egizio Museum Turin) standing beside a seated Amen. His first wife Amenia had previously died and on becoming ruler the general married thirty year old Mutnedjmet, the daughter of Ay and sister of Nefertiti, to legitimize his position. He was close to the veteran state treasurer Maya and Viceroy Paser but introduced two of his own men as
viziers based at Thebes and Memphis. It was originally thought that Horemheb had actually erected a statue in Amarna in his early years, but the earlier Egyptologists had confused him with paaten emheb who was Comander in Chief for Akhenaten. The first mention of Horemheb came during the reign of Tutankamen; a text in Viceroy Huy's tomb states he was the king's royal spokesman for foreign affairs.

Horemheb soon started a Damnatio Memoriae style purge of the previous rulers, who were tainted by Aten worship. The kings Akhenaten, Smenkhkare, Neferneferuaten, Tutankhamen and even Ay were all erased from the king lists and Horemheb made the imaginative claim that he was the immediate successor to Amenhotep 3. Their names were completely lost until mid Victorian times when archeologists began to discover traces of the names of these unknown forgotten rulers. Horemheb and later Ramesses 2, dismantled the Amarna buildings to build their own temples at nearby Hermopolis on the west bank. At Karnak the Aten temples were systematically dismantled by Horemheb and the talatat blocks used for his huge new building projects. The blocks, with their texts and colored reliefs left intact, were used as fill for his massive west entrance pylon two and as foundations for his south entrance pylons nine and ten.

His Karnak pylon reliefs show campaigns against the Hittites in Syria, but no details, as well as action in Nubia and a trading expedition to Punt.

The Hittite royal achives are more helpful. In year seven of the reign of his Hittite comtemporary Mursili 2 1321-1295BC, Horemheb in his regnal year fourteen was alleged to have supported a revolt of Hittite-controlled north Syria, incuding Kadesh.These dates are quite accurate due to the reported solar eclipse in Anatolia at mid day on June 24th 1312BC.

At the Luxor temple he inscribed his own name on top of that of Tutankhamen and defaced Ay's names and images in Ay's unfinished West Valley tomb WV23. It is thought that he only spared Tutankhamen's tomb because he was indebted to him for being chosen as his successor. Horemheb also adopted and enlarged Ay's mortuary temple by Medinet Habu on the west bank opposite Thebes. Here he erased all reference to Ay and over wrote his name on this imposing, seventeen feet high, colossal statue (right) of Tutankhamen now in the Oriental Institute of the University of Chicago.

**Domestic reform stele.** By far the most important extant monument is the famous 'Edict of Reform' stele' that he erected in Karnak at the foot of his tenth pylon and copied on a stele at Abydos. It is a sixteen-feet by ten-feet stone tablet of his domestic reforms, intended to correct abuses of state power that had been prevalent since the reign of Akhenaten, possibly due to the concentration of power in the hands of too few Aten officials. It was directed against tax inspectors, police, militia and judges the penalties for abuse were severe. Horemheb also reformed the army, the judiciary and the tomb workers at Deir el Medina. Lawlessness had broken out at Thebes during the Amarna period and tomb robbing was rife, it had even spread to the Valley of the Kings. In regnal year eight, treasurer Maya recorded on the wall before the burial chamber of Thutmose 4 that he had to restore the robbed tomb of the king, who had been buried only sixty eight years before. The great builder, Horemheb could well have planned to build a copy of Amenhotep 3's Luxor Great Colonnade concept and may have commenced work on the Great Hypostyle Hall at Karnak but died before the foundations were completed.

In year thirteen, his wife Mutnodget, at forty three, died during childbirth, he was to leave no children. There is now a fourteen gap in the royal annals, the last record is some hieratic graffiti on a statue in his mortuary temple from year twenty seven. He went to his destiny after reigning for thirty important years. His Saqqara noble's tomb was superseded by his unfinished royal tomb in the Valley of the Kings KV57 (left).

Horemheb had lived at court and seen at first hand the unfolding succession turmoil of four kings from Akhenaten onwards. He was acutely aware that all the consolidation and progress made during his thirty year reign would be jeopardized if there was not a clear strong heir to the throne. With this in mind, and having no children of his own, around year twenty nine, he appointed his old friend, army general, vizier and high priest of Amen, as his co-regent. His name was Pa Ra-messu. This rewarded his friend's loyalty but more importantly made absolutely sure of a smooth succession, as his heir had both a thirty-year old son, Seti I, and a three year old grandson, Ramesses 2, to guide Egypt for the next three generations.

# CHAPTER TEN

# The Ramessids

**Ramesses I** 1298-1296BC (men pehty re) was the first king of the 19th Dynasty which marked the beginning of one-hundred years of the same blood line. General Pa ramessu took the throne name Ramesses but ruled for less than two years. He was a non-royal but the member of an influential military family from the Delta, near the old Hyksos capital of Avaris. As a vizier and high priest of Amen he was a solid choice as a proven enemy of the heresy of Akhenaten. Already an old man in his sixties when he was crowned, Ramesses I appointed his son, the later king Seti I, as the Crown Prince, immediately on gaining the throne. In the second regnal year, thirty-two year old general Seti I led minor campaigns into Canaan to maintain the flow of tribute and in Nubia as a show of force. Ramesses I himself focused on domestic issues, particularly the completion of Horemheb's enormous west entrance pylon two at Karnak, and the start of a new temple at Abydos completed by his son Seti I. His sixteen month reign was to see the last traces of Amarna art. He was buried inside a pink sarcophagus, in a small hastily finished tomb KV16, which gives the impression of having been decorated quickly. There is only one room; its wall scenes were painted rather than carved, the hurriedly-written texts also contained errors. His mummy was returned to Luxor from Niagara via Atlanta in 2003

**Seti I** 1296–1279 BC (men maat re) The name Seti refers to 'of Seth' the patron god of his home town of Avaris, in full it was Seti Merneptah, meaning 'man of Seth, beloved of Ptah'. As being a military man, his main objective was to recover the Syrian provinces and restore the Asiatic boundary to that of Thutmosis 3. He is shown (right) in a relief from his temple at Abydos.

**Miliatary campaigns.** On coming to power he immediately commenced preparation for the forthcoming campaigns by rebuilding and strenghtening the key fortress of Tjaru (Sile) on the route out of the east Delta. In regnal year one he led the army out of Tjaru along the 'Way of Horus', the coastal road that led from the Delta to southern Canaan. He reached Gaza in ten days. The 'Way of Horus,' consisted of a series of military forts, each with a well. They are shown in the king's war scenes on the north wall of the Karnak Great Hypostyle Hall. He then crossed the top of the Sinai, defeated the Shasu (Bedouin) and moved north into Retjenu (Canaan). There he took the walled cities of Beth Shan near the Dead Sea and Yenoam *'the forest girt city'* near Megiddo. At Beth Shan he erected a stele recording his victory, the first combat lead by an Egyptian king in fifty years, over the 'habiru' bandits.

Later he proudly celebrated this in battle reliefs on the walls of the Great Hypostyle Hall (right). He then proceeded up the coast into Lebanon to Tyre and Sidon. They sent cedar logs to Thebes, as tribute, for the giant pylon flagpoles. He may have advanced beyond Horemheb's border at Byblos and reached Sumur, the old Egyptian provincial governor's base, before returning home to Thebes in triumph. The campaign had stabilized Canaan and Lebanon; even distant Cyprus is recorded as paying tribute.

In year two, he spent the first half of the campaigning season expelling Libyan tribes from the west Delta, before continuing his Syrian campaign. In this action, he first punished the pro Hittite Amorite kingdom west of Damascus and took the Galilee town of Kadesh (not the one on the Orontes). Having secured Canaan and south Syria, he proceeded north to the Orontes and with his field commander, Mehy, engaged a part of the Hittite army outside Kadesh. Despite the propaganda of the Karnak inscriptions, the battle was indecisive, the city may have surrendered for a short time but Seti I, like Horemheb, had found the Hittites too strongly entrenched in Syria and he could not hold Kadesh or extend the border beyond Sidon. He returned to Thebes and celebrated his victory. This was the first time an Egyptian king had personally engaged the Hittite army and he proudly displayed his Hittite captives in the Karnak reliefs.

Since the Empire days of Thutmosis 1 and 3 the Asiatic territories had been merely seen as vassal states, not worthy and too costly to be governed full time as part of Egypt. The Hittite stategy, however, had been to make the north Syrian states colonies under direct control, with a permanently established army in the region. Hence, they were now firmly entrenched and for Egypt to take and hold north Syria would require incessant warfare. So in year six Seti, accepted the balance of power and formally agreed with the Hittite king Muwattalli 2 (1295-1272BC) that the border would be set along a southeast line between Kadesh and Byblos. Year seven saw the king and crown prince Ramesses 2 in action against the Libyans (Tjhenu). These peoples were to present an ever increasing threat to Egypt over the next sixty years. The following year the army, accompanied by the crown prince, put down a revolt at Irem (Nubia), and an expansion of the Nubian and Eastern Desert gold mines took place.

By regnal year nine, Seti I, at the age of forty one, had completed his military campaigning and he appointed his fourteen-year old son Ramesses 2 as his chosen successor. There is however no evidence of a formal co regency. The Abydos temple reliefs linking the two rulers were carved after Ramesses 2 himself came to power. The remaining eight years saw prince Ramesses using a royal title but he did not start his regnal years until his father had died.

**Restoration building program.** Seti 1 is credited with the bulk of the resoration of the Amen temples; everywhere that the name of Amen had been removed during the Amarna period, it was restored. He also had an ambitious building program of his own, particularly focused on the four religious centers of Karnak, Abydos, Mempis, and Heliopolis as well as his family city of Avaris. At Karnak, he completed the Great Hypostyle Hall, only just started by Horemheb. He also built his mortuary temple at Gurnah in a new location north of the previous mortuary temples built on the west bank. The temple reliefs there are very highly regarded for their superb execution. In year nine, Seti personally opened new Aswan granite quarries, two rock stelae there commemorate granite obelisks being cut. However, most of Seti's obelisks such as the Flaminian in Rome and that at the Luxor temple, were only partly decorated by the time of his death and were completed by his son. Seti 2 built a temple at Heliopolis with two obelisks flanking the entrance pylon; the unique scale model made during its design has been found intact. He commenced the great Nubian rock-cut temple at Abu Simbel which his son would later make his own.

Although Seti I is given a reign of seventeen years there are no records beyond the year eleven sandstone stele at Gebel Barka (Nubia). Ramesses 2 had to complete the decoration of many of his father's unfinished monuments, including the southern half of the Great Hypostyle Hall at Karnak, his mortuary temples at Gurnah and the exquisite Abydos temple (see Chapter 2). There is speculation that his reign may have been as short as fifteen or even only eleven years. Seti I's huge tomb KV17 was found in 1817 by Belzoni in outstanding condition. It  is of truly gigantic proportions almost four hundred feet long, the longest and the deepest in the valley. All of the internal walls were covered in exceptionally fine painted reliefs and texts; it is a fragile treasure.His 5ft 7 inch mummy (left) was discovered in the 1881 royal mummy cache at Deir el-Bahri. His huge sarcophagus, highly decorated with blue inlay, was removed by Belzoni and since 1824 has been in the Soane Museum in London.There is speculation he may have suffered from, and eventually died of, a congenital heart disease.

Seti I's military exploits have been given high importance by some Egyptologists because of the extensive coverage of his two Syrian campaigns on the walls of the Great Hypostyle Hall at Karnak. Although he decisively took the fight to the Hittite vassals in two campaigns and achieved important victories, he was no more successful in recovering the territories lost during the reign of Akhenaten in north Syria than was Horemheb. North Syria was now permanently lost to Egypt.

### Ramesses 2 'The Great' 1279-1212BC (user maat re)

At age fourteen, Ramesses 2 was appointed prince regent by his father Seti I, eight years later he became king. He changed the spelling of his name in year twenty from that of his grandfather Ra-messu, to Ra-messes; it is not known why. His father's family had originated in the east Delta and they still retained estates near Avaris the old Hyksos capital. He was to become one of Egypt's most notable kings. Because of his long reign of sixty seven years, he was able to complete one of the most extensive and impressive building programs ever seen (Luxor temple statue right). He has also been associated by some traditional religious scholars, since Diodorus c60BC first mooted the hypothesis, as being the ruler associated with the Old Testament Exodus legend; although there is no archeological evidence whatsoever to support this. He was to become most renowned for the battle of Kadesh against the Hittites. Before he ascended the throne he married thirteen year old commoner Nefertari meaning 'most beautiful companion'. She remained the most important of  his eight wives for twenty five years. Nefertari had many children but none succeeded to the throne. It was Prince Merneptah who succeeded him, his thirteenth son by wife, Isetnofret. In total Ramesses 2 had over fifty sons, they are buried together in the most extensive Valley of the Kings tomb KV5. Although Burton, in 1825, and Carter, in 1902, had penetrated the first few rooms, it was not until 1989 that the full extent of the tomb was appreciated. Since 1995, Weeks has been excavating the estimated one hundrd and fifty rooms, so far less than twenty have been fully cleared.

**Military campaigns.** He grasped that the main threats to his kingdom were his powerful and aggressive neighbors. In the northwest, were the expanding Libyans, and in the northeast were the expansionist Hittites who were now reaching the peak of their empire. Thebes and even Memphis were clearly too remote from these northern threats and he made a strategic decision to build a new northern capital in an area he knew well, the east Delta where his family had originated.

During regnal years one to three he concentrated on building his new Delta capital city of Pi-Ramesses once his father's royal summer palace, which was to be the main military base for his campaigns in Syria and was built over the Hyksos site of Avaris. Pi-Ramesses, meaning the domain of Ramesses, was mentioned in the Old Testament story of Exodus as the site where ' ..(the children of Israel) built for the Pharaoh treasure cities, Pithom and Raamses'. Today its foundations lie below ground, only the colossal feet of a statue of Ramesses 2 remain above ground. The ancient city comprised magnificent temples and the royal palace, which even included a zoo. The city was a military capital and contained extensive chariot horse stables also described in the Old Testament story of Exodus.

**Pirate incursions** In regnal year two, he led a campaign to defeat the northern

Mediterranean Sherden (Shardana) pirates later called by king Merneptah the *'sea peoples'* who had been disrupting shipping along the Egyptian and Levant coasts. The Sherden originated from the coasts of Ionia and western Anatolia (Turkey). The action was one of stealth, he tempted the bulk of the pirate fleet by offering easy pickings, and then launched a surprise attack, defeating them decisively at the mouth of the Nile; the victory was commemorated on his Tanis stele. The fighting skills of the Sherdan were highly respected by the Egyptians, and the survivors were to form a permanent part of the king's bodyguard. They can be seen on reliefs at Karnak and later at Medinet Habu, easily identified by their helmets, adorned with a ball and horns, and their characteristic round shields and curved swords. Also defeated in the action were the Lukka, and Shelekesh, who returned with a vengeance seventy years later.

In regnal year three, to fund his coming military campaigns Ramesses 2 expanded the gold mines in el Alaki in the south eastern desert of north Nubia, and erected a stele at Kuban south of Aswan describing the particularly deep well he constructed on the road to the mines, for the benefit of the mining community there. In year four he conducted his first campaign into Syria commemorated in the badly eroded stele on the Dog River near Beirut. It was a scouting raid in preparation for the following year. He consolidated the towns of Megiddo, Tyre, Sidon and Byblos controlled by his father, and ended with an action in west Amurru near Kadesh. In retrospect this may have been rash; by personally getting so close to the Hittite border he probably triggered a warning to king Muwattalli 2 over his future intensions.

**Battle of Kadesh.** In regnal year five, the records describe his military preparations. In a single two-week period, his armory in Pi Ramesses produced *'250 chariots and 1,000 shields'*. His objective was the permanent occupation of the strategic border town of Kadesh and then to extend the Egyptian border northwards. The walls of his temples and palaces throughout the kingdom are adorned with the reliefs (Pictorial Record) and inscriptions (Bulletin) describing the campaign and the final *'victory'* at Kadesh. It is a fiction. In late spring the 20,000 strong army left his father's rebuilt fortress at Tjaru (Sile) and marched along the 'Way of Horus', then north along the coast road to Tyre. They turned inland along the Litany River and north into the Orontes valley. As the army approached Kadesh, in 1275BC, Ramesses (right) allowed himself to believe two Hittite-planted Shasu (Bedouin) spies who deliberately misled him concerning the exact location of the Hittite army. The king allowed the four divisions (named Amen, Re, Ptah and Sutekh)  of his army to become separated along the road north to the city, and was hopelessly unprepared when the Hittite king Muwattalli 2 sprung his trap. The Hittite chariots attacked the center of the unsuspecting division of Re, which was moving casually north to join the king, and was put to flight. Seeing their plight the division of Amen joined them, deserting Ramesses 2. Now with only his own personal bodyguard, and his pet lion, he bravely resisted the brunt of the enemy and only escaped with his life when the Hittites overran his baggage train and stopped to loot. The enemy was finally driven off the battlefield and into the Orontes River, when by good fortune, some of the Egyptian auxiliary troops arrived from the west coast. Thinking that the main Egyptian army had finally caught up with their king, the Hittites withdrew. The next day the two armies fought to a draw and Ramesses 2 returned home leaving the Hittites still firmly in control of Kadesh. In fact Muwattalli 2, later that year, expanded south into the Upe territory taking Damascus.He stopped just short of the Egyptian regional capital at Kumidi, north of Sidon.

Reliefs and descriptions of his *'great victory'* decorate all of his temples and palaces including the Ramesseum, the Abydos temple (right), the Karnak Great Hypostyle Hall, the Luxor temple and his great temple at Abu Simbel. The Bulletin text makes the vain boast *'.. his majesty slaughtered the armed forces of the Hittites in their entirety, their great rulers and all their brothers...their infantry and chariot troops fell prostrate,...His majesty killed them... and they lay stretched out in front of their horses.*

*But his majesty was alone, nobody accompanied him...'*. In contrast, the Hittite annals simply record *'..Muwattalli defeated him (the King of Egypt)'*. Listed as one of the Hittite allies on the Egyptian reliefs was Dardany believed to be the Homeric city of Troy and known to have been a client state of Hati at the time.The great Hittite king, Muwattalli 2, was to die in 1272BC only a few years after the battle of Kadesh and was succeeded by his weak son, Uhri Teshub. In regnal year eight, Ramesses 2 conducted a policing campaign in the east; he defeated the Shasu (Bedouins) in the Negev desert east of Sinai and then pacified the territories of Edom, Moab and Galilee further north.

Ramesses 2 took the opportunity in year ten (1269BC) to test the Hittites under their new king. Leaving his base at Pi Ramesses he travelled along the 'Way of Horus' to Gaza and then north along the 'Via Maris' past Megiddo, Tyre , Sidon across the Dog river to Byblos and then to his base at Sumur. He proceeded to raid the Hittite vassal cities in the Orontes valley and Amurru region. The high point was the siege and capture of the fortified double-walled city of Dapur across the Orontes from Tunip and well north of Kadesh. The commemorative reliefs on the east wall of the hypostyle hall in the Ramesseum show that on this campaign he was accompanied by six of his young sons; although Ramesses 2 celebrated this as a triumph over his enemy the two armies did not engage. In the same year (ten), Egypt aware of the growing Libyan threat, started a series of protective forts along one hundred and ninety miles of the western border and along the Mediterranean coast.

By year twelve, the Hittite royal family was in disarray. After only five years, the young king Uhri Teshub was deposed by his uncle, the future great Hittite king Hattusili 3 1267-1237BC, and Uhri Teshub fled to Egypt. Hattusili

3 demanded that Ramesses 2 extradite his nephew, but he did not. War was only averted because Assyria, the new regional superpower in the east, chose that very moment to launch an attack. Assyria had expanded into the vacuum created by the Hittite destruction of the Mittani heartland in north east Syria. Shalmanesser I (1274-1245BC) of Assyria, seeing the Hittites at a weakness, marched west crossed the Euphrates and raided the Hittite-controlled north of Syria. Ramesses 2 after twelve years of warfare, had decided like his father, that Egypt was no longer strong enough to take and hold northern Syria against the Hittites or Assyrians; from this time onwards his was to be a peaceful reign.

These were the beginnings of very troubled times in the Middle East. From c1300BC the first massive waves of new Indo-European migrants were moving out of southern Russia, whole peoples were seeking permanent homes in Anatolia, Greece, and the eastern Mediterranean lands. Greece was about to enter a period of four-hundred years of chaos called the 'Greek Dark Age'. These mass migrations threatened the existing civilizations, including the Mycenaean Greeks, Troy, and the Hittites. Hattusili 3 was well aware of the threat these migrants posed on the stability of the west of his empire. In addition Assyria was expanding very aggressively to his east. He wisely sought reconciliation with Egypt. Ramess 2 was also in a conciliatory mood he was very conscious of the growing Libyan threat to Egypt's north western border.

**Hittite Peace Treaty.** In regnal year twenty-one (1258BC), Ramesses 2 and Hattusili 3 therfore concluded a formal peace treaty, the oldest surviving between superpowers in the world. A reproduction hangs in the United Nations headquarters in New York. The two originals were in the form of silver tablets, both written in Akkadian cuneiform, the international language in the Middle East at this time; they have both been lost. However each side made a copy; one in Egyptian hieroglyphs, the other in Hittite cuneiform,

both versions survive. Although the majority of the text is the same, each side modified its version to record that the other side had originally sued for peace. A partial Hittite copy is in the Istanbul Archaeological Museum (left), an almost intact Egyptian version can be seen on the south wall of the Great Hypostyle Hall. It contains eighteen articles defining the peace, including the first reference to mutual extraditon. The exact border was not geographically defined in the treaty but can be inferred from other records which list the Levantine cities under Egyptian control. The furthest north was the traditional Egyptian regional capital at Sumur, north of Byblos, which had been garrisoned by Egyptian crack advance troops since Thutmosis 3's reign. It would seem that the border was roughly the traditional one of the past hundred years, running between Egyptian Sumur and Hittite Kadesh. This peace in Syria was to last for almost one hundred years. Egypt and Hati were destined never to go to war against each other again.

**Building program.** In year twenty four the king accompanied by queen Nefertari traveled south into Nubia to inaugurate the new wondrous temple of Abu Simbel (right) which was dedicated to himself as a living deity. It had been started by his father Seti 1 and was a reprise of Amenhotep 3's Soleb (Kush) temple also dedicated to himself as a god, one hundred years before. Four colossal rock cut sandstone statues in his image, each seventy feet high, guard both sides of the entrance to the rock cut temple. It is considered

to be the most impressive temple in all of Egypt. It was a giant exercise in intimidation, being located strategically just north of the Kush border on the main Nile trade route into Egypt. It was a warning to Nubian and Kushite tribes not to threaten Egypt's southern border. Ironically, the construction of the temple was mostly carried out by by Nubian captives. Seven years after it was dedicated, an earthquake, cracked the southern inner seated statue at waist level; its head and torso fell to the ground, oddly it was never restored. Nefertari has a similar but smaller temple at Abu Simbel, also dedicated to her as a living god. In choosing Abu Simbel, Ramesses 2 followed the caution of Amenhotep 3 in only being worshiped as a deity outside of Egypt proper.

Shortly after her return from the temple dedication, Nefertatri is presumed to have died, as she is not heard of again, and Isetnofret became his principal wife. Nefertari was one of only a few wives to be deified in her own life time; her tomb is the finest in the Valley of the Queens. It contains magnificent, but fragile, highly colored wall paintings, and is regarded as one of the greatest art achievements of Egypt. Following major restoration work, public access to the tomb today has been restricted to prevent damage to the wall paintings that humidity brings. About this time Ramesses 2's eldest son, and crown prince, died, the start of a succession of twelve sons to predecease him. In year thirty he celebrated his jubilee with even more building projects. The highlights were his Ptah temple at Memphis, with the two colossal flanking staues discussed in Chapter 2, and a new temple at Heliopolis with customary obelisks. Ramesses 2 erected more obelisks than any other king, twenty-three were erected at Pi Ramesses alone. However they all bear dedication inscriptions of a general nature, unfortunately containing no reference to the royal jubilees for which they were erected.

**Ramesseum.** Also in this jubilee year he completed his mortuary temple and nearby palace which have been known as the 'Ramesseum,' since European travelers rediscovered it in the nineteenth century. The first stone entrance pylons, now partly ruined, are decorated with Kadesh battle scenes. The north tower shows the Hittite chariots breaking into the Egyptian camp, the south tower shows the king driving the enemy into the river. They stand in front of the first court with the private royal palace at the left and the remains of the colossal Aswan granite seated statue of the king at the rear. Only parts of the base and feet remain in situ, the torso has fallen into the inner court; it was toppled and badly broken after an earthquake. The colossus was fifty seven feet high and weighed over 1,000 tons. It was the largest statue to survive, although Petrie at Tanis found fragments of another colossus of Ramesses 2, which would have been even taller at ninety two feet. In his history of Egypt, Diodorus c60BC, repeated the inscription, originally reported much earlier by Hecateus of Abdera c300BC, from the base of the now fallen colossus. This led to the colossus being referred to as Ozymandias. It stems from an alledged transliteration by Hecateus into Greek of his throne name User Maat Re Setep en Re. Shelley's sonnet of the same name paraphrases the questionable inscription reported by Hecateus. *'King of Kings am I, Osymandias; if any would know how great I am, and where I lie, let him surpass one of my works'.* It is not surprising that Ramesses 2 is considered the greatest builder, but in fact he usurped many existing statues by inscribing his cartouche on them. The shallow cartouches of previous kings such as Amenhotep 3 were easily overwritten by his, which were very deeply engraved, making them less likely to be usurped, and more distinguishable in the bright sun. Around the inner court only a handfull of impressive Osiride pillars survive to give a hint of its former grandeur.

In year thirty-four his second principal wife Isetnofret died and to fill this important court role his daughter Bintanat became his royal wife in the following year. She is shown (right) standing at the feet of the kings colossal statue now outside pylon two at Karnak. The records of the next twenty years of his reign have been regrettably lost, however between the years 34 to 42, to cement the Hittite peace treaty, he married a series of Hittite princesses at Pi Ramesses. In year fifty five crown prince and high priest of Ptah, Khaemwaset, died at over fifty years of age, Ramesses was continuing to outlive his children; he then appointed his next oldest and thirteenth son Merneptah (Merneptah) as crown prince and heir.

Twelve years later, one of the greatest kings of Egypt went to his destiny at the age of ninety; he had reigned for a remarkable sixty seven years. By the time of his death, Ramesses 2 (left) was suffering from extensive dental decay, extreme arthritis, hardening of the arteries and his red haired mummy showed he had suffered battle wounds. He was buried in his tomb KV7 near the entrance to the valley and opposite the tomb for his many sons, KV5. The location for KV7 was badly chosen; it lay on the floor of the valley and over the years became ruined by the ingress of storm water and debris from flash floods which occur every half century or so.

Nine more kings took the name Ramesses in his honour, but none ever equaled his achievements. Less than one hundred and fifty years after Ramesses 2 died, the Egyptian empire permanently collapsed. His descendants were unable to hold the country together; Asia was lost for all time and the New Kingdom came to an end.

**Merneptah** 1212-1201BC (Baenre Merynetjeru) came to the throne at between fifty five and sixty years of age and ruled for eleven years. Now that there was peace with the Hittites he was able to return the seat of government from his father's military capital, Pi Ramesses back to Memphis, where he (right) constructed a new royal palace next to the temple of Ptah. He is recorded as  having erected a red granite obelisk at Heliopolis but regrettably commenced to dismantle Amenhotep 3's magnificent mortuary temple, then only one hundred and fifty years old. He quaried the stone to build his own mortuary temple, one hundred yards to the northwest. However, Amenhotep 3 was to have his revenge. Later the mortuary temple of Merneptah was also quarried; today nothing remains of it either.

**The Libyans** were now supported by 'northern' migrant sea peoples, probably Greek and Anatolian, who had moved progressively southwards and had settled on the north African coast. They began to invade the border lands of Tehenu (east Libya) and reached the western Delta town of Perire The 'Great Karnak Inscription' consists of eighty lines of text on the inside of the east wall connecting the Karnak temple with pylon seven. It, and the Athribes stele, describes how in regnal year five Merneptah engaged the western invaders '... *the foreign countries (or 'peoples') of the sea....* '. He won in *'six hours a great victory'* at Perire over the Libyan king Meryey, who escaped, and a Northern coalition. The text reports six thousand dead and nine thousand prisoners taken. It lists the Northern coalition members as the Meshwesh, the Sherden now settled in north Africa, the Lukka from south west Anatolia, the Ekwesh, perhaps from the Greek islands/Turkey, the Teresh from northwest Anatolia and the Shekelesh from Sicilly. These, and others, are referred to generically as the Sea Peoples when they attempted to over run Egypt again, thirty years later, during the reign of Ramesses 3.

There is also an account of the same battle in the form of a poem from the 'Merneptah Victory Stele' (right) also known as the 'Israel Stele' found by Petrie in the ruins of Merneptah's mortuary temple opposite Thebes in 1896. The inscription was written on the back of a stele of Amenhotep 3 taken from his massive mortuary temple nearby. On it are twelve lines of text which gave the state of the nation and refer to a previous campaign of Merneptah

in Canaan. The following four lines electrified the Old Testament historians when they were translated and first published. *'..wasted is Tehenu (Libya) ,Kheta (the Hittites) is pacified, plundered is Pekanan (Canaan). . .carried off is Askalon, seized upon is Gezer, Yenoam is not exiting , '-s-r-'-r (Israel?) is desolated, his seed is not: H'-rw (Gaza area ?) has become a widow.'.* Petrie wrote *'won't the reverends be pleased'* and added *'this stele will be better known in the world than anything else I have found'.* Although this text appears to be the first recognized Egyptian record of the existence of the Kingdom of Israel, it is not. The hieroglyphic context of '-s-r-'-r is very clear. This was not a kingdom, country, or even a city, but a tribe of nomadic people comparable to the Bedouin at that time..

At this time the Hittite Empire was in its death throes its towns and lands were being overwhelmed by the Sea Peoples, order was breaking down and there was famine from disastrous crop failures. Merneptah recorded that in 1207BC, regnal year five, he sent relief grain shipments *'to keep alive the land of Hatti'* aiding their old Hittite enemy, but it was too late.

After only eleven years on the throne, Merneptah died at the age of around seventy and was buried in KV8, in an unusual humaniform stone sarcophagus (right). His mummy, found in the 1898 royal mummy cache, shows he suffered from arthritis and arteriosclerosis and died of natural causes. The facial features resemble his father Ramesses 2, but more so his grand father Seti I.

**Chaotic succession** Merneptah's son, with Isisnofret, and successor was **Seti 2** 1201-1195BC, who by now was in his mid fifties. Little is known of his short reign; however from his tomb came one of his favourite library papyri referred to as Papyrus D'Orbiney (British Museum,London). It tells the tale of 'The two brothers' considered one of the finest examples of Egyptian narrative literature much loved in ancient times for its didactic overtones. Although he ruled for six years his half brother **Amenmesse** 1200-1196BC, the son of Merneptah and Takhat, seized control over south Egypt and Kush around year three. Seti 2 was able to reassert his authority over Thebes in his fifth year after defeating Amenmesse. Both were buried in the Valley of the Kings in KV15 and KV10 respectively; however Seti 2 erased the name of Amenmesse in his burial chamber and elsewhere.

Succession confusion continued. A little-known twelve-year old, **Siptah** 1195-1189BC became king for six years he may have been an obscure son of Seti 2. Due to his youth and a severely polio deformed left foot, he was placed under the regency of his stepmother **Tawosret**, Seti 2's minor royal wife. Chancellor Bey, of Syrian extraction, claimed in several inscriptions that he was responsible for setting Siptah on the throne. Bey did not last long at court. Siptah had Bey executed and he disappeared in year four being replaced by the Viceroy of Kush also called Seti. We only know of this execution from a most unusual text discovered in 2000AD. The letter was directed to the Deir el Medina tomb workers who were told to stop work on Bey's tomb since he had been deemed *'a traitor to the state.'* On the early death of Siptah (tomb KV47) queen Tawosret ruled on as female king but for only two further years, her hurriedly built tomb was KV13.On her death the country erupted into a full blown civil war, **Setnakhte** 1187-1185BC emerged as the new ruler he was a usurper who seized the throne during a time of crisis and political unrest,although he may have been a member of the family of Seti 2 or even a grandson of Ramesses 2. To secure the throne he married Tiy the daughter of Merneptah. He appointed his son Ramesses 3 as co regent on becoming king but ruled for only two more years. He initiated the 20th Dynasty as recorded by Manetho.

**Ramesses 3** 1185-1153BC (User maat re mery amen).

Ramesses 3 is considered to be the last great New Kingdom ruler; he reigned for thirty two years and is best known for bringing stability to the country after the sucession civil war, and saving Egypt from the combined threat of the Libyans and the Sea Peoples; the latter expression was coined by king Merneptah (p. 166). The main sources for his reign are the extensive well preserved inscriptions from his mortuary temple (right) at Medinet Habu. However, his conflicts were not recorded in the detailed and logical way that the military scribes of Thutmosis 3 reported his campaigns. The poetic style of the texts and lack of proper order have meant we have only approximate chronological records.

**Libyan invasions.**The first few years of the reign of Ramesss 3 were spent in consolidating the kingdom after his father's success in the civil war. His first military test came in regnal year five, with the first of two Libyan invasions. In the first, the Libyan king Themer joined with their western neighbors the Meshwesh and segments of the Sea Peoples. The coalition consisted of the two *'northern countries'* of Thekel and Peleset, for a time they occupied the west branch of the Nile and raided as far south as Memphis. The army of Ramesses 3 won a decisive victory in the west Delta where 12,535 of the enemy were killed and 1,000 prisoners taken as the invaders were repelled.

**Sea Peoples** This regnal year five incursion proved to be only the advance guard of the Sea Peoples, who had sent ships to fight in support of the Libyans. These Sea Peoples migrating en masse with their families in ox-drawn carts had already overwhelmed the Hittites and pressed on into north Syria, accompanied along the coast by their supporting fleet. Ramesses 3 recorded the strength of the Sea Peoples and the destruction of the Hittites at Medinet Habu in regnal year eight. '...no one stood before them neither the Keti (Hittites) or Kode (Carchemish) or Arzawa (west Anatolia) or Alasiya (Cyprus)...' That year their movement south had reached Arvad, just north of the Egyptian regional capital of Sumur in north Lebanon. The main tribes identified in this Sea Peoples coalition against Egypt, included the Peleset, Thekel (Tjeker), Shekelesh, Denyen and Wesesh. Ramesses 3 went on the offensive. He went with his war fleet to Sumur and nearby destroyed the ships of the Sea Peoples; he went on to personally lead a decisive victory on land. These engagements proved to be decisive, the Sea Peoples were not to trouble Egypt again. The Harris Papyrus, dated to just after the king's death, mainly reports the wealth the king had given to the various Amen temples during his regn. However, of much greater historical interest at the end of the papyrus, is a tantalizingly but brief reference to the destiny of the remaining Sea Peoples. It states that the Sea Peoples in their 'hundred thousands' were settled by Ramesses 3 'in his strongholds' where they were taxed. This is interpreted to mean that to avoid the Sea Peoples continuing to make incursions into Egypt he allowed the Peleset and others to settle in south Canaan which eventually became known as Philistia and then later as Palestine. This settlement concept was to be repeated later in history c300-400AD when the Romans were forced to allow the barbarian invaders to settle across the Danube in Roman territory.

In year eleven the weakened Libyans joined with their dominant western neighbors, the Meshwesh, and carried out a second invasion this time penetrating only to Heliopolis. Ramesses 3 recorded another victory, killing two thousand and capturing the same number. He then harried them for 'eleven miles' expelling them out of the Delta. They were not to return during the remaining twenty one years of his reign. However, this was to be only a temporary respite. Over the years they continued to migrate peacefully into the Delta, growing in number until two hundred years later they become the kings of Egypt as Manetho's 22nd Dynasty 948-715BC.

By year twenty seven, 1158BC, Ramesses 3 had appointed his son crown prince Ramesses 4, as regent. This coincided with the beginning of a long period of significant economic decline accentuated by a series of bad harvests. The tree ring growth in the northern hemisphere in this period supports the possibility of a regional climatic cooling period between 1160 and 1140BC. Yurco, in 1999, speculated that this was linked to the major Hekla volcanic eruption in Iceland. This, coupled with the high cost of the military operations earlier in his reign and declining tribute, from Syria and Canaan, weakened Egypt's reserves to such a low that at one point the tomb workers living in Deir el Medina did not receive their food rations. This led to the world's first recorded labor- strike in year twenty nine. However the regular food rations were quickly re-instated and the incident did not stop the king ordering vizier Ta to commence planning for his Heb Sed jubille festival.

**Medinet Habu.** Ramesses 3 carried out a very significant building program during his long reign. Most notable was the rebuilding of Amenhotep 3's Karnak Temple of Khonsu, the erection of his Amen temple in the great courtyard at Karnak and the construction of the vast Medinet Habu complex on the west bank. Medinet Habu was ostensibly a fortified mortuary temple, royal palace and administration complex all in one. It is by far the best preserved of all of the Thebes west bank mortuary temples. Not only is it truly enormous, it is also very important

artistically and historically. The temple is five hundred feet long and is very similar in layout to the Ramesseum' it is surrounded by a now partly ruined massive mud brick wall. The entrance is through a fortified gate, known as a Migdol, (above) after a typical Syrian fortress gate design of the time.

The second pylon leads into an open peristyle hall of closed bud columns (left), to this day the roof displays are a riot of beautifully colored reliefs some of the best preserved from all of ancient Egypt. The site was next to the earlier so called 'Small Temple' decicated to Amen built by Hatshepsut and Thutmosis 3 but usurped by later rulers. It stood on one of the most sacred spots in Egypt being the site of the primeval mound and the burial site of four pairs of gods. Ramesses 3 also built at Pi Ramesses, Heliopolis, Memphis, Asyut, Abydos and Edfu.

**Conspiracy plot.** The very last year of his reign was tumultuous. The Turin Judicial papyrus and the Lee/Rollin papyri tell in graphic detail of the trial, following a failed conspiracy plot to kill the king, which took place in the royal harem at Medinet Habu. The conspiracy was led by principal wife Tiye, the lesser wife being Isis, over whose son would succeed his father. Isis's son, Ramesses 4 had already been appointed crown prince and heir; he had been chosen in preference to Tiye's son 'Pentawere'. The two main conspirators were supported by at least fifteen ficticiously named senior officials of the court and army. In total thirty-eight people were found guilty of the conspiracy and were executed, the senior ones were allowed to take their own lives, those more junior were most likely burnt alive to prevent an afterlife. The tombs of Tiye and Pentawere were defaced and their names erased so thoroughly that the papyri are the only record of their existence. There is no mention that the assassination attempt on the king was successful; he was present at the initiation of the trial but from the wording of the text he knew his health was failing and he would not live long enough to see the result. Ramesses 3 died in regnal year thirty-two his mummy shows no wounds. He was buried in KV11, one of the largest Valley of the Kings tombs. It is well preserved and often open to the public.

The conspiracy plot failed to prevent his son **Ramesses 4** 1153-1146BC from becoming king; however, the reign lasted only seven years, and he was buried in tomb KV2, which is unique as it is the only tomb to which there is an extant original construction drawing. The drawing was made on a papyrus, now in the Turin Museum. The dimensions shown in the detailed engineering drawing compared to those of the built tomb are accurate to within a fraction of an inch. Although only of short duration his building program was substantial and left some interesting records. He doubled the Deir el Medina tomb builder's village to one hundred and twenty and expanded the stone quarries at Wadi Hammamat and the turquoise mines in the Sinai. In year three, his Wadi Hammamat rock cut stele recorded that out of nine thousand workers employed there, fully ten percent died during the year. Some of the sand stone blocks weighed forty tons which had to be dragged sixty miles west to the Nile mainly for statues of the king. Ramesses 4 was the last king of the New Kingdom to be able to afford such a substantial building effort. In year three there came the last reference to the Sea Peoples regarding an unsubstantiated reference to a naval victory gianst them.

There are two important surviving papyri from his reign. The hieratic Harris Papyrus relating to his father's temple gifts and settling the Sea Peoples, mentioned above, is now in the British Museum, London. It is the longest ever found at one hundred and thirty three feet. The Turin Map Papyrus contains the oldest suriving map of topographical interest. It is eight feet long and shows a ten mile section of Wadi Hammamat and its geology. It includes routes to the mines, distances, the location of gold deposits, types of stone and gravel beds, and makes use of legends and colors. The details shown in the map have been identified in modern times and found to be astonishingly accurate, it is dated to c1150BC.

The end of the reign of Ramesses 4 was to see the start of one hundred years of decline in the New Kingdom which ultimately led to the 3rd Intermediate Period. There were, in total, seven more kings who carried the Ramesses name; they each generally had short reigns and ruled over a kingdom that was collapsing from poor harvests, high grain inflation, smallpox outbreaks, lost gold income and diminished Asiatic tribute revenue. In despair tomb-robbing became endemic, as central control eroded and corrupt local officials and priests took advantage of the situation. Little of significance is known of the very short reigns of Ramesses 5,6,7 and 8.

**Ramesses 9** 1123-1104BC There are two important papyri from his more substantial reign. The Abbott papyrus now in the British Museum, London records the official investigation into ten royal tombs that had been robbed. The Amherst Papyrus, from later in the reign describes the trials of those caught robbing Theban noble tombs; senior officials from Thebes were heavily implicated. During the reign of Ramesses 9 the high priest of Amen at Thebes, Amen Hotpe, became a very powerful individual, even producing a relief at

Karnak which shows him as the same size as the nearby figure representing the king, a portent of things to come. The Mayer Papyri from early in the reign of **Ramesses 10** 1104-1094BC records court proceedings where the vizier of the south cross-examined six suspects charged with noble tomb robbing at Deir el Bahri. Five were found innocent, demonstrating that a guilty verdict was not necessarily a forgone conclusion. **Ramesses 11** 1094-1064BC had a longer thirty-year reign, but he was not strong enough to stop the country disintegrating around him. He was to be the last king of the 20th Dynasty and the New Kingdom; he died without an heir. He spent most of his rule in Memphis and in the north. In year twelve, a power struggle erupted in Thebes. The powerful high priest Amen Hopte attacked the king's temple complex at Medinet Habu and civil war broke out. Medinet Habu was eventually relieved by the Viceroy of Kush, Panehsy, but he then chose to remain in Thebes and rule south Egypt, as well as Nubia and Kush. It was seven years later before the king's loyal general Piankh managed to expel Viceroy Panehsy from Thebes, who then returned to Nubia. In 1075BC Herihor the brother of the high priest of Thebes, appointed himself Viceroy of Kush and then unchallenged became king of the whole of south Egypt until his death in 1069BC. Ramesses 11 then rewarded his loyal general Piankh by appointing him to the then vacant, yet highly influential post, of high priest of Thebes. Based on the disturbing events of these volatile times in Thebes, it is not surprising that Ramesses 11 was the last king to build a royal tomb in the Valley of the Kings. The tomb workers, in danger of their lives, themselves moved their one hundred and twenty families out of their workers village at Deir el Medina and took refuge in the now heavily fortified Medinat Habu complex nearby. The workers village was later ransacked, never to be occupied again. Control of Nubia, Kush and the Asiatic territories had by now been lost.

The New Kingdom was the climax of the ancient Egyptian civilization; it created a World Empire and then allowed it to wash away *'like tears in rain'*. In the long slow painful disintegration that followed, there were to be flashes of brilliance and the temporary recovery of lost territories and occasional glories reflecting past times. However, the history of ancient Egypt, and the rest of the countries of the ancient middle east, from now onwards would be decided not by the kings of Egypt but by the other great civilizations now waiting in the wings.

# CHAPTER ELEVEN

# Assyria, Babylon, Israel and Persia

The four hundred year period from the death of Ramesses II in 1064BC, to around c660BC, is characterized by the country's fractured kingship and is referred to as the 3rd Intermediate Period. Ramesses II had ruled over a divided country; he had lost power in Thebes whose priests were becoming increasingly more powerful.

**Tanis rulers.** When Ramesses II died in 1064BC, the country appeared to split completely. His royal successor **Smendes 2** was the son-in-law of Ramesses 9 and ruled the north from his new capital city of Tanis, his 21st Dynasty ruled until 948BC. Tanis was built out of the stone robbed from the buildings and temples that Ramesses 2 constructed at Pi Ramesses. During this Dynasty, the High Priests of Amen at Thebes actually ruled the south of the country, however, both they and the Tanis kings were interrelated by blood. For example, for fifty years, from 1034 to 981BC, the following two heads of state were full blood brothers. The king in Tanis was **Psusennes I**, he was the chief robber of Pi Ramesses and was buried in a fabulous silver coffin with a gold mask, discovered in 1939AD, Egyptian Museum, Cairo. His brother **Men kheper re**, was high priest and ruler of Thebes. The overall decay in law and order led to ongoing widespread looting of tombs, particularly in the Theban necropolis. Around 1034BC the high priest of Amen at Thebes, **Pinedjem** (the father of Psuennes I above), gathered many of the already robbed royal mummies from the tombs in the Valley of the Kings and sealed them for safe keeping in the tomb of Amenhotep 2 ,where they were discovered intact as the 2nd royal mummy cache in 1898.

**Libyan Bubastis ruler –Shoshenq I.** The whole country was reunited again by the 22nd Dynasty founder Shoshenq I 948-927BC. He was descended from the Libyan/Meshwesh immigrants who fought against Merneptah and Ramesses 3. The Meshwesh were originally 'northerners' who settled in the lands along the coast of northeast Africa and took control of Libya during the reign of Ramesses 3, two hundred and fifty years before. This Egyptian reunification brought one hundred years of stability. Shoshenq I, who reigned for twenty one years, is generally believed to be the Shishak of the Old Testament book of Kings, from now on the history of Egypt and the history and the chronology of the Old Testament begin to converge. Prior to ascending to the throne, Shoshenq I had been the commander in chief of the north Egyptian army and vizier, he also held the title of Great Chief of the Meshwesh. He came from the east Delta town of Bubastis south of Tanis, and was the nephew of a previous king from Tanis, Osorkon the elder. On coming to the throne he named his eldest son, Osorkon I, as his heir to ensure his smooth succession as king of both Tanis and Thebes. To strengthen his control over the whole country, but particularly Thebes, he appointed his other son Iuput to be the High Priest of Amen at Thebes as well as Governor of south Egypt and Commander in Chief. In year eleven, Iuput rescued more robbed royal mummies from the Valley of the Kings tombs and hid them for safe keeping in the remote Deir el Bahri tomb of high priest. Pinedjem. This first-to-be-found royal mummy cache, was discovered in 1881, when the abu Rassul brothers, who had been caught selling artifacts from the cache, agreed under persuasion, to lead officials to the site. The location was very well hidden, two hundred feet high in the vertical cliffs overlooking Hatshepsut's mortuary temple.

**Palestine campaign.** Now for the first time in two hundred years, since Ramesses 3, the king of Egypt went on the offensive in the previously held vassal territories in Palestine. In 926BC, regnal year twenty, very late in his reign, he led a major campaign into Palestine, Canaan and Lebanon which was recorded on the south east corner (left) of his beautiful colonnaded Great Courtyard at Karnak now known as the Bubasite portal. Its damaged inscription lists the capture of around fifty towns and villages in the north of Canaan and one hundred in the south. Although Jerusalem is not specifically mentioned, 1 Kings 14,25 records the terrifying Egyptian raid on the region. Jerusalem may have avoided being taken only when king Rehoboam paid Shoshenq 1 huge tribute from both the temple and palace. However, within a year of this historic campaign, Shoshenq 1 died. He was unable to complete his building projects at Karnak and left no trace of his tomb. It is reasonable to speculate that he was buried at either Tanis or Bubastis. There then followed a period of stability, when a succession of little known 22nd Dynasty kings progressed smoothly. This continued until **Osorkon 2** 877-838BC came to power and ruled at the same time that a new regional super power appeared on the scene, the Assyrians.

**The New Assyrian Empire.** It was at this time that the New Assyrian Empire started to threaten the whole of the Levant down to Egypt. The previous Assyrian empire, under their king Ashur Urbalit, had allied itself with Horemheb in 1336BC to unsuccessfully challenge the Hittites. Assyria had by 1,000BC, shrunk to a tiny shadow of its former self, only one hundred miles by fifty miles in area, in modern north Iraq. Assyria was to grow and dominate the Middle East for the next three hundred years. Assyria possessed the greatest army the world had yet seen, it had the best siege engine technology, superior iron weapons and benefited from an almost unbroken royal succession of gifted military kings for a period lasting over ten generations.

The great Assyrian military king **Ashurnasirpal 2** 884-859BC (top-right page) founded in 879BC a magnificent new capital at Nimrud (Kalhu), in

present day north Iraq. The city was surrounded by a
fortified perimeter wall five miles in length.In a series
of nine brilliant campaigns, not unlike Thutmosis
3, he expanded the state, which had no natural
boundaries, in all directions. In the spring of 876BC
he turned his attention to north Syria. His army
crossed the Euphrates river and attacked Carchemish,
this time payment of tribute avoided its destruction

and the army moved on to the *great deep sea* unopposed. At the shores of the
Mediterranean, the king ceremoniously and ominously *washed his weapons* in its
waters. The great independent Phoenecian sea ports and trading city states of
Tyre, Sidon and Byblos (Egypt's main ally during its Empire days) were taken by
surprise at the speed and strength of this new aggressor and paid Ashurnasirpal
2 tribute to avoid being taken. Satisfied for now, the Assyrian army returned
to Nimrud where the king saw to the consolidation of his new Empire for the
remaining seventeen years of his reign. At the inauguration of the new city of
Nimrud in 864 BC, the king invited seventy-thousand dignitaries to celebrate
with feasting which was recorded as lasting a whole week.

The Assyrians returned to Syria under their new king
**Shalmaneser 3** 858-825BC. In his first regnal year he
(left) marched on Syria but underestimated the strength
of the now-prepared coalition of Syrian kings, and could
only extract tribute from Tyre. For now, Egypt did not
need to become involved and in regnal year twenty-two,
855BC, Osorkon 2 celebrated his jubilee. However, the
following year Shalmanesser 3 returned to Syria and took Allepo and moved
south to the Orontes river. Again the Syrian kings formed a strong coalition.
This time Osorkon 2 sent one thousand Egyptian troops to support them.
Under the abe leadership of King Ahab of Israel and King Adad of Damascus
the Assyrian army was surprisingly stopped at Qarqar(853BC) on the Orontes
river, eighty miles north of Kadesh.

It was to be ten years later that Shalmaneser 3 returned again to Syria, this
time with the whole Assyrian army and its siege divisions. In 842BC the
Syrian coalition collapsed internally and the Assyrians were able to penetrate
southwards and besiege the walled city of Damascus,
but the strong defenses held out. The army swung west
to the coast; Tyre, Sidon and Jerusalem all then sent
tribute as did Osorkon 2. The cities giving tribute are
each recorded on a panel on the eight feet high Black
Obelisk (right) of Shalmanesser 3 which was erected in
825 BC in the central square of the Assyrian capital,
Nimrud, now in the British Museum,London.The dark
limestone obelisk features twenty reliefs, five on each
side. They depict five different subdued kings, bringing

tribute and prostrating themselves before Shalmanesser 3. The kings shown are Sua of Gilzanu (Iran), Jehu of Bit Omri (Israel), the king of Musri (Egypt) probably Osorkon 2, Marduk-apil-usur of Suhi (middle Euphrates), and Qalparunda of Patin (Anatolia). The second register from the top on one side shows the earliest surviving picture of a king of Isarel, Jehu, or his ambassador; it describes how Jehu brought or sent his tribute c841 BC. Jehu was forced to sever Israel's alliances with Phoenicia and Judah, and became a vassal subject of Assyria. The text reads: *'The tribute of Jehu, son of Omri: I received from him silver, gold, a golden bowl, a golden vase with pointed bottom, golden tumblers, golden buckets, tin, a staff for a king and spears.'* After this four year campaign, the Assyrians turned their attention northwards to Tabal and Que and the silver mines of Anatolia and left Syria in relative peace for thirty years; they were later preoccupied by a protracted civil war 827-822BC

The Assyrian king **Adad Nirari 3** (810-783BC) raided Syria in 805BC to punish the vassal city Damascus which had ceased to pay tribute, after a siege the city fell and he was able to consolidate the region. The Egyptian Osorkon 2 had by now been succeeded by his son, Shoshonq 3 838-798BC, who ruled Egypt for forty years, although for much of that time the country was split again into two states; with Shoshenq 3 controlling north Egypt and Takelot 2 (23rd Dynasty) ruling middle Egypt and Thebes.

Revolts and plague preoccupied Assyria until in 775BC, the Assyrian king Shalmaneser 4 campaigned in Syria and Lebanon; little is known of this tribute gathering action. Thirteen years later Assyria's Commander in Chief led a military coup against the all powerful Ashur priesthood and usurped the throne. He was to become their greatest military ruler his name was **Tiglath Pileser 3** 745-727BC.

He easily conquered his southern neighbor, Babylon, in his first regnal year and extended the Assyrian empire down to the Persian Gulf. He is also known in the Old Testament (1 Chronicles 5.26) as the hated king Pul, the throne name Pulu was given to him when he was later, 729BC, proclaimed king of Babylon.

He introduced far reaching state reforms which allowed Assyria to dominate the region (Empire map right) for the next one hundred and fifty years, He followed many of the reforms of the kings of the Egyptian Middle Kingdom. He reduced the status of high officials, governors and generals, he appointed eunuchs as provincial  governors, to avoid dynastic succession, and made provinces smaller to prevent any one governor from being able to threaten the king. His army reforms allowed conquered peoples into the infantry who, unlike the patrician cavalry and chariotry, would campaign all year round.

The Syrian vassals ceased their annual payment of tribute on the ascension of Tiglath Pileser 3, a not uncommon practice in the ancient world, and felt strong enough to declare full independence three years later in 742BC. This was a serious tactical mistake, as it brought the whole weight of the Assyrian war machine to bear down on the region. The royal Assyrian annals record that the major sea port of Arpad north of Sumur resisted but fell after a three year siege. By 740BC, tribute was extracted from every major town in east Anatolia (Carchemish, Que) and Syria/Lebanon (Byblos, Tyre, Sidon, Damascus). This time Samaria, the capital of Israel, and Jerusalem, the capital of Judah, could not escape and had to pay tribute to avoid destruction. For the first time, all the major cities north of Gaza and the Egytian border came under Assyrian control. Most of Syria was then turned into full Assyrian provinces they each had a permanent military governor and militia to keep the peace and collect annual taxes and tribute, which went to support the huge building program of palaces, temples and gardens at both the capital, Numrud, and the religious center of Ashur. The first governor of Zimirra, one of the new Syrian provinces, was crown prince, and future king, Shalmaneser 5.

Eight years later (734BC) the region erupted in revolt, led by Rezon, the king of Damascus, and Pekah, the king of Samaria, who pressured Ahaz the king of Jerusalem to join them. Ahaz declined and fearing imminent attack from his neighbors, called to the Assyrian king Tiglath Pileser 3 for help supplying him with temple gold and silver as an inducement. (2 Chronicles 28.20). The Assyrian army swept in and besieged, captured and then destroyed Damascus; the rebel king Rezon was executed. The Assyrians then proceeded south and started to destroy the other major rebel cities of Israel one by one. The first was Hazor in Galilee, then south to Megiddo and then to the gates of Samaria the capital, itself. The rebel king of Samaria, Pekah, then died and the city sued for peace, which was granted only after a huge tribute was paid. Assyria then placed a vassal king, Hoshea, on the throne. Many inhabitants of Damascus and Megiddo were transported to the northeast of the Assyrian Empire. Finally in 732BC the Assyrians captured Gaza as a base from which to control Palestine and invade Egypt if necessary. Assyrian advance troops were now less than one hundred miles from the Egyptian border, however they tuned for home, their first priority was to invade Babylon. There was peace in the region for the next five years.

## The Nubian kings of Egypt.

The ongoing divisions in Egypt, from c850 to c750BC and consequential economic weakness had created an opportunity for the Nubian Kushite kingdom with its capital at Napata at the fourth Nile cataract. Their King **Piye** (Piankh) 752-721BC was descended from Viceroy of Kush, Panehsy, who in 1075BC had temporarily taken control of Thebes. Piye took advantage of the lack of central control and political instability in Egypt to build on the growing influence his predecessor Kashta had already exerted at Thebes. In 740BC, regnal year twelve, Piye peacefully appointed his sister to the position of Gods Wife at Thebes. Then, in year twenty c732BC, Piye took more aggressive action. He marched north and temporarily pacified the combined north Egyptian rulers, taking Lisht and Memphis in the process. In 728BC he marched north again, taking Herakleopolis and he retook Memphis. Although he received tribute from the Delta princes of Sais and Tanis they later revolted and were defeated, but to bind the country together were appointed as provincial governors. Piye was now the undisputed king of all of Egypt and Nubia and became the founder of the 25th Dynasty, sometimes called the 'Black Kings of Egypt'. However, Egypt's standing and strength in the international community was a pale shadow of its glorious past. Egypt's old Asian allies and vassals had by now fallen firmly into the sphere of influence of Assyria and it now became just a matter of time before Assyria and Egypt would clash. Despite the now united Egypt's size and prosperity, Assyria had by far the more powerful army, better war-hardened generals, and more advanced siege engine technology. With the expanded Assyrian Empire came a plentiful supply of superior iron weapons, because of easy access to wood and charcoal needed for iron production.

**The lost ten tribes of Israel.** In 727 BC the great Assyrian military king Tiglath Pileser 3 died and was succeeded by his son and governor of Zimirra (Syria), Shalmaneser 5, for a short reign of only five years. The peace in the region was shattered when the Assyrian-appointed vassal king Hoshea of Samaria revolted. The revolt was the result of Egyptian intrigue, Piye wanted to create a buffer zone between Egypt and Assyria and so supported the breakaway of the southern part of the Assyrian province including Tyre, Sidon, Acre, and Samaria. The new Assyrian king wasted no time and led the army west in 726BC. With the unexpectedly rapid approach of the Assyrians the Syrian coalition collapsed again, only Tyre refused to offer tribute and was besieged. After five years, the siege was called off and a compromise was reached. Meanwhile, Shalmaneser 5 had also besieged the ring leader Samaria. After a siege lasting three years Samaria the capital of the northern kingdom of Israel fell to the Commander in Chief of the Assyrian army, who later usurped the Assyrian throne and was crowned as **Sargon 2** 722-704BC. He ordered the deportation of the Samarian leaders. The Assyrian annals boast of the dispersion, across the Assyrian Empire, of 27,290 belonging to the *'ten tribes of Israel.'* Most were settled in the north of modern Iraq and the extreme northwest of modern Iran; they then disappeared from history. The Old Testament, 2 Kings 17.6, quotes the following specific dispersion locations *'Halah,Habor,Gozan and the cities of the Medes'* which fit reasonably well with the Assyrian records. Samaria was turned into the Assyrian province of Samerina.

Piye died in the following year, 721BC, and his brother **Shabaka** 721-707BC succeeded to the throne and continued the consolidation of the unified Egypt deep into the Delta. Like his brother, he hoped to keep the Asyrians at bay by supporting the Syrian princes. They Asiatics seized their opportunity in 720BC and 'cast off the Assyrian yoke' on hearing that Sargon 2 had just been held to a draw by the king of Elam (modern south west Iran) at Dur. Sargon 2 remained in Elam to conclude the campaign and sent his western army to capture and punish Qarqar and Hamath north of Kadesh. Sargon 2 then joined the army as it swept south to take Arpad, Sumur, Damascus, Tyre, and Samaria. He then started preparations to invade and punish Egypt for supporting the

revolt. The Assyrians captured and burnt Gaza and were able to defeat Shabaka's Egyptian force at Raphia, the last fortified town before Egypt. However Sargon 2 in 719BC had to return rapidly to his new capital at Khorsdabad (left) to put down a major revolt in the far north of his empire. He left his field generals to punish Egypt. However they correctly assessed that Shabaka was too strong an opponent to take on at this time; Egyptian tribute mentioned in the Assyrian annals may also have been a factor.

Over the next few years, many of the kings of the major cities that had revolted were replaced by Assyrian governors, as Sargon 2 consolidated the provinces. However, in 714BC the king of Ashdod, just north of Gaza, withheld tribute and others followed suit. Sargon 2 retaliated quickly. He sent his bodyguard to apprehend the king of Ashdod, a Greek called 'Iamani', who fled to Egypt but later as a friendly gesture was extradited by Shabaka. In 711BC Ashdod was absorbed into the Asyrian Empire as Asdudu province, its poulation was deported.

Shabaka died in 707BC, his reign had consolidated the Kushite Kingdom's control of Egypt and saw a significant building program at Karnak where he erected this pink granite 'Donation stele' now in the Metropolitan Museum, NY. He can be seen here (right) wearing the traditional twin crowns of Egypt, making a donation to a pair of Egyptian gods

Shabaka was succeeded by his nephew **Shabatka** (Shebitku) 707-690BC, who initially continued his predecessor's policy of conciliation with Assyria. In 705BC Sargon 2 died in battle against the Cimmerians at Tabal in east Anatolia and was succeeded by his son the 'mighty' **Sennacherib** 704-681 BC 'the wolf on the fold' of Old Testament notoriety. King Sennacherib ruled for twenty-three years and is considered one of the greatest kings of Assyria. He moved the royal capital to the ancient site of **Nineveh** (Ninua), opposite modern Mosul on the Tigris. His new palace there was a wonder of the ancient world. It contained a zoological park and artificial irrigation for the extensive gardens. Some historians believe that Nineveh was the true location for what later became the legend of the 'Hanging gardens of Babylon'. It was the largest of all the Assyrian palaces with eighty rooms and a huge royal library; it rivalled the palaces of the Egyptian rulers of the New Kingdom. In 690BC Sennacheib constructed a fifty mile aquaduct to provide water all year round for his palace, parks and gardens. The city was protected by eight miles of thirty feet high walls containing fifteen fortified gates and a deep wide moat. The population grew to almost three hundred thousand inhabitants. Today it is mostly ruined, but three of the toweing gates have been reconstructed, one still protected by its giant stone winged-bulls.

In Egypt, Shabatka appeared to have taken the death of Sargon 2 as a sign of weakness and adopted a more aggrersive new policy of now actively supporting Tyre, Jerusalem and Ashdod in withholding tribute. In response Sennacherib led the Assrian army into Syria in 702BC. The reliefs from his palace at Nineveh (British Museum, London) describe the campaign in graphic detail, not unlike those that the Egyptian kings created to mark their own military victories. The army took and burned the cities in the hills behind the Dog river near Beirut. Tyre and Sidon are also shown being besieged; the Assryian army then continued south taking the port of Joppa (modern Tel Aviv). The Egyptian king Shabatka sent his military commander and nephew, crown prince Taharqa, with elements of the Nubian army to support king Hezekia of Jerusalem. In 701BC the Assyrian and Egyptian/Jerusalem armies met at Eltekeh west of the city, where the Assyrians won a commanding victory, Ekron was taken and Sennacherib delegated his 'Tartan' (Commander in Chief) to invest Jerusalem while he and the bulk of his army moved on to take other key cities of Judah and then Gaza. The best-recorded, and most famous, is the siege of Lachish, the second stongest walled city in Judah.

**Campaign Prism.** The siege is described in 2 Kings18:14 and beautifully depicted in the Nineveh palace reliefs. The city fell and the population was later deported. Sennacherib recorded the whole campaign on the 'Sennacherib Prism' dated to 689BC. The original was found intact and is now in the British Museum, copies were kept in the various temples. One of these copies (right) was purchased in Baghdad by Breasted in 1919 for the Oriental Institute at the University of Chicago. Sennacherib first describes the general assault on the cities of Judah '......*because Hezekiah, king of Judah, would not submit to my yoke, I came up against him,....I took 46 of his strong fenced cities....from these places I took and carried off*  *200,156 persons...*' Sennacherib then records the attack on Jerusalem. '...*and Hezekiah himself I shut up in Jerusalem, his capital city, like a bird in a cage, building towers round the city to hem him in, and raising banks of earth against the gates, so as to prevent escape...*

*Hezekiah...sent out to me the chiefs and the elders of Jerusalem with 30 talents of gold and 800 talents of silver, and diverse treasures, a rich and immense booty... All these things were brought to me at Nineveh, the seat of my government.'*

**Battle of Pelusium - Egypt versus Assyria.** Sennacherib now having pacified Judea and secured his back, felt confident to invade Egypt. The army led by Sennacherib himself, followed the 'Way of Horus' to Pelusium east of Sile (Tjaru) the gateway to the Delta. Shabatka hurriedly sent the combined Egyptian and Nubian army in a last ditch effort to stop the Delta being overrun by the Assyrians and the two armies met near Pelusium. What followed next is a matter for much speculation to this day. On the day before the battle the 6th August 700BC there occurred a total solar eclipse. In 2 Kings 19:35 the Old Testament writers take up the story *'...the angel of Yaweh went out and smote in the camp of the Assyrians an hundred four score and five thousand (185,000)... early in the morning they were all dead corpses'.* Herodotus writing two hundred and fifty years later gave a different explanation.*'..there came in the night a multitude of field mice which devoured all the quivers, bow strings and shield thongs of the Assyrians.'* As proof he referred to later seeing a statue, or relief, of Shabatka with a mouse in/by his hand. He was not to know that the mouse was a sign of peace in Ancient Egypt. It might have been the eclipse being interpreted as a bad omen, or an outbreak of bubonic plague raging in Syria at the time, in any case, Sennacherib abandoned the invasion and peace was agreed. Both Sennacherib and Shabatka placed their seals on the treaty, later there was a royal marriage to seal the peace and Sennacherib returned to Nineveh. Peace descended on the region for twenty years. Sennacherib was proccupied campaigning in Elam and Babylon, culminating in the sacking of Babylon in 689BC.

In 690 BC, Shabatka died and was succeeded by crown prince **Taharqa** 690-664BC. Now that there was peace with Egypt, Taharqa indulged in a significant building program in Nubia and Egypt. He rebuilt the temple at Kawa, south of the third Nile cataract; this granite sphinx (left), bearing his face, has been recoverd from the site. He also erected a stunningly elegant open colonnade in the great coutyard of the Amen temple at Karnak. It consisted of ten sixty-five-feet slender columns with ten foot wide open papyus capitols; only this one (right) is still standing.

Nine years after Taharqa ascended to the throne of Egypt, Sennacherib was assassinated by his two sons in the religious center of Ashur, 681 BC. After a short civil war his youngest son, the governor of Babylon, defeated his brothers and with the support of the army became king **Esarhaddon** 680-669BC. Taharqa now made a strategic political blunder which was to incur the wrath of the strongest superpower in the region and ultimately result in the invasion and sack of Egypt. Taharqa wrongly believed that he could take advantage of the civil war in Assyria and chose to support Sidon when it rebelled in 680BC. Esarhaddon had been occupied for his first three regnal years rebuilding Babylon and putting down successive invasions by the Cimmerians and the Medes. He finally reached Lebanon in 677BC and easily captured Sidon, its king was beheaded and the city sacked and renamed 'The harbor for Esarhaddon'. It became the province of Sidunu in 676BC, its people were deported. All the other cities in the region proved loyal to Assyria, the king of Tyre was especially rewarded along with Gaza. Esahaddon departed to campaign in the northwest and left his Tartan 677-6BC, to secure the coastal area around Gaza and Raphia and pacify the Bedouin, to avoid being harried on the way into the Delta. A stele in the western desert records that Egypt was at this time put on a war footing in preparation for the expected Assyriain punitive invasion. The details of the subsequent Assyrian unsuccessful battles with Taharqa are naturally not mentioned in the Assyrian annals. It seems that Esarhaddon's Tartan only succeeded in reaching the so called 'Brook of Egypt' east of Pelesium before the combined Egyptian and Nubian armies stopped him. Taharqa had been able to delay the inevitable punishment for three further years.

**The Assyrian conquest of Egypt.** With Egypt's connivance, in 673BC, the previously loyal city of Tyre revolted against Assyrian rule. This resulted in the return of Esarhaddon himself in 671BC. The siege of Tyre draged on for four years, and he left the investment to lead the invasion of Egypt personally. In anticipation of the invasion of Egypt, king Taharqa had sent troops to strengthen the fortified city of Ashkelon near Gaza. To avoid a delay Esarhaddon bypassed the city and rapidly moved on to Raphia. The Assyrian annals record that it took the army a full fifteen days, instead of the expected three, to cross the Sinai desert in the middle of summer. They arrived at the fortified east Delta city of 'Ishhupri' (perhaps Quantarah) where Taharqa's army was drawn up against them. During the ensuing battle, the Assyrian army soundly defeated the combined Egyptian and Nubian armies who proceded to retreat and then regroup a total of three times on the 3rd, 16th and 18th of July 671BC, being defeated on each occasion. A wounded Taharqa then fled south to Thebes leaving the Assyrians to take Memphis on the 22nd July. The city was looted and the spoils taken to Nineveh. Esarhaddon now gave himself the title 'King of Egypt and Kush' and managed to capture most of the members of the royal family including Taharqa's wife and children. Before returning to Nineveh he appointed the Assyrian governor Sha nabu shu as ruler of the new Assyrian province Musru (north Egypt). He also established prince Necho I as ruler of Sais, taking Necho's son, Psametek I, to Nineveh as a guarantor of loyal behavior. Following the departure of Esarhaddon, Taharqa based at Thebes, took advantage and promoted numerous revolts. In 670BC he quickly was able to retake Memphis. In resonse, in 669BC, Esarhaddon set off from Nineveh to return to Egypt but died on the journey in the city of

Harran east of Carchemish.

The Assyrian crown prince **Ashurbanipal** 668-627BC had been left in charge of the government while his father had been campaigning in Egypt. Although he was the younger of two brothers, he was the darling of the army and proceeded smoothly to the throne. He was to be the last great king of Assyria, building a magnificent new royal palace beside that of his grandfather, Sennacherib, at Nineveh. The palace walls were lined with exquisite bas reliefs recording his military victories and the famous lion hunts (right, British Museum, London) which are considered to be the pinnacle of Assyrian art. He was also a man of letters and assembled one of the finest libraries of the ancient world. In 667BC he invaded Egypt meeting little resistance. This time, Memphis was thoroughly

sacked and he pursued Taharqa to Thebes, which was then captured but not sacked. Ashurbanipal returned to Nineveh and Taharqa retreated to his native homeland Nubia, where he died three years later in 664BC and was succeeded by his heir **Tanutamen** 664-656BC the son of Shabaka. As soon as he came to power, Tanutamen left Nubia, moved north to invade Egypt and took back both Thebes and Memphis. Ashurbanipal returned immediately, expeled Tanutamen and this time sacked Thebes as punishment. His annals recorded curtly the catastrophy which had befallen the city and ancient Egypt. '*The golden statues of Amen and two golden obelisks..*' were looted and taken to Nineveh but have not survived.

## The Saite Dynasty.

Ashurbanipal took the Egyptian prince **Psametek I** 664-610BC, who had been living in Nineveh for six years, and appointed the trustee as vassal king of Sais and most of the Delta. Psametek I became the founder of the 26th Saite Dynasty. He ruled for fifty-four mostly peaceful and prosperous years. Assyria was heavily preoccupied at home during his reign, which allowed Psametek I to slowly and carefully expand his kingdom. In regnal year nine, 655BC, he dispatched a fleet south to Thebes and forced the Theban Governor Montuemhet to accept his daughter Nitocris I as heir to God's Wife of Amen, recorded on the 'Adoption Stele' there. With the help of Greek mercenaries, based in the Greek Delta colony of Dafnia, he was ultimately able to rule the whole country and take it independent, but was careful to be very sympathetic to his mentors the Assyrians who were distracted by a prolonged war with Elam and later Babylon. In 653BC his Saqqara stele records a victory over the Libyans as he pushed the border west. There is a break in the annals until regnal year thirty-four (630BC) when the Cimmerian invasion penetrated deep into Syria. Egypt under Psametek I, sent troops to Ashdod, where they were victorious.

In 646BC Assyria finally destroyed its old enemy Elam. Although not appreciated at the time, this inadvertently created a power vacuum in the south east of the Fertile Crescent which ultimately spelled the downfall of Assyria. The aggressive Medes were able to expand into the old Elamite territories and in 630BC started to raid the Assyrian homeland itself. Led by their king Cyaxares, the Medes penetrated even as far as the royal capital Nineveh. In 627BC Ashurbanipal, the last great king of the Assyrian Empire died and Babylon took the opportunity to gain its independence from Assyria. The Assyrian Empire was exhausted after three hundred years of constant warfare, having no natural boundaries and now without a strong military king, the Empire began to fall prey to the attacks of both the Medes and the Babylonians.

**The fall of Assyria.** All four of the grand capitals of the Assyrian Empire Nineveh, Nimrud, Khorsabad and Asshur, were threatened in 616BC, when the powerful Babylonian king, Nabopolasser, raided north up the Euphrates. Seeing the potential danger to Egypt of an Assyrian collapse, the loyal Psametek 1 led the Egyptian army to the north of Syria and moved down the Euphrates to engage the Babylonians. Nabopolasser withdrew, but returned the next year, this time unsuccessfully besieging the religious capital Ashur. The Medes invaded east Assyria and again reached the walls of Nineveh, but the stout defences proved too strong. Instead they swung south and captured Ashur. The Babylonians and Medes then formed a coalition; Assyria was now fighting an all out war for survival. The overwhelming might of the coalition was proving to be too strong for the exhausted Assyria and in June 612BC, the Assyrian army faced the combined Babylonian and Median armies outside the walls of the royal capital of Nineveh. The out-numbered Assyrian army held the coalition troops in three successive battles but in the end could not stop the walls from being breached in the northeast corner, the city was over-run and the magnificent palaces, temples and libraries were thoroughly sacked. The surviving elements of the Assyrian army retreated north west to make a last stand at Harran east of Carchemish. Nabopolasser was not able to take Harran on his own and called on his ally the, Medes; together they captured Harran in 610BC. A remnant of the Assyrian army escaped and joined with the newly crowned king of Egypt **Nekau 2** (610-595BC) and the Egyptian army which had marched north to meet them. In 609BC they combined but were unsuccessful in recovering. Harran. The following year spelled the end for Assyria. Their army was completely destroyed by the Babylonians and their last king was killed. The Egyptian king Nekau 2 led his army north with the navy moving in tandem along the coast, but arrived too late to save them. He was tragically delayed in arriving, having first to defeat Josiah, king of Jerusalem who obstructed him at Megiddo on his march north. The Assyrian Empire thus disappeared from history. In 1891 Winckler wryly observed '... *no effort to recover herself was possible, the country was in the hands of an army of mercenaries ....there was no longer an Assyrian people. It was a matter of complete indifference in the provinces whether the (Assyrian) governor exacted his extortions in the name of the king of Assyria , or in that of the king of Babylon'*

**The Babylonian threat.** After the fall of Assyria her conquerors divided the empire between them. The Medes took all the lands east of the Tigris, north of Elam, Babylon took all lands west of the Tigris to the Mediterannean Sea including Syria, and kept Elam in the south east. For three years, from 609-606BC, the Babylonians and Egyptians disputed control over the region around Carchemish in a number of indecisive actions. Nekau 2 of Egypt was able to maintain control of both Syria and Palestine but this was not to last. In 605BC crown prince prince Nebuchadnezzar, now the Babylonian Commander in Chief moved north up the Euphrates to recover the old Assyrian provinces of Phoenica, and Nekau 2 was defeated at Carchemish. He regrouped south at Hamath on the Orontes but was defeated again. Prince Nebuchadnezzar was now poised to invade Egypt when his father died in 604BC and he returned to Babylon to be crowned. Nekau 2 thus gained a three-year respite. Under the now king Nebuchadnezzar, the Babylonian army returned in 601BC and scythed through Syria and Palestine but were unexpectedly held at the Egyptian border by Nekau 2 who was then able to retaliate and recover Gaza. The Babylonian army withdrew leaving Egypt at peace for fourteen years. The focus in Babylon was now the rebuilding and the beautification of the city. It was during this time that the legendary Walls of Babylon were constructed and

the beautiful blue glazed tile gates built. Shown right is the fabulous Ishtar gate reproduced in the Berlin Museum. The most notable building project during the reign of Nekau 2 was the widening and extension of the Ramesses 2 navigable canal from the east Nile to the north of the Red Sea.

Nekau's son and successor was king **Psametek 2** ,595-589BC. He conducted a policing campaign to the fourth Nile cataract in year four and a year later joined with the king of Jerusalem and the Phoencian cities in holding off a Babylonian invasion of Palestine. However four years later the Babylonians returned in earnest (586BC) and this time even support from the new Egyptian king **Apries** (589-570BC) could not stop Nebuchadrezzar taking and sacking Jerusalem and carrying off the remaining two tribes to captivity *'by the rivers of Babylon'*. The Egyptian army, once again, was able to hold the Babylonians at the Egyptian border in 581BC, regnal year eight. In regnal year fifteen Apries went on the offensive, he led campaigns into Phoenicia from 574-570BC and manged to take Tyre and Sidon and even won a naval victory over Cyprus. However the expanding Greeks invaded Libya and when Apries came to the support of their neighbour, the Greeks inflicted a heavy defeat at Kyrene (Cyrene) in 570BC. King Apries lost two further battles that year to the Egyptian usurper, General Amasis (later king Ahmose 2), supported by Greek mercenaries from the Delta, and he fled to Babylon.

In 567BC the new king **Ahmose 2** (570-526BC) defeated ex-king Apries, accompanied by the Babylonians, who never threatened Egypt again. The short lived Babylonian Empire was now in rapid decline. In 560BC Ahmose 2 conducted a naval campaign and took the southern Cyprus sea ports. Greece had by now become a major trading partner and supplier of mercenaries and Ahmose 2 allowed the Greeks to set up a colony at Naukratis, in the west Delta, in the same year. Under Ahmose Egypt was to experience a period of unparalleled peace and prosperity, lasting for thirty years. The Egyptians could well have thought that they had put the bad days of the Assyrian and Babylonian threats behind them. However it was was the calm before the storm; a new regional super power was emerging ominously in the Near East, Persia. By the end of the reign of Ahmsoe 2, the one hundrd and forty year old Saite Dynasty had run it's course and had almost collapsed; the Egyptian state was isolated and entirely dependent on fickle Greek mercenaries for survival. As Breasted put it *'the character and policies of Amasis (Ahmose 2) clearly disclose the fact that the old Egyptian world…..has already ceased to be. Its vitality,which flickered again into a flame in the Saite age, is now quenched forever'*.

## The Perisan conquest

In 560BC **Cyrus 2 'The Great'** 560-526BC became the king of the Persians, and ten years later had integrated the powerful Medes into his Archaemenid Empire and his expansion accelerated. In 548BC he took the old Hittite capital of Hatussas and then in 547BC defeated Croeses of Lydia at Sardis in south west Anatolia. He took Egyptian-held Cyprus in 545BC and in 539BC he captured Sippar on the Euphrates and then took nearby Babylon in 538BC, without a struggle. This ended the 'captivity' as he allowed the Jews to return to rebuild Jerusalem. The Cylinder of Cyrus (right), British Museum,London, is a milestone in  political and religious tolerance for such turbulent times. Cyrus was planning the invasion of Egypt when he died in 526BC, having single-handedly created ther greatest empire the world had yet seen.

The unfortunate **Psamtik 3**, 525BC, had succeeded his father Ahmose 2 for only six months before he had to face the new, but short-lived, Persian king, **Cambyses** 2 525-522BC, and the might of the enormous Persian Empire (right page) at Pelusium on the border. Egypt was no match, and Psamtik 3 was routed, but escaped to Memphis which was besieged and captured. He was caught and later executed at the Persian capital Susa. Egypt was then integrated, along with Cyprus and Phoenicia, into the sixth satrapy of the Achaemenid Empire. Thus began the first period of Persian rule over Egypt, known as the 27th Dynasty. Cambyses 2 in his short three-year reign led three unsuccessful military campaigns; in Africa against Carthage, in the oases on the Libyan border and in Nubia. He infamously lost a whole army of c50,000 troops on the way to the Siwa oasis and in 522 BC died from gangrene on the way back to Persia to quell a revolt. Cambyses 2 was reported to have burned

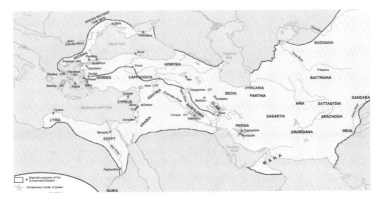

and destroyed the religious center of Heliopolis, which never recovered; Stabo, c24BC, recorded it as a ruin. The Heliopolis temple complex was the greatest the world has seen, the temple to Re alone was the size of all of Karnak. Its protective walls were fifty feet thick and even as late as 1898AD they were still forty feet high. Nothing except a solitary obelisk remains.

From 522 to 404BC Egypt was ruled by a series of Persian governors or Satraps. During this period, the Persian Empire was ruled by a series of powerful kings who expanded the Empire and then tried to invade and conquor the mainland city states of Greece, on a number of occasions, but without long-term success.

**Darius I** 'The Great' 522-485BC expanded the Persian Empire into Libya, west India, Thrace and parts of Afghanistan. This was the greatest extent of the Empire; in total it covered twenty provinces, each with a Satrap. The central government minted national coin currency and constructed a network of roads, the extent of which was not to be seen again until mid way through the Roman Empire c180AD. In expanding westwards as far as the Ionian Sea, Darius I had absorbed a number of major independent Greek city states into the Persian Empire. These cities rebelled during the 'Ionian Revolt' of 499-493BC and were supported by their mentor, Athens. Darius I crushed the revolt and decided on a full blown invasion of the Greek mainland to punish the Athenians. In 490BC Darius I landed an army of 20-40,000 trooops north of Athens. On the 12th of September the Persian army, still on the beachhead, was engaged in battle by an Athenian force less than half it's size. However, the Greeks on home territory with their Phalanx method of fighting, won a decisive battle that day at **Marathon**. The defeated invasion fleet returned home and five years later Darius I was assassinated. During his reign the expansion of the navigable waterway from the Nile Delta to the Red Sea, started by Nekau 2 was completed. It was marked along the way by four great bi-lingual 'Canal Stelae' inscribed in both hieroglyphics and cuneiform. Darius was popular in Egypt as he continued the early Persian policy of religious tolerance defined in the Cylinder of Cyrus.

**Xerxes I** 485-465BC was the son of Darius I and in contrast to his father was most unpopular in Egypt. In 484 BC he cruely put down an Egyptian revolt and one in Babylon, both of which had broken out on his succession. His ambition was to avenge his father's defeat at Marathon and conquer the Greek mainland. In 483BC he led an immense c60,000 strong Persian army and crossed the Hellespont on a bridge made up of floating boats. He then moved south and invaded Greece, where in 480BC he won a costly victory at the battle of **Thermopylae** against only 7,000 assorted Greeks led by the legendary king Leonidas, with his 300 Spartans. Xerxes burned Athens but his navy was later cleverly defeated at Salamis. The next year, an alliance of united Greek city states won decisive land victories at Platea and later at Mycale. This ignited the remaining Greek cities into action and the Delian league was formed against the Persians who were finally expelled three years later.

A much more serious and extensive Egyptian revolt took place c460BC during the reign of the Persian king **Artaxerxes I** 465-424BC. It was led by the Libyan/ Delta prince Inarus with support from Sais and Athens. Inarus defeated a Persian force in the Delta and with an Athenian fleet of two hundred ships sailed up the Nile as far as Memphis. He won a naval victory there and killed the Persian Satrap, the brother of Xerxes 1, However, the Athenian admiral was also killed and Inarus was wounded. After eighteen months of guerilla warfare in the Delta, Inarus was defeated and captured in 454BC. He was taken to the Persian capital Susa and executed. With this the revolt collapsed; however, Herodotus writing at this time claimed *'Inaros had done the Persians more hurt than any man before'*.

**Egypt's last independend king.** Egypt managed to gain a brief sixty year period of independence from 404 -343BC led by Amyrtaeus supported by Spartan and other Greek mercenaries who by now made up most of the Egyptian army. There were two significant Egptian kings during this era. **Nectanebo I** 380-362BC (right), was successful in holding off the Persians, with the help of Athens and Sparta, for the whole duration of his eighteen year reign. His most notable victory came in 374BC and was due to the Persian army's Greek mercenary officer's dissent in the midst of the battle. Nectanebo 1 was able to carry out a major building program and is mostly known for his many monuments and temples. He erected a small kiosk at the entrance to the Temple of Isis at Philae which would become one of the most important religious sites during the Ptolemaic period. He also built at el Kab, Memphis and Tanis and erected a stele in front of the the pylon of Ramesses 2 at Hermopolis. Most notably, he built the giant first pylon at the western entrance to the Karnak complex and the enormous outer mud brick walls which still surround most of the whole complex today. Visitors to Karnak can see that Nectanebo was not able to complete the northern of the two entrance pylons, which stopped short at a height of sixty five-feet. He also left the construction ramp in place to the ninety five feet high southern pylon as a valuable illustration of how these huge pylons were built. Finally, at Luxor he constructed an avenue of sphinxes, decorated with his face, which still line the interconnecting road (at the Luxor end) between the Karnak and Luxor temple complexes. From c365 BC, Nectanebo 1 ruled with his son **Teos** as co-regent who three years later was to succed him for a short reign.

**Nectanebo 2** 360-343BC was the nephew of Teos. He was the last king of the 30th Dynasty and also the last native Egyptian ruler of the country. Nectanebo 2 ascended to the throne with the support of the Spartan king who helped him overthrow his uncle Teos, while he was out of the country campaigning in Syria. In 351BC, Nectanebo 2 managed to halt a major Persian invasion, again only with Greek help. However after a reign of seventeen years, in 343BC, his exhausted Egyptian army was eventually outnumbered and soundly defeated by the Persian king Artaxerxes 3 (358-338BC) and his alledged '330,000 Asiatics plus 14,000 Asian Greek troops' strong army. Artaxerxes 3 had already gained a reputation for excessive cruelty even for those times. Soon after becoming king he murdered all of his Persian royal family to secure his place as king. Nectanebo 2 fled into exile in Nubia, where he vanished from history. Artaxerxes 3 destroyed the walls of Memphis, looted its temples and applied punitive taxes. Egypt once again was reduced to being only the 6th Satrapy of the Persian Empire. For the next ten years it suffered under Persian rule, its religion was persecuted and its sacred books were stolen. Nectanebo 2's sarcophagus (right, British Museum, London) was found in a mosque in Alexandria, it had been used as a water container or as a bath, judging by the twelve drain holes.

**Alexander 3 'The Great'** 332-323BC. Ten years after the conquest of Egypt, the ruthless Persian king Artaxerxes 3 was murdered by Bagoas, one of his senior generals, and was eventually succeded by king **Darius 3** 336–330BC. Soon after coming to power, Darius 3 was to be confronted by the twenty-year old recently crowned king of Macedonia, Megas Alexandros. After the assasination of his father and the consolidation of his domestic kingdom, Alexander crossed the Hellespont with a rerlatively small army of 42,000 soldiers in 334BC. He easily defeated a small part the Persian army at the Granicus river in northwest Anataolia near Troy. In November of the next year at Issus near Antioch, Alexander outnumbered two to one, delivered a severe defeat to Darius 3. Darius had personally led the Persian army which, incidentally, contained cohorts of Egyptian troops. In 332BC Alexander approached the Egyptian border; the Persian Satrap Mazaces handed over the country to him without a fight. Alexander began restoring the temples damaged during the Persian conquest which endeared him to the Egyptians. The following year in 331BC he defeated Darius 3 for the final time at the great battle of Gaugemela (near Mosul), putting an end to the Achaemenid Empire which had dominated the known world for a brief, but notable, two hundred years.

It was customary for past historians from Manetho onwards to end their account of the history of Ancient Egypt at the conquest of Alexander. However, this would exclude one of the most important eras particularly with regard to the monumental building programs of the Ptolemaic dynasty, which makes up the best preserved of the Egyptian temples.

# Chapter Twelve

# The Last Years Under Greece and Rome

In 332 BC **Alexander** was welcomed by the Egyptians as a deliverer. He went directly to the capital Memphis, followed by a pilgrimage to the reknowned ancient Egyptian oracle of Amen at the Oasis of Siwa, close to the Libyan border. Curious about his destiny and parentage, he asked the oracle *'who is my father?'* in response the oracle declared him to be the son of the god Amen Re. Macedonians were appointed to command the main military garrisons at the capital Memphis and at the strategically important border town of Pelusium; otherwise Alexander left the civil administration in local control. He founded a new Greek city, Alexandria, which was quickly to become the major commercial port in the Mediterranean. He visited major religious sites, such as the Serapeum at Saqqara, in respect of the traditional Egyptian

religion. The wealth of Egypt could now be harnessed for Alexander's conquest of the rest of the Persian Empire and beyond. The famous Roman c50AD mosaic (right), found at Pompei, shows Alexander fighting Darius at the battle of Issus. Early in 331 BC he was ready to depart, and led his forces out of Egypt never to return.

He left instructions for the rebuilding of one of the two inner sanctuaries of Amenhotep 3 at the Luxor temple. The beautiful colored cartouches and reliefs of Alexander's sanctuary are clearly visible today.

**Ptolemy I** (323-283BC) Soter (Saviour). Eight years later Alexander died in Babylon without naming an adult heir, and a succession crisis erupted among his generals. Initially, Perdiccas ruled Alexander's empire as regent on behalf of the Macedonian joint royal leaders. He appointed Ptolemy, Alexander's childhood friend, general and closest companion to be Satrap of Egypt in 323BC. Ptolemy I cleverly intercepted Alexanders's body in Syria, while it was on its way from Babylon to Macedonia. Initially it was kept in Memphis reputedley at the Serapeum, Ptolemy 2 in 280BC moved it to it's permanent tomb in Alexandria where it became a popular Greek and Roman tourst attraction until it became lost during the Roman Christian pagan purges. It was last mentioned c450AD. Under the traditional Macedonian sucession convention, possession of the dead king's corpse imparted an extra level of legitimacy to the regime of the successor, in this case Ptolemy I. Perdiccas soon grew to consider Ptolemy I to be his greatest rival and launched an invasion of Egypt in 321BC. It failed at the Nile and Perdiccas was killed by his generals. Ptolemy I was then offered the regency but declined, choosing to keep his power base of Egypt instead. Ptolemy proceeded to consolidate his position in Egypt and managed to hold Cyprus, Syria and Judah during the long drawn out Wars of the Diadochi, meaning succesors (322-301BC), to decide who was to be the successor to Alexander. In 305 BC, Ptolemy assumed the full title of King of Egypt. As Ptolemy I Soter he founded the Ptolemaic dynasty that was to rule Egypt for three hundred years and began an astonishingly peaceful and prosperous period to end the previous four hundred years of invasions, occupation and civil wars. The Ptolemies did not threaten the religion or customs of the Egyptians, quite the opposite; they like the early Persians kings and Alexander, embraced the Egyptian culture.

They built magnificent new temples dedicated to the Egyptian gods most notably at Dendera, Esna, Edfu, Kom Ombo and Philae. They even adopted the dress style and appearance of the traditional kings of Egypt. Ptolemy I is shown (right) in this bust now in the British Museum, London, complete with the royal Nemes headdress and uraeus.

In 285BC, Ptolemy I made his son Ptolemy 2 Philadelphus his co-regent and died two years later at the remarkable age of 84. Shrewd and cautious, he had a stable and well-managed kingdom to show at the end of forty years of consolidation. The Ptolemies limited the number of Greek cities in Egypt to only three, namely Alexandria the state capital, Ptolemais, the capital of the south (near Thinis) and Naucratis the west Delta port which was the first Greek colony in Egypt founded c560BC. During Ptolemy I's early reign, Macedonian troops were granted land in Egypt and they brought with them their families. Consequently tens of thousands of Greeks settled and became the new ruling class. Local Egyptians were only allowed minor roles in the Ptolemaic government; this was to become a constant source of irritation and friction.

**Great Royal Library.** Ptolemy I was not only a military leader and statesman he was also a man of learning. He founded at Alexandria the Great Royal Library and museum, named the *'house of muses'*. or Museion. The library became by far the the most important center of learning and depository of knowledge in the world. It had an acquisitions department, close to the harbor, along with an extensive cataloguing section. The library contained shelves for the collections of papyrus scrolls, known as bibliothekai, above the shelves was carved the famous inscription *'The place of the cure of the soul'*. It was the first known library to seriously acquire books from across the known world; it was charged by Ptolemy I with collecting all the world's knowledge. It conducted regular well funded sourcing visits to the literary centers of Rhodes, Pergamon and Athens. One unsubstantiated and perhaps exaggerated practice, was to remove books from each ship that berthed at the harbor, keeping the originals and returning copies. Thanks to the Pharos lighthouse (see right), trade from both east and west grew. As Alexandria became the hub for international trade it also became the leading producer of papyrus and scrolls. As well as being a depository for a reputed 500,000 historical scrolls, the library became the focus for international scholars who received royal support for travel and accommodation. It was a leading research institution for mathematics, astronomy, physics, natural sciences and medicine; scientific methodolgy was first applied there. The precise nature of the decline of the library is unclear. There is evidence to support that 'some books' were destroyed accidentally during a fire when Julius Caesar took Alexandria and Egypt in 48BC. However the main library survived for another three hundred years before it was largely destroyed in a fire following Emperor Aurelian's attack on Alexandria c270AD. The smaller Serapeum library nearby, escaped destruction. The final destruction of the Serapeum and its library took place in 391AD when Emperor Theodosius decreed that all pagan temples had to close. Pope Theophilus of Alexandria encouraged the Christian Copts to destroy the pagan Serapeum temple; in the ensuing fire the library was consumed. The myth that the library survived until it's destruction during the Arab conquest in 642AD has been dismissed as anti-Islam propaganda.

**Pharos Lighthouse.** Ptolemy I started the construction of a huge four hundred feet high lighthouse on the island of Pharos in the harbor of Alexandria. It utilized sunlight reflected form a bronze mirror to guide ships to the harbor by day; later a flame was added to provide the same service at night. It was completed by his son in c280BC but was mostly destroyed in the catastrophic earthquakes which rocked Alexandria in both 1303 and 1323AD.It was said that the port of Alexandria during the time of Ptolemy I was the largest in the world and boasted it could berth twelve hundred ships simultaneously.

Ptolemy I was Alexander's great boyhood friend and companion throughout all the travels and battles that led to the creation of his Empire. As a tribte to his friend, he wrote a history of Alexander's campaigns that sadly has not survived. It was considered by contemporary writers as the best objective work on the subject and became the principal source for the best surviving account by Arrian of Nicomedia, c130AD 'Anabasis of Alexander'. During the reign of Ptolemy I, the Egyptian chief priest of Heliopois Manetho, who spoke and wrote Greek, was encouraged by the king to start a monumental work, the writing of the history of Egypt from the earliest times to the conquest by Alexander. The objective was to create a 'modern' history to correct and replace the 'Histories' written by Herodotus two hundred years earlier. The work was completed during the reign of his son Ptolemy 2.

**Ptolemy 2** (284-246BC) Philadelphus The coin on the right shows Ptolemy 2 and his wife Arsinoe 2. He began his thirty-eight year reign as co-regent with his father, living at the royal palace in the capital Alexandria. Egypt was involved in several wars during his reign. Magas, the Greek king of Cyrene (Libya) opened with an invasion from the west in 274BC which failed and on his

death Egypt absorbed Cyrene. The Seleucid kings, Antiochus 1 and 2 both contested the control of Syria with Ptolemy 2 during three years of warfare in 275BC and again in 260BC, the so called 1st and 2nd Syrian wars. Egypt's victories solidified Ptolemy 2's control over most of Syria and Egypt became the dominant naval power of the eastern Mediterranean. The victory won by Antigonus 2, king of Macedonia, over the Egyptian fleet at Cos in 258BC did not significantly affect Ptolemy 2's command of the Aegean Sea. The extravavgance of the Alexandrian court was at its height under Ptolemy 2 it bordered on decadence in the extreme. Ptolemy 2 deified his parents, and his wife, after her death in 270 BC. He staged a procession in Alexandria in honor of the Greek god Dionysus led by tens of chariots drawn by elephants and an exotic procession of wild animals in 276BC.

**Old Testament translation.** Callimachus, the keeper of the Great Royal Library, increased the size of the Museion building and the scroll collection and extensively encouraged the sciences, mathematics and medicine. Ptolemy 2 called a meeting of seventy-two Jewish Scholars (six from each of the twelve tribes), the so-called 'Septuagint', to translate the books of the Old Testament from Hebrew into Greek for the library at Alexandria. This translation became a milestone. It was used exclusively by the early Christians until Jerome, in c400AD, translated the Hebrew directly into Latin. The 'Septuagiunt' Old Testament is still utilised by the Eastern Orthodox Church to this day. It is likely that the translation of the whole of the Old Testament was actually made progressively in Egypt during the reigns of the subsequent Ptolemies. Probably only the Pentacheuch itself, the first five books, were actually translated by the 'Septuagint'. Ptolemy 2 also conducted an extensive building program; the highlight was the commencment of the great entrance pylons and temple of Isis (right, Robert's 1838AD lithograph) at Philae which was completed and decorated by his son and Ptolemy 5.

**Ptolemy 3** (246-222BC) Euergetes is noted for his military campaigns in north Syria during the 3rd Syrian War, he advanced as far north as Antioch and may have even have raided Babylon. Ptolemy 3 was responsible for the first of a series of three surviving decrees by successively, Ptolemy 3, 4 and,5 all published as tri-lingual inscriptions on stelae. His is known as the **Canopus Stone** of 239BC. The seven-feet high stele contains a number of decrees referring to famine relief, military campaigns, religion, government structure, donations to temples, and the return of statues of deities recovered from the Persians. In the text he boasts about keeping the peace and his generosity to the people by reducing taxes during a year of low-inundation. It is historically very important, as it introduced the innovation of having 365¼ days per year; however the addition of a leap year failed and it was left to Julius Caesar ,in

45BC, to implement it for the Roman Empire. The Canopus text (see Chapter 4) also initiated a memorial festival in honour of his deceased daughter Berenice, and ordered that the Decree was to be written in Hieroglyphic, Demotic and Greek, and that copies of the stele be displayed in the 'top ranked' temples for public inspection.

Ptolemy 3 is credited with the foundation of the new Serapeum Temple in Alexandria and was responsible for erecting the imposing extant southwest portal at Karnak, as well as the western portal there. The most notable building project however was without doubt the temple of Horus at Edfu. He started construction over an exsiting 18th Dynasty temple in 237BC and the inner temple was finally completed by his son in 212BC. It was expanded and decorated by their successors, culminating in the erection and decoration of the two magnificent giant outer pylons one hundred and twenty-five feet high

(right), by Ptolemey 12 in c70BC. After almost two hundred years of work, the temple was formally dedicated in 42BC. The Horus temple of Edfu is widely regarded as the finest and most intact Ptolemic temple in Egypt. It was fortified by a twenty foot high brick wall parts of which are still present. The ten story high pylons are partly hollow containing rooms with windows, serving as dormitories for the temple priests. The nearby mound Tel Edfu covers the city which grew up to become the capital of the 2nd Nome of Egypt, dating back to the Old Kingdom. The temple was closed after 391AD and became deserted and buried in forty feet of sand and silt; thus it remained protected until its rediscovery in 1798AD. The body of the temple was cleared in 1859/1860 but the local villager's houses on the temple roof remained until 1901.

**Ptolemy 4** (222-205BC) Philopator, was chiefly known for his tri-lingual Memphis Stele or Memphis Stone, bearing the 'Decree of Memphis' dated to c216 BC. His reign also saw a series of nationalist riots which continued sporadically for the next twenty years. The underlying grievances were to be a constant feature of the second half of the Ptolemaic period. At the end of his reign he lost control of parts of the country. Aswan was lost to the Kushites from 218-190BC. He was responsible for constructing the tiny yet beautifully proportioned temple at Deir el Medina, by the tomb workers village, on the west bank at Luxor. The temple was dedicated to both Hathor and Maat and contained chapels to Amen, Hathor and Osiris.

**Ptolemy 5** (205-180BC) Epiphanes became king as a young child of four; his reign had to contend with attacks from both the east and west. Antiochus 3 took Syria and Phillip 5 of Macedonia captured Cyrene (Libya). The internal strife during the reigns of his two predecessors continued, it is beleved he died of natural causes at the young age of 29. He is most noted for the third and most famous of the tri-lingual decree stelae erected in his ninth regnal year in recognition of his success when he recovered most of the parts of the country lost at the end of his father's reign, particularly the suppression of the Delta rebellion. It is now called the 'Rosetta Stone' and can be dated to March 27th 196 BC; it is more properly known as the 'Decree of Memphis by Ptolemy 5'. It is rather a vebose document, see Chapter 4. The essence includes a tax amnesty for the temple cult priests, from the boy king, restoring the tax privileges they had enjoyed from the past. In line with the the two other tri-lingual decrees, described above, many copies would have been erected in temples throughout the country. Two whole or part copies have been discovered for each of the three stelae. In addition the text of the Rosetta Stone is inscribed on the walls of the temple at Philae. As we saw in Chapter 4, it is the Rosetta stone found in 1799AD, which was a key to the early decipherment of hieroglyphics, the other stelae were disovered much later between 1866 and 1923, too late to assist in the decipherment process. He was responsible for the 1st pylon at Philae built around Nectanebo Gate.

**Ptolemy 6** Philometor (180-145BC) became king as a child aged six. His mother, Cleopatra 1 ruled as co regent until her death four years later. The following year he married his sister, Cleopatra 2. In regnal year ten, Antiochus 4 began the 6th Syrian War. He invaded Egypt and was even crowned as king in 168BC before Rome intervened, wishing to protect its grain supply. Egypt was then jointly ruled by three kings Ptolemy 6, his sister and younger brother **Ptolemy 7**. There followd a period of rivalry between the two brothers and civil unrest, however Rome continued to support Ptolemy 6. Even though his reign was disturbed, Ptolemy 6 was able to carry out a significant building program. He built the birth house between the first and second pylons at Philae and the hypostyle hall. He started the magnificent hypostyle hall at the 18th Dynasty temple at Esna which was completed by the Roman emperors, Tiberius and Claudius. The eighteen columns each thirty-seven feet high, were decorated later by Trajan and Hadrian, and the hall was finally dedicated by Emperor Vespasian in 75AD. His most notable project, however, was the start of the unique dual temple at Kom Ombo, dedicated to both Sobek and Horus, it was added to by his succesors and mostly finished by the Roman Emperors Tiberius c20AD and Claudius who added the entrance courtyard and collonade. Trajan c100AD, built the ambulatory outer wall and had it decorated with reliefs. The Nileometer at Kom Ombo in the west courtyard is one of the deepest and best-preserved in Egypt.

On his death in 145BC, internal rivalries broke out again. The Alexandrian mob continued to be disruptive and Rome had to step in to preserve the peace as she was becoming more and more heavily dependent on Egyptian grain. There were six more rulers who carried the dynastic name. **Ptolemy 8** (145-116BC) Physcon, meaning pot-bellied, was responsible for the tiny Opet temple at Karnak. During the reign of **Ptolemy 9** (116-80BC). Philae was such a very popular destination for visitors to the tomb of Osiris, that the priests petitioned Ptolemy 9 to prohibit government staff from staying at the temple and living at their expense. The fallen obelisk (see Chapter 4) on which this petition was engraved c112BC in both Hieroglyphics (on the obelisk) and Greek, (on the base) was discovered by Bankes in 1815AD. He had it brought to England in 1821, where it still stands in the grounds of Kingston Lacy, in Dorset. Its hieroglyphics,were to prove invaluable as a critical addition to those on the the Rosetta stone in unlocking the Egyptian alphabet. Ptolemy 9 made the terrible error of replacing the gold sarcophagus of Alexander the Great with one in glass, and used the original to mint state coins. The mob of Alexandria was incensed at this vandalism and soon after Ptolemy 9 was killed. **Ptolemy 10** (110-88BC) competed for the throne with his predecessor and the next king **Ptolemy 11** ruled for only a few days in 80BC before he was lynched by the Alexandrian mob.

**Ptolemy 12** (80-51BC) was a great builder but like all the kings after Ptolemy 2, he was corrupted by decadence and administered the state badly. He believed he was an accomplished flute player, shades of the Emperor Nero, and competed in open competitions. The magnificent peristyle court and giant entrance pylons to the Edfu Temple were completed by him c70 BC. In 55BC he started to rebuild the Dendera temple of Hathor, it was complted and decorated by Cleopatra 7. He also added the outer hypostyle hall to Ptolemy 6's Kom Ombo temple. During his reign, he conducted a successful pro-Roman policy culminating in 59BC when he made financial contributions to two of the Triumverate members Julius Caesar and Pompey. However the resultant hoped for long term alliance only lasted until the following year and broke down over the Roman conquest of Cyprus. He fell ill in 51BC but before he died he appointed his seventeen year old daughter Cleopatra 7 as his co-regent. In his will he declared that she and her twelve year old brother Ptolemy 13 should rule the kingdom jointly with Rome being executors.

**Ptolemy 13** (51-47BC) and **Cleopatra 7** (51-30BC) The first three years of their joint reign were fraught with domestic calamities, famine, poor Nile inundations and political conflicts. Although Cleopatra was married to her young brother, she had no intentions of sharing power. In August of their first year relations between the joint sovereigns completely broke down her face appeared alone on coins. A court conspiracy, however, removed Cleopatra (right, Altes Museum, Berlin) from power thus making Ptolemy the sole ruler c50BC. Two years later, her attempted counter coup in the east Delta at Pelusium  failed and she was forced to flee to Syria. While Cleopatra was in exile, Pompey was defeated by Julius Caesar at Pharsalus in Greece in 48 BC, and he fled to Alexandria to seek the support of the young Ptolemy 13 to fight on against Caesar. On September 28th, 48BC, Pompey arrived in the harbor of Alexandria without a bodyguard and was murdered by one of his former officers, who was now working for Ptolemy, as he stepped off his ship. He was then gruesomely beheaded in front of his wife and children. It is believed that Ptolemy 13 had ordered the death to win favor with the new strong-man of Rome, Julius Caesar, hoping in the process to clear his debts. Caesar followed Pompey to Egypt; when he arrived in Alexandria Ptolemy 13 presented him with Pompey's severed head. Caesar was saddened and then enraged that Pompey, a Consul of Rome, had been so treacherously treated. His forces occupied Alexandria and he moved into the royal palace where he began arbitration between the two rulers. Cleopatra 7, now twenty, hurriedly returned to the royal palace hidden in a Persian carpet. Caesar at fifty-two years of age was charmed by the bright witty and entertaining ruler and she became his mistress.

There then followed a seven month processional Nile, cruise consisting of a flotilla of four hundred ships. Cleopatra gave birth to their son the next year and named him Caesarion meaning 'little caesar'. Caesar now supported Cleopatra's claim to the throne and after a brief conflict, Ptolemy 13 was drowned during the Battle of the Nile. Cleopatra 7 then raised her younger brother Ptolemy 14 (42-44BC) to become her short lived co-regent. Cleopatra and Caesarion visited Julius Caesar in Rome between 47 BC and 44 BC where she dwelt at Caesar's country residence outside the city. Although of

Egyptian royal blood, she was not a Roman citizen and her close relationship to Caesar made her rather unpopular at Rome. It is not known if she was in the city at the time that Caesar was assassinated on the Ides of March 44 BC. Back in Egypt, Cleopatra made Caesarion her co-regent and successor. On the outside wall at the rear of the temple of Hathor at Dendera, there is a unique relief (left) which shows Cleopatra 7 and her young son Caesarion making offerings, both are shown as the same height.

Mark Antony, the chief deputy to Julius Caesar during the Gallic wars, and Octvaian, Caesars's heir, plus Lepidus were appointed by the senate as the 2nd Triumvirate in 43BC to jointly rule Rome after the assassination. Mark Antony was given Rome's eastern provinces to govern and in 42BC summoned Cleopatra to travel to Tarsus (south east Turkey) to examine her loyalty. Cleopatra now twenty-six, so charmed Antony that he wintered with her in 41/40BC in Alexandria, she later gave birth to his twins. In 37 BC, Antony again visited Alexandria on the way to the Parthian war. He then settled in Alexandria and 'married' Cleopatra in 35BC, according to Egyptian custom. However, this act was not recognized in Rome, as she was not a Roman citizen and he had already married Octavia c40BC, the sister of the powerful Octavian. Antony and Cleopatra subsequently had another child.

In 34BC, Antony made a fatal error of political judgement which was to seal his fate. He appointed Cleopatra to became co-ruler of the Roman eastern provinces and even produced coins (right) with both their heads.It became known from his will, that Antony's children with Cleopatra were to become rulers of Rome's eastern provinces on his death. In Rome,

it was feared that Cleopatra planned to unite the eastern provinces against Rome, with her as ruler.The Roman Seanate considered these events to be treasonable and a threat to the Republic. Octavian easily convinced the Senate to revoke Antony's power and he was recalled to Rome and war was declared on Cleopatra and Egypt. In 31BC, Antony's fleet accompanied by that of Cleopatra, was narrowly defeated off the coast of Actium (western Greece). Octavian then invaded Egypt. As his legions approached Alexandria, in August 30BC, to engage the combined armies of Antony and Cleopatra, Antony's army deserted to Octavian.

According to Plutarch (46-120AD), writing one hundred and thirty years later, fearing the rage of Antony, following his defeat, Cleopatra had a false message sent to Antony that she was dead. To avoid capture he fell on his sword and was dying when Cleopatra had him brought to her where he died in her arms. The contemporary Roman authors are in concensus that Cleopatra, at the age of thirty nine, now poisoned herself by the bite of an asp.The historian and traveller Strabo (64BC-23AD), who may even have been in Alexandria at the time, wrote that she either used a toxic ointment, or that she was bitten by an asp on the arm.She died on August 12th 30BC. Plutarch wrote that after she was found dead an asp was found concealed in a basket of figs nearby. He added that on Octavian's later triumph through Rome accompanying him was an an effigy of Cleopatra with the asp.Caesarion now seventeen was captured and executed at Alexandria, Octavian is quoted as saying 'Two Caesars are one too many.' So died Ptolemy the 15th, the last to bear the dynastic name. This ended not just the Hellenistic line of Egyptian kings, but the line of all ancient Egyptian kings. The three children of Cleopatra and Antony were spared and taken back to live in Rome where they were taken care of by Antony's wife Octavia, but were never to visit Egypt again.

It is ironic that right to the very end of the now exhausted three hundred year Ptolemaic dynasty the worn out kings of Egypt still aspired to associate themselves with their noble ancient predecessors. They religiously copied the traditional style of the magnificent regal reliefs first produced three thousand years previously. That on the right, adorns the imposing entrance pylons at Edfu, created by one one of the last Egyptian kings,Ptolemy 12, c70BC. He is seen in the the traditional regal pose 'smiting the kings enemies' just as as king Narmer had been depicted on the Narmer Palette over three thousand years before.

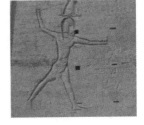

## Roman Domination

So it was that Egypt became a province (Aegyptus) of the Roman Empire in 30BC, following the defeat of Antony and Cleopatra 7 by Octavian. He was later to become one of the greatest of all of Rome's leaders as the Emperor Augustus (30BC-14AD). Alexandria became an increasingly important center on the trade route with the orient, as exotic luxuries were in high demand in Rome. The important grain province was governed by a Prefect selected by the Emperor himself, not a Governor who could be influenced by the Roman Senate. The main Roman interest in Egypt was always the reliable daily delivery of grain to the inhabitants of Rome. Rome did not substantially change the Ptolemaic system of government. Roman officials replaced Greeks in the highest offices but Greeks continued to fill most of the administrative offices. The Greek language remained the language of government in Egypt and the Eastern Roman Empire except when conducting communications with Rome itself. Unlike the Macedonians and Greeks under the Ptolemies, Romans did not settle in Egypt in large numbers. Although those that did, like the Ptolemies, respected Egyptian religion and customs, for example, a temple dedicated to Isis was even built near the Roman Forum. In Egypt many temple sites were enhanced by the construction of Roman additions, reliefs and decorations. Traditions such as mummification thrived and the art of mummy portraits flourished as can be seen in this typical example (right) of Fayum Roman mummy decoration. Some of the Roman emperors had themselves depicted as pharaohs, though not to the extent that the Ptolemies had. From the mid first century AD, Christianity took root in Alexandria and spread throughout the country. As a consequence, Egypt's pagan culture and religion began its decline. While the local population continued to speak their language, the ability to read hieroglyphic writing slowly disappeared, as the role and number of Egyptian temple priests declined. As we  have seen in Chapter 2 and 4, the temples themselves were finally abandoned and the Egyptian hieroglyphic writing which had been in daily use for almost four thousand years finally expired. The last hieroglyphic inscription is dated to August 24th 394BC at Philae.

## The Roman building legacy.

Because of its strategic importance, the Roman emperors often visited Egypt and the tradition of invaders and foreign rulers building in the ancient Egyptian style continued for almost four hundred more years, until the Roman Emperor Theodosius made Christianity the state religion of the Empire in 380AD and then banned pagan temples and worship in 391AD. The final blow came c545AD when Emperor Justinain introduced his sweeping legal and religious reforms, which led to the closure of the remnants of the temple of Isis at Philae; it had only survived that long as it was so remote from Rome and Alexandria.

**Augustus** (27BC-14AD) added the west and east collonades on the approach to the entrance pylons of the temple of Isis at Philae. The thirty two columns in the west colonnade were all completed, but curiously six of the seventeen capitols on the east colonnade were left only roughed out. He also constructed a small temple to Hathor there, which has now gone. He built the tiny 'Iseum' at the rear of the Hathor temple at Dendera and the bath house outside the main entrance. He added a walled courtyard at Kom Ombo. In Nubia he built at Kalabsha and Dendur (Metropolitan Museum, NY).

**Tiberius** (14-37AD) arranged for the construction at Dendera of the stunning outer hypostyle hall containing eighteen fifty-foot high columns. Each of the four sides of the capitals has a beautifully carved face of Hathor. Although the Coptic Christians later defaced the outer Hathor capitols, most of the inner ones are close to their original condition. The beautifully-colored astral ceiling is currently undergoing cleaning to expose the original colors which had become blackened over the years by smoking torches. At Kom Ombo he completed the southern peristyle courtyard of Augustus, which has been mostly lost.

**Claudius** (41-54AD) Despite his cartouches, it is not certain that he was responsible for the magnificent Roman Pronaos of eighteen columns at Esna; Tiberius may have started it. It was later decorated by Trajan and Hadrian.

**Trajan** (98-117AD) built this beautiful open kiosk (right) at the Roman period entrance to the Philae temple on the eastern approach to the island. The kiosk, however, was not completed; some of the reliefs on the inside lower walls were only sketched out. In earlier times the approach to the island was from the south where Nectanebo I had built his kiosk. **Hadrian** (117-138AD) later constructed the western water gate at Philae.

**Antoninus Pious** (138-161AD) built the outer entrance pylon and courtyard to the Medinet Habu small Amen temple. The last major Roman builder was **Diocletian** (284-305AD), who visited Egypt once in 301-2AD. He ordered the construction of the northeast gateway to Philae He was a religious conservative and was responsible for the last major persecution of the Christians. At Luxor he converted a portion of the the inner temple and dedicated it to the worship of the cult of the Roman Emperors. The painted frescoes in the so-called Roman vestibule there have been uncoverd and restored to expose part of their original extensive colors. The main scene shows the Tetrachy, meaning leadership by four, which include images of the two emperors Diocletian (east empire) Maximian (west empire) and their two deputies, the caesars Galerius and Constantinus I. It is ironic that although under Diocletion the Luxor temple became the core of a Roman Legion fortress, this transformation may have protected it from further damage. The remains of his fort can be seen to the north west of the temple.

**Septimius Severus** (192-211AD) repaired the earthquake, c27BC, damage to Amenhotep 3's north colossus at Thebes. The Libyan emperor was a great builder and arranged for his engineers to bring the large blocks used in the the repair, c199AD, from Edfu along with the stone platforms on which both colossal statues now stand.

## Removal of Obelisks

The impact of the Roman emperors on Egypt's buildings and artifacts was not always beneficial. Many Roman emperors removed Egyptian sculptures and reliefs to add to their own art collections at their country estates outside Rome. Hadrian visited Egypt in 130AD and assembled an extensive collection of Egyptian artifacts at his two hundred and fifty acre Tivoli Villa outside Rome. Some of the items removed by the Roman Emperors have been recovered and are now on display in the Egyptian collections of the world's museums. However, the emperors also carried out wholesale looting of Egyptian obelisks which were ultimately taken to decorate the public areas in Rome and Constantinople. Today there are more tall Egyptian obelisks standing in Rome, eight, than those that remain standing in all of Egypt. There are in total six; two at Karnak, one at Luxor, two in Cairo and one at Heliopolis.

**Augustus** (27BC-14AD) removed a pair of red seventy-feet high granite Thutmosis 3 obelisks from Heliopolis; they never reached Rome and remained at Alexandria. One now stands in London on the Thames Embankment, the other in New York in Central Park behind the Metropolitan Museum of Art. Augustus also removed a seventy-six feet Seti 1/Ramesses 2 decorated obelisk from Heliopolis; it was taken to Rome in 10BC and erected on the central island, the 'spina', of the Circus Maximus. It was later found broken in two pieces and was finally moved to the Piazza del Popolo in 1589AD, where the lion fountains were added in 1818.

**Caligula** (37-41AD), in 37AD, brought to Rome an eighty-three feet undecorated obelisk. It may have been from Heliopolis but as it has no decoration it could also be the obelisk cut by Augustus and erected in Alexandria. In Rome, it was erected on the 'spina' of the Gai Circus near the present day Vatican and was relocated slightly in 1586AD. It is the only obelisk in Rome that has not toppled since ancient times.

**Constantine** (312-337AD) removed one of the pair of the giant ninety-five feet red granite obelisks of Thutmosis 3 which stood in front of his pylon seven at Karnak. It was transported to Alexandria and later to Athens, finally **Theodosius** in 390AD had it cut into three pieces to ease transportation and had the largest section erected on the 'spina' in the Hippodrome at Constantinople (Istanbul), where it stands on his decorated marble pedestal to this day. The hieroglyphic texts describing the great Egyptian king's Syrian victories decorate the obelisk and are still in outstandingly crisp condition.

Emperor **Constantius 2** (337-361AD), in 357AD, removed the famous red granite 'single' obelisk of Thutmosis 3, at one-hundred and six feet tall it was the tallest obelisk ever erected. It was moved from the extreme east gate area of Karnak first to Alexandria and then to Rome where it originally stood on the 'spina' of the Circus Maximus. The obelisk broke into three pieces and was repaired in 1587AD although twelve feet were lost. It was then relocated to its current site outside the Lateran Cathedral in Rome.

# Chapter Thirteen

# *Our Inheritance from Egypt, an A to Z*

---

The following is a non exhaustive list which provides a catalogue of Ancient Egyptian achievements that have passed down through the Millennia to our lives today. In some case they may not be absolute documented 'firsts' but are close enough to warrant inclusion.

**Administration.** The King was the absolute ruler of the country and had complete control of the land and all its resources. As in many countries today, he was the commander in chief and head of the government. He relied on a bureaucracy of officials to manage his state affairs and appointed one or more viziers, or prime ministers, to act as the king's representative. The vizier co-ordinated the land, treasury, building projects, the legal system, and the archives. The country, towards the end, was divided into forty two administrative regions called Nomes (or counties) each governed by a Nomarch (governor), who was accountable to the vizier. The Nomarchs were responsible for collecting and storing the nation's wealth in both granaries and treasuries administered by overseers, who then redistributed grain and goods.

**Agriculture** The ancient Egyptians were able to consistently produce sufficient food for their own use and in later times had a regular annual surplus for export. Land management was crucial as taxes were based on land ownership and food production. Farming was completely dependent on the annual inundations of the river Nile. Crops included emmer,barley,and other cereal grains. Flax plants were cultivated for linen clothing and papyrus plants were used to make writing materials. Vegetables and fruits were grown in gardens close to homes, produce included leeks, garlic, melons, squashes, lettuce and grapes for wine.

**Archaeology.** King Djoser of the 3rd Dynasty c2550BC was the word's first identified archeologist, like all of his predecessors he possessed a deep respect for his ancestors. He collected hundreds of clay pots from earlier royal cemeteries which had decayed from neglect, and stored them carefully in rooms beside his burial chamber, ninety feet below his towering stepped pyramid. He decorated some of these rooms with magnificent blue faience glazed tiles, representing reed matting, with yellow stars painted onto the ceilings. Later king Thutmosis 4 c1390BC cleared the Sphinx which had over the years been buried up to its neck in sand; he commemorated this work by erecting his 'Dream Stele' between its paws.

**Architecture.** Ancient Egyptian architecture includes some of the most famous structures in the world: the Great Pyramids of Giza and the temples at Luxor, Karnak Edfu and Philae. Building projects were planned and paid for by the state partly for religious and commemorative purposes, but also to reinforce the power of the king. Builders used simple but effective tools and instruments made from stone, wood, copper, and later bronze and iron. Royal architects and engineers built enormous stone structures with the highest precision by making use of huge populations of highly organized labor. They were often farmers who were expertly trained and managed to efficiently repeat simple tried and tested processes.

**Animals.** Cattle were the most important
livestock, the state levied taxes on livestock;
based on the regular 'cattle count' conducted
every one or two years. Egyptians also kept
sheep, goats, and pigs. Wild poultry such as
ducks, geese, and pigeons were captured in
nets by the river, then bred on farms, where
they were force-fed to fatten them. There were abundant supplies of fish from the Nile and bees were kept for honey and wax. They relied on donkeys and cattle for transport and plowing. Horses were only introduced later by the Hyksos and the camel, although known from the New Kingdom, was not used until much later. Dogs, cats and even monkeys were common family pets. Pet lions were reserved for royalty only. Ramesses 2 was accompanied by his pet lion during the battle of Kadesh.

**Art.** For over 3,000 years, Egyptian artists followed formal
styles that were developed during the Old Kingdom, and
hardly changed. These standards provided a sense of order
and balance, Maat. The one exception is the Amarna period,
where art dramatically changed for a few decades from the
traditional to the humanistic style. This late Amarna period
Neferetiti bust demonstrates the abilities of the sculptor if
not restricted by the traditional style.

**Astronomers.** Nabta Playa was a large permanent settlement, sixty miles west of Abu Simbel. Its people constructed an arrangement of large megalith stones that is considered to be the oldest astronomical configuration and is dated to c6200BC. The orientation is set to align with the stars in Orion's belt and accurately points to the summer solstice. A later astronomical stone circle is considered to be the worlds earliest, and predates the Stonehenge circle by c2000 years. There was a fascination with celestial activities as seen in the tomb inscriptions of the Old Kingdom which continued into Ptolemaic times. Certan priests were designated as the 'keepers of time'; they watched the nightly movement of stars, planets and the moon. They recorded their rising and setting and their orbits. One set of stars were known as ikhemu seku the 'stars that never fail'; these were the polar stars. A second set were the ikhemu weredu, the never resting stars which followed specific orbits. The most important stars were Sirius the Dog star, called Sopdu or Sopdet, which signaled the coming inundation and Orion (Sah), Ursa Major, Cygnes and Cassiopeia. The planets were considered to be forms of Horus; the priests knew and tracked Jupiter, Saturn, Mars, Mercury and Venus. On the ceiling of the tomb of Senenmut, Hatshepsut's adviser, was an astronomical map, which is considered the world's first known star chart dated to c1460BC.

**Boats.** The Old Kingdom developed the world's finest river craft. They were originally used for transporting food and goods between the river side townships. By the time of the pyramid builders they had been developed into vessels that could transport massive granite stone blocks weighing over a hundred tons from the Aswan quarry to Giza in the north. In the New Kingdom, they were capable of transporting huge obelisks from Aswan to Karnak, Luxor and Heliopolis. These obelisks were over one hundred feet long and some weighed over four hundred tons. Examples of these marvelous craft have survived, the most notable being those found buried at Khufu's Giza pyramid. One of these has been reassembled and was found to be completely river worthy, it probably had been used to transport the king's coffin and its mummy across the Nile to its final resting place inside the pyramid.

**Book of the Dead.** Beginning in the New Kingdom, books of the dead were included in the tombs, along with shabti statues that were believed to perform labor for them in the afterlife. Typically for one year's salary, middle-class Egyptians were able afford to have a colored scroll made especially for them to ward off evil spirits on the way to and during the afterlife. (See Chapter 2)

**Burial customs** Ancient Egyptians maintained an elaborate set of burial customs that they believed were necessary to ensure immortality. Religious custom dictated the preservation of the intact body by mummification (see below), followed by specific burial ceremonies which included placing with the body, items to be used by the deceased in the afterlife. Before the Old Kingdom, bodies buried in desert pits, were naturally preserved by desiccation. Desert burials for the poor continued however, the middle-classes buried their dead in mud brick and then stone tombs.

**Calendar.** The Ancient Egyptians established a momentous breakthrough in record keeping associated with the movement of the stars which was to lead to the invention of the calendar. It was driven by the need to be able to predict accurately the start of the annual inundation. Astronomers of the Delta used precise observations and mathematic calculation to match the start of the inundation with the exact day that, one of the brightest stars, Sirius rose. It is believed from modern celestial calculations, that the Egyptian calendar was established as early as 4242BC, when they first started to use the heliacal rise of Sirius as the start of their new year. Their calendar year consisted of exactly 365 days, it was divided into twelve thirty-day months plus five feast days at the end. Each month was sub divided into three weeks each of ten days. The leap year concept was a much later Ptolemaic and Roman invention; hence the Egyptian calendar year was a quarter of a day shorter than the solar year and the months therefore moved slowly through the seasons on a 1,460 year cycle. However divergence from one year to the next was so slow as to be imperceptible to the general population. This remarkable calendar was to become the basis of our time recording to the present day.

**Chemistry.** An analysis of Egyptian ingredients has shown they were using technology to produce blue pigments as early as 2500 BC. Chemists have identified the main organic and mineral ingredients used in ancient Egyptians' make-up powders, the two main mineral ingredients being the naturally occurring ores, galena and malachite. However, laurionite and phosgenite have been analyzed, both of these rarely occur naturally implying that Egyptians synthesized the compounds. The entire process would have taken several weeks of continual purification to complete. The manufacturing of these compounds has revealed a previously unknown level of sophistication of ancient Egyptian chemistry.

**Confessions** Part of the early mortuary temple rituals was a text to aid the deceased when being judged in the presence of the judges of Osiris. These negative confessions 'the declaration of innocence' deal with ethical and moral concerns. They start with 'I have not....' and then typically list the following sins '....stolen from man or god, plundered, slain people, committed crimes, lied, cursed, copulated with a man or man's wife, caused anyone to weep, indulged in despair, led anyone astray, gossiped, slandered, been contentious, terrorized, become angry or made others angry, eavesdropped or made anyone hungry. These confessions empahsized the spirit of co-operation and Maat. They predate all the early ancient law codes including Hammurabi c1760BC and Moses and some religious scholars refer to them as the 'twenty commandments'.

**Conspiracy trial.** The minor wife and son of Ramesses 3 c1150BC plotted in the royal harem to have the king killed and conspired to have her son take over the kingdom. Before the act could be carried out one of the conspirators informed on the group and they were rounded up by the royal guards. The king was not directly involved in the trial, leaving it to the courts and the due process of law. A specially arranged series of courts tried the accused and they were found guilty and faced the death penalty. Senior members of the royal family and court were allowed to take their own lives, others were less fortunate. Some of the judges were unduly influenced by the harem members and were found guilty of undue leniency and were themselves punished. The precise details of the failed plot and the subsequent trials were carefully recorded by the royal scribes on papyri which have survived to the present day.

**Cosmetics** When the ancient Greeks visited Egypt they remarked that both women and men wore, what seemed to them, extravagant amounts of facial cosmetics. This is confirmed in numerous intact colored tomb reliefs and paintings. Egyptian cosmetics can be traced back to the earliest periods, the Narmer ceremonial palette c3100BC was used for grinding and mixing cosmetics for application to the cult statues of the temple gods. Three noble ladies at the court of Thutmosis 3 c1450BC were buried with costly cosmetics contained in purpose-made decorated containers, two of these jars still contained a cleansing cream made of oil and lime. Egyptians used a brush, doubling as toothpaste, from the salvadora persica tree. To improve their breath the Egyptians chewed herbs, gargled with milk, and chewed frankincense. The most common facial make up was black 'kohl' as an eye liner and mascara, and green malachite as an eye shadow. Lipstick and blusher were made from ochre. Eye make-up was kept in lumps and was ground on a palette to a fine powder. The powder was poured into vases from which it was extracted with a moist application stick. Eye makeup was also beneficial in curing or preventing eye diseases caused by the ever present wind-blown organisms prevalent in the dry dusty climate. The heavy metals copper and lead in the make-up also killed bacteria. Red lip gloss made from fat with red ochre was applied with a brush or spatula. Facial rouge consisting of red ochre with resin has been discovered in a tomb c2000BC having survived satisfactorily for four thousand years. Chalk and white lead pigment were used to provide the sought-after traditional white skin appearance for women. Some Egyptians appear to have dyed their fingernails using henna.

**Columns.** The most inspiring aspect of Egyptian temple architecture are the spectacular temple columns. The Great Colonnade at Luxor and the Hypostyle Hall at Karnak are unequalled in size and decoration anywhere else in the world. The columns represented nature; they alluded to prehistoric times when vast forests covered the land before the climate changed; they also symbolized the Nile reed marshes. The world's first columns were constructed at Djoser's pyramid complex c2600BC and were engaged into the walls of the structure for support. Three hundred years later, free standing limestone columns were in use in the Giza plateau noble's tombs, for example, in that of the king's 'Overseer of the house of life' Sesh em nefer 4 of the 6th Dynasty. Much harder-to-work granite columns were in use by the time of king Sahure, 5th Dynasty. The most common types were those representing papyrus bundles, papyrus stems, lotus stems and palms. Their capitals were often of open or closed bud design and highly colored. Egyptian columns were extensively copied for the later Greek and Roman equivalents.

**Dyes.** The ancient Egyptians commonly used natural plant and mineral based dyes for clothes, inks and tattoos. The most common were indigo from plants or sea snails, carthamin red and yellow from the seeds of the safflower, purple from the murex snail, green from malachite ore and black from crushed antimony.

**Egyptomania** describes the western fascination with Ancient Egyptian culture and history. This fascination originally goes back to Greek and Roman times but specifically refers to the renewed interest in Egypt during the nineteenth century, as a result of the extensive scientific study and popularization of Ancient Egyptian remains and culture at that time. In addition to its aesthetic impact on literature, art and architecture. It also played a role in the discussion about race, gender and national identity. Consequently, Ancient Egypt has had a significant impact on the cultural imagination of all western cultures for example the Washington monument obelisk and the pyramid on the US one Dollar bill.

**Eye of Horus.** The 'Sacred eye of Horus' was called the 'wedjet', its hieroglyph is meant to represent a human eye, the teardrop markings below it (right) are those of the Peregrine falcons eye. The eye was considered to be a strong lucky charm, originating from the Osiris- Isis legend. Eastern Mediterranean sailors still frequently paint the 'wedjet' symbol on the bow of their vessels to ensure safe sea travel. Often worn in the form of a necklace or earring, the 'wedjet' is still worn in Greece, Turkey, North Africa and parts of the Middle East. It is called the 'eye of Horus' or the all seeing 'evil eye'. In the west the simplified version of the decorative eye hieroglyph has become simplified as the RX symbol of the pharmacist and can be seen every day on prescriptions and prescription packaging.

**Forts** The Egyptian military was responsible for maintaining fortifications along important trade routes and along national frontiers. The most notable were the chain of huge Middle Kingdom mud brick forts built along the Nile in Nubia and those protecting the western border with Libya. Massive brick forts were also constructed during the New Kingdom to serve as military bases, such as the those at Sile and Pelusium, which were used as bases for operations and campaigns into Canaan and Syria.

**Games** The ancient Egyptians enjoyed a variety of leisure activities, including games and music. Senet, the board game where pieces were moved according to the throw of something similar to dice was particularly popular from the earliest times. There are wall reliefs showing the game being played by Nefertari and complete sets used by the royal family of Amenhotep 3 have been discovered.

**Glazed pottery and glass.** Even before the Old Kingdom, the ancient Egyptians had developed a glassy material called faience, which was used for decoration and as a type of semi-precious stone. The material was used to make beads, tiles, figures, and other small items. The Ancient Egyptians were able to craft a wide range of glass objects, such as delicate perfume bottles and attractive containers to hold cosmetic oils. These items have survived for thousands of years and have been mostly recovered from burial tombs.

**Homes** Houses were constructed from mud-brick and were primarily designed to remain cool. Each home had a kitchen with an open roof, which had a stone for making flour and a wood-fired oven for baking bread. Walls were painted white and covered with dyed linen wall hangings. Hygiene and appearance were both very important. Most of the population bathed in the Nile and used a soap paste made from animal fat and chalk. Clothes were washed in the river and beaten against stones. Men shaved their whole bodies for cleanliness, both men and women shaved their heads to avoid lice. Clothing was made from simple linen sheets bleached white, and both men and women of the upper classes wore wigs, jewelry, and cosmetics. Children went without clothing until maturity and mothers were responsible for taking care of the children, while the father provided the family's income.

**Irrigation** The Nile in ancient times was one of the most predictable rivers in the world. The duration of the annual inundation averaged more than a hundred days each year. Egyptian agriculture along the Nile was based on planting autumnal crops after the annual inundation had subsided. The river was too powerful to control so irrigation works were set high along the river bank and dealt only with the peak of the flood. Irrigation schemes could initially not carry water any great distance away from the river, so the ancient Egyptians built large basins for growing crops along the river banks, and simple gates that diverted water into them.Silt that settled in the basins was extremely beneficial as it brought fresh nutrients each year. It is estimated that up to ten feet was deposited in a good year, the inundation also washed harmful salts out of the soil. Herodotus c450BC wrote that the Egyptians *'get their harvests with less labor than anyone else in the world.'* Egypt flourished during periods of strong central government when the state irrigation system was properly maintained.

**Jubilee.** The Ancient Egyptians invented the Royal Jubilee. The kings had to prove to their subjects during the jubilees that they were worthy and competent to rule the land. These jubilees known as Heb Sed festivals were celebrated from the earliest times, King Djoser is seen running the Heb Sed race in his burial chamber reliefs. This ancient festival was instituted to replace the ritual of murdering a king who had reached an age that he was unable to continue to rule. The later Heb Sed festivals were jubilees celebrated after a ruler had held or been nominated to the throne for thirty years. In the pyramid complex of Djoser there are two boundary stones in the great courtyard for him to run the Heb Sed race.Several kings deviated from the traditional thirty-year period, notably Hatshepsut and Akhenaten, Hatshepsut counted her Heb Sed from the passing of thirty years after the death of her father. Akhenaten celebrated his first Heb Sed festival in his third regnal year, wishing to establish his authority over the powerful Amen priesthood. It was intended to reinforce the king's divine powers and religious leadership during a time of religious change.

**Karnak** became the religious center of Egypt during the New Kingdom centered on the cult of Amen along with Mut and Montu. Today it is a vast complex of partially ruined temples, chapels, pylons and other buildings on the north east outskirts of modern Luxor. It's ancient name was Ipet-isut meaning *'the most selected of places'*. It is the largest ancient religious site in the world. It is particularly famous for its one hundred and thirty four columns in the Hypostyle Hall some almost seventy feet tall. What differentiates Karnak, founded in c1900BC, from most of the other Egyptian temple complexes is the sixteen hundred years over which it was constructed. Its main period of growth was the New Kingdom particularly the 18th Dynasty commencing c1500BC. The last major change was the addition of the first pylon and the massive brick enclosure walls that surround the whole precinct constructed by Nectanebo I c370BC. The two-hundred and fifty acre site of Karnak was mostly abandoned with the establishment of Christianity as the state religion of the Roman Empire. Some of the temples were converted into Coptic Christian churches, the most notable example was the reuse of the Festival Hall of Thutmosis 3 for that purpose, the decorations of saints and Coptic inscriptions can still be seen. The older religious temple complex of Heliopolis was close to modern Cairo. At its height it was significantly larger; the temple of Re at Heliopolis, alone was twice the size of that of Amen at Karnak. Tragically the Persian conqueror Cambyses 2 c525BC sacked Heliopolis It was never fully rebuilt, only the solitary obelisk of Senusret I c 1944BC remains. Being close to Cairo its stone buildings were quarried to make more modern structures. So it is only by good fortune, because the major centers of later Egyptian population were based in the north at Cairo and Alexandria, that Karnak and Luxor have survived so well.

**Language** The Egyptian language has the longest documented history of any, having remained in written use from c3200BC to late Roman times and as a spoken language for longer. It was the forerunner of Philistine, Phoenician, Greek, Latin and English.(See Chapter 4).

**Law** The ancient Egyptians viewed men and women, except slaves, as essentially equal under the law, and even the lowliest farmer was entitled to petition the vizier and the courts for justice. Both men and women had the right to own and sell property, make contracts, marry and divorce, receive inheritance, and pursue legal disputes in court. Married couples could own property between them and protect themselves from divorce by agreeing to marriage contracts, which stipulated the financial obligations of the husband to his wife and children on the occasion of a divorce. Although no legal codes from ancient Egypt survive, court records show that the law was based on a common sense view of right and wrong that emphasized reaching agreements and resolving conflicts rather than strictly adhering to a complicated set of decrees. Local councils of elders, known as Kenbet, were responsible for ruling in court cases involving small claims and minor disputes. More serious cases, involving murder, major land transactions, and tomb robbery were referred to the Great Kenbet, over which the vizier or king could preside. Aggrieved individuals were expected to represent themselves and were required to swear an oath that they had told the truth. In some cases, the state took on both the role of prosecutor and judge, and it could torture the accused with beatings to obtain a confession and the names of any co-conspirators. Punishment for minor crimes involved either imposition of fines, beatings, facial mutilation, or exile, depending on the severity of the offense. Serious crimes such as murder and tomb robbery were punished by execution, carried out by burning, decapitation, drowning, or impaling on a stake. Punishment could also be extended to the criminal's family.

**Libraries**, called the *'houses of papyrus'* were part of the center of learning called per ank the *'house of life'*, which included a facility for medical training. The libraries were vast storehouses of accumulated knowledge and records. In the New Kingdom, the rulers of previous times were much admired indicating they had a profound knowledge of their own history, which sadly became lost. Prince Khaemweset in the 19th Dynasty studied the past, examining the necropolis sites of earlier dynasties and recording his findings with care. The priests of the per ankh recorded the enterprises of the government, levels of the Nile, movement of celestial bodies and the biannual cattle count census. Because this documentation was recorded on papyrus most has not survived. For The Great Library of Alexandria see Chapter 12.

**Literature** Writing was first used simply for labels and tags and to record commercial transactions. Later, tomb texts appeared, narrating the past lives of individuals such as Harkhuf and Weni. There were also instructions, sebayt, developed to communicate teachings; for example from a king to his son or to nobles. The Ipuwer papyrus poem describes natural disasters and social unrest. The Middle Kingdom 'Story of the Sinuhe' is considered a classic of Egyptian literature, it tells of a court official who flees Memphis following the king's assassination but after a series of adventures returns to a royal welcome. The Westcar Papyrus is a series of five apocryphal stories told by Khufu's sons, but in fact written much later, describing the marvels performed by priests. The 'Story of Wenamun' tells the adventure of a court official who is robbed on his way to buy cedar from Lebanon and his struggle to return to Egypt. Ancient Egyptian Literature in modern terms is neither pastoral nor lyrical, but mostly didactic, meaning teaching, and rather unromantic although not lacking in personal feelings. Most stories deal with personal themes concerned with the heart. Mankind's ethical life is their central concern not personal emotions, such as romatic love. Late copies of the classics of Egyptian literature show that the stories were read in some cases for at least seven hundred and fifty years, twice as long as we have read the Shakespeare plays.

**Maps.** The Turin Map Papyrus from the reign of Rameses 4 contains the oldest suriving map of topographical interest. It is eight feet long and shows a ten-mile section of Wadi Hammamat in the Eastern Desert of Egypt and its geology. It includes routes to the gold mines, distances, the location of gold deposits,types of stone and gravel beds and makes use of legends and colors. The details shown on the map have been identified in modern times and found to be astonishingly accurate, it is dated to c1150BC.

**Mathematics.** The earliest examples of mathematical calculations date to the predynastic Naqada period c3500BC, and show a fully developed number system. Mathematics were used every day to calculate accounts, taxation, farming and labor matters. The Rhind Mathematical Papyrus c1535BC and the Moscow Mathematical Papyrus show that the ancient Egyptians could perform addition, subtraction, multiplication, division and were able to manipulate fractions, compute the volumes of rectangular structures and pyramids, and calculate the surface areas of rectangles, triangles, circles and even spheres They understood the concepts of algebra and geometry, and could solve simple sets of simultaneous equations.They used the power of ten up to one-million. Egyptian mathematicians had a grasp of Pythagoras's theorem, they knew that a triangle had a right angle opposite the hypotenuse when its sides were in a 3,4,5 ratio. They did not have the concept of pi but were able to estimate the area of a circle by subtracting one ninth from its diameter and squaring the result, as a good approximation of the formula $\pi r2$. Pythagoras trained in Egypt and Herodotus claimed that geometry was first known in Egypt and then passed into Greece.

**Medicine** (see also Chapter 5). The medical problems of the ancient Egyptians stemmed directly from their environment. Living and working close to the Nile brought hazards from windblown dust, malaria and debilitating parasites, which caused liver and intestinal damage. The hard physical labor of farming and building put stress on the spine and joints, and traumatic injuries from construction and warfare were common. The presence of grit and sand from stone ground flour severley wore teeth, leaving them susceptible to abscesses. The diets of the wealthy were rich in sugars, which promoted tooth decay. Overweight mummies of many of the upper class show the effects of a life of over indulging. Adult life expectancy was about thirty to thirty five for men and around thirty for women. However infant mortality was extermely high; it is estimated that about one-third of the population died in infancy. Egyptian physicians were renowned in the ancient Near East for their healing skills, and some, like Imhotep, remained famous long after their deaths. Herodotus remarked that there was a high degree of specialization among Egyptian physicians, with *'some treating only the head or the stomach, while others were eye-doctors and dentists'*. Training of physicians took place at the per ankh or House of Life where they learned of anatomy, injuries, and practical treatments. Wounds were treated by bandaging with raw meat, white linen and swabs soaked with honey to prevent infection, while opium was used to relieve pain. Egyptian surgeons stitched wounds, set broken bones, and amputated diseased limbs, but they recognized that some injuries were so serious that they could only make the patient comfortable until he died. The University of Manchester, England reported in 2008 that 'seventy percent of the ingredients they used are still found in medicines today'. Egyptian Medical care was much sought after by their neighbors; the Hittite king Hattusili wrote to Ramesses 2 requesting an Egyptian physician to help his fifty or sixty year old sister become pregnant. Ramesses replied that a physician could not help, but he would send one anyway.

**Military** The ancient Egyptian military was responsible for defending Egypt against foreign invasion, and for maintaining control of Egypt's vassals in their ancient Near East Empire, as well as putting down internal revolts. Typical military equipment included bows and arrows, spears, and round-topped shields made by stretching animal skin over a wooden frame. In the New Kingdom, the military began using chariots (see Chapter 7) that had earlier been introduced by the Hyksos invaders. Weapons and armor continued to improve after the adoption of bronze. Shields were now made from solid wood, spears were tipped with a bronze point, and the Khopesh curved sword was adopted from Asiatic soldiers. The king was usually depicted in art and literature riding at the head of the army, and there is evidence that at least a few pharaohs, such as Seqenenre Tao 2, Thutmosis 3 and Ramesses 2 did do so. Thutmosis 1 is credited with creating the first standing army c1500BC. Soldiers were recruited from the general population, but during, and especially after, the New Kingdom, mercenaries from Nubia, Kush, and Libya were hired to fight for Egypt. At the time of the Persian invasions, Greek mercenaries made up the bulk of the Egyptian army.

**Money** Egyptians did not use coins until the Late period, instead they did use a money-barter system with standard sacks of grain weighing around seventy pounds, and the deben, a weight of roughly three ounces of copper or silver. Workers were paid in grain; a simple laborer might earn five and a half sacks of grain per month, while a supervisor might earn seven and a half sacks. Prices were fixed across the country and recorded in government lists to facilitate trading; for example a shirt cost five copper deben, while a cow cost one hundred and forty deben. Grain could be traded for other goods, according to a fixed price list.

**Monotheism** the belief that only one deity exists, is a concept common to the world's three largest religions Judaism, Christianity and Islam. The first recorded monotheist in human history was the Egyptian king Akhenaten c1360BC. In year five of his reign, he established the Aten as the exclusive monotheistic god and began to disband the priesthoods of the other gods particularly of Amen, and diverted the income from these cults to the Aten. He later officially changed his name from Amenhotep 4 to Akhenaten, meaning 'Servant of the Aten. He founded as new capital, Akhetaten meaning

'Horizon of Aten', now Amarna. Uniquely, the Aten was worshipped in the bright day light rather than the dark temples of traditional gods. He composed the Great Hymn to the Aten which religious scholars have observed shows a remarkable similarity to the later Old Testament Psalm 104. By year nine of his reign, Akhenaten declared the Aten was the only god and ordered inscriptions referring to the plural word 'gods' to be removed. Monotheism died with Akhenaten and Egypt returned to the worship of multiple gods. Some have speculated, but without any evidence, that Moses was an Aten priest who left Egypt and fathered Judaism when Akhenaten died.

**Music and dance.** The ancient Egyptians maintained a rich cultural heritage complete with feasts and festivals accompanied by music and dance which were very popular (right) entertainments. Early instruments included flutes and harps, while instruments similar to trumpets, oboes, and pipes developed later and  became popular. Later the Egyptians played on bells, cymbals, tambourines, and drums and imported lutes and lyres from Asia. The sistrum was a rattle-like musical instrument that was especially important in religious ceremonies.

**Mummification** (see also Chapter 2). The dry hot desert had provided a natural process for the preservation of dead corpses. The use of tombs by the wealthy changed this and artificial mummification developed into an art. It involved removing of the internal organs, wrapping the body in linen, and burying it in a rectangular  stone sarcophagus or wooden coffin. Some parts were preserved separately in canopic jars. The most thorough technique took seventy, or sometimes ninety, days and involved removing the internal organs, removing the brain through the nose, and desiccating the body in a mixture of salts, called natron, for forty days. In the New Kingdom, the body was coated or filled with resin or aromatic balm. The word embalm comes from the Latin 'to put into aromatic resins', the process was called ut by the Egytians. The body was then wrapped in linen, with protective amulets inserted between layers and then placed in a decorated coffin. The Late period used painted cartonnage mummy cases made from stiff paper, linen and plaster in place of wood. Actual preservation practices declined during the Ptolemaic and Roman eras, greater emphasis was placed on the outer appearance of the mummy, the faces of which were highly decorated.

**Natural resources.** Ancient Egypt and Nubia was rich in building and decorative stone, copper and lead ores, gold, and semiprecious stones. These natural resources allowed the Ancient Egyptians to build monuments, create statues, make tools and weapons and fashion jewelry. Embalmers used salts from the Wadi Natron for mummification. It also provided the gypsum needed to make plaster. The Wadi Hammamat in the Eastern Desert was a significant source of greywacke stone and gold. The Egyptians worked deposits of the lead ore galena at Gebel Rosas to make fishing net weights, plumb bobs, and small figurines. Copper was the most important metal for tool making in Ancient Egypt and was smelted in furnaces from malachite ore, mined extensively in the Sinai. Workers collected gold by washing the nuggets out of sediments or by the dangerous and labor intensive process of mining, grinding and washing gold-bearing quartzite. The principal sources of gold were the south of the Eastern Desert but mainly Nubia and Kush, both in the extreme south. Iron deposits found in the south were only used very late in its history. Tin was imported from Anatolia.

**Nileometers** measured water levels in the Nile; records were primarily used to set tax levels for the coming year. Every summer melting snow and rain in the mountains of Ethiopia caused the inundation (akhet); the Nile overflowed its banks and covered the flood plain. When the waters receded, around September or October, they left behind a rich alluvial deposit of exceptionally fertile black silt over the fields. Nileometer records were carefully recorded and kept in the royal libraries. A moderate inundation was a vital part of the agricultural cycle; however, a light inundation could cause famine, and too much flooding would destroy the riverbank farming villages. Ancient records show that on average, one out of five inundations was either too low or too high. The ability to predict the height of the coming inundation was important to determine the levels of tax to be paid, usually in the form of grain. The oldest form of nileometer design comprised a flight of stairs leading down into the water, with depth markings along the walls. The finest surviving example is at Elephantine by Aswan, being in the extreme south it was the first to detect the rising Nile waters. A few nileometers were located some distance from the river within a temple complex, the finest example is at the temple of Kom Ombo below Aswan.

**Obelisks** The Greeks gave the name obelisk ,meaning a meat spit, to the tall, thin four-sided tapering columns which end with a pyramid shape. They were always made from a single monolith, usually from the red granite quarries at Aswan. Obelisks were normally placed in pairs at the entrance to temples. Twenty-nine Egyptian obelisks have survived along with the giant flawed 'unfinished obelisk' still in the Aswan quarry. These obelisks are now dispersed around the world, and only a few remain in Egypt (see Chapter 12). The earliest obelisk still in its original position is a sixty eight feet high red granite obelisk of Senusret I at Heliopolis. The obelisk symbolized the sun god Amen Re, and during the brief religious reformation of Akhenaten was said to be a petrified ray of the Aten, the sundisk. It was also thought that Re existed within the structure. Talcott believes pyramids and obelisks were derived from naturally occurring sun pillars (right).

**Paints** were obtained from minerals such as iron ore (red and yellow ochres), copper ores (blue and green), lamp soot or charcoal (black), and limestone (white). Paints could be mixed with gum Arabic as a binder and pressed into cakes which could be moistened with water when needed.

**Papyrus** is a paper like material produced from the pith of the papyrus plant, a wetland sedge that was once abundant in the Nile Delta. Papyrus was first used as early as the 1st Dynasty c3100BC, for boats, mattresses, mats and most notably writing material. In the first centuries BC and AD parchment began to compete, it was prepared from animal skins which were tougher and could be cut into pages and bound into book-like Codices. The book form was much more practical to read and store. However, papyrus had the advantage of being relatively cheap and easy to produce, but it was fragile and susceptible to both moisture and excessive dryness. Unless the papyrus was of good quality, the writing surface was uneven. The latest certain dates for the use of papyrus are 1057AD for a papal decree and 1087AD for an Arabic document. Papyrus therefore overlapped with the start of the use of paper in Europe in the 11th century.

**Peace Treaty** the world's first recorded peace treaty between superpowers was between Ramesses 2 and the Hittite king Hatussili 3 in 1258BC; it interestingly includes the first extradition agreement. A reproduction hangs in the United Nations headquarters in New York. (For more details see Chapter 10.)

**Quarrying.** Unlike the Mesopotamian civilizations of Babylon and Assyria, Egypt was fortunate to have extensive, conveniently located deposits of varying types of stone which produced quality masonry for the construction of massive permanent monuments, such as pyramids, temples, sculptures and obelisks. Eighty percent of the ancient quarry sites lay in the Nile valley close enough to the Nile to be able to drag the stone blocks to the river and float them downstream. At Aswan there was red, black and gray granite for burial tombs, specialized pyramid casing and obelisks. There were also major quarries at Gebel Silsila (sandstone), Edfu, Wadi Hammamat (basalt) Amarna (alabaster) Koptos (black slate), Qurna (limestone) and the famous fine white limestone from the quarries at Tura south of Cairo.

**Religion.** (See also Chapter 2) Beliefs in the divine and in the afterlife were ingrained in ancient Egyptian culture and religion from the start. Royal rule was based on the divine right of kings. However, the gods were not always viewed as benevolent, and Egyptians believed they had to be appeased with offerings and prayers. Gods were worshiped in cult temples, administered by priests acting on the king's behalf. Only on select feast days and celebrations was a shrine carrying the statue of the god brought out for public worship. Normally, the gloomy forbidding god's domain was sealed off from the outside world and was only accessible to temple officials.

**Social organization.** Egyptian society was highly stratified, and status was deliberately displayed. Farmers made up the bulk of the population, but agricultural produce was owned directly by the state, temple, or noble family that owned the land. Farmers were also subject to a labor tax and were required to work on irrigation projects or alternatively on construction projects during the inundation. Scribes and officials, who formed the upper class in ancient Egypt, displayed their social status in art and literature. Below the nobility were the priests, physicians, and engineers with specialized training in their field. Slavery was known in ancient Egypt, but not extensive.

**Sprirt.** The Egyptians believed that each human being was composed of a number of physical and spiritual parts. In addition to the body, each person had a šwt (shadow), a ba (personality or soul), a ka (life force) and a name. The heart, rather than the brain, was considered the source of thoughts and emotions. After death, the spiritual aspects were released from the body and could move, but they required the physical remains or a substitute, such as a Serdab statue as a permanent home. The ultimate goal of the deceased was to rejoin his ka and ba and become one of the 'blessed dead', living on as an akh, or 'effective one'. In order for this to happen, the deceased had to be judged worthy in a trial, in which the heart was weighed against a 'feather of truth'. If deemed worthy, the deceased could continue their existence on earth in spiritual form in the so called after life (see Chapter 2).

**Stone building.** King Kasekhemwy c2600BC made a truly significant breakthrough in construction techniques. He and his architect chose to construct the king's mastaba tomb not out of traditional mud brick, but out of quarried small blocks of limestone. This became the world's first masonry building.(See Chapter 3).

**Strike** The first recorded labor strike occurred during the reign of Ramesses 3 cI150BC, when due to the severe economic crisis at the time the tomb workers could not be fed and they withdrew their labor. (See Chapter 10).

**Surgical instruments.** It is ironic that surgical skills in ancient Egypt were perfected primarily for the benefit of the dead. Embalming necessitated the careful removal of organs to ensure preservation of the corpse for the after life. Trepanning procedures into the skull to remove pressure were known and were occasionally successful based on skulls which have been discovered showing healing having taken place after the operation. Surgeons had available to them a remarkable array of instruments, evidenced by the fine relief at the rear of the temple of Kom Ombo (see Chapter 5). We have clear evidence that Egyptian physicians used knives, scalpels, retractors, lances, bone saws, suction cups, forceps, tweezers and clamps as they do today. Although they did not have the technology to produce the surgical steel scalpels of modern times, knives with obsidian blades have been found with exceptionally sharp cutting edges. Unlike surgical steel obsidian has the advantage of a non-corrugated microscopic surface and is still used today to reduce tearing in delicate skin surgery.

**Trade** The Ancient Egyptians engaged in trade with their foreign neighbors to obtain rare exotic goods not found in their own country. They established the gold trade with Nubia and cedar wood trade with Byblos. They sent marine expeditions to trade with the distant Land of Punt (Ethiopia), which provided aromatic resins, ebony, ivory, and wild animals such as monkeys and baboons. Anatolia provided tin, Afghanistan provided blue stone lapis lazuli and Greece and Crete, provided olive oil. In exchange Egypt exported grain, gold, linen, and papyrus as well as other finished goods, including glass and stone objects and medical knowledge.

**Upper and Lower Egypt.** The two early kingdoms of Egypt, Red in the north and White in the south, were unified by Menes c3200BC. Because the Nile flows from south to north, the southern part of the country was designated as Upper Egypt, while the north including the Delta as Lower Egypt.

**Valley of the Kings.** For a period of nearly five-hundred years, tombs were constructed for the kings and a few very privileged nobles of the New Kingdom notably the 18th to 20th Dynasties. The valley lies on the west bank of the Nile opposite the New Kingdom religious capital of Thebes (modern Luxor). It actually consists of two valleys, the East Valley where the vast majority of the royal tombs are located and the West Valley, which contains only two royal tombs. The valleys contain sixty two tombs, one of the smallest (only four rooms) insignificant king's tomb belongs to Tutankhamen, the largest belongs to the sons of Ramesses 2 containing over 120 rooms. Most of the the royal tombs are decorated with religious scenes and funerary rituals of the period. All of the tombs were reopened and at least partially robbed in antiquity.

**Vizier** called a djat, in Ancient Egypt was the prime minister of the state. In the Old Kingdom viziers were usually relatives of the king and trusted with affairs of the nation. Over time the office was divided with one each for the north and south; the boundary was set at Asyut. Viziers heard all domestic territory disputes, conducted the cattle counts, controlled dykes and irrigation works and monitored food and Nile levels. All government documents had to be stamped with the seal of the vizier, During the New Kingdom, the vizier of the south lived at Thebes and served as its mayor, with an assistant for the important west bank mortuary temples and necropolis. The other two important senior state officials were the treasurer and chancellor; they both reported to the vizier who met or communicated with the king almost daily. The best detailed account of his duties is that inscribed on the walls of vizier Rekhmire, from the reign of Thutmosis 3.

**Viceroy.** As Egypt extended is influence south during the reign of Ahmose I the king reorganized his cabinet structure. Because of is remoteness from Thebes, Ahmose I now needed a trusted senior figure to manage Nubian affairs on his behalf and to continue with the expansion into Kush. He founded the office of Viceroy and appointed Si tayit to the position. The position was later expanded during the reign, when the decision was made to actually colonize Nubia. Ahmose I upgraded the Viceroy position adding the impressive titles of 'Kings Son of Kush' and 'Overseer of the gold lands for the lord of the two lands'.

**Water clock.** During the reign of Amenhotep I c1520BC, there is the first mention of the water clock, implying an accurate measurement of the hours in a day was now being made.

**Women's empowerment** Ancient Egyptian women had a great range of personal choice and opportunities for achievement. Women such as Meryetneith c 2900BC, Khentawes c2385BC, Hatshepsut (1479-1458BC) and Cleopatra (51-30BC) even became great female kings, while others wielded great power as Great Royal Wives or Divine Wives of Amen. Despite these freedoms, ancient Egyptian women did not take part in official roles in the administration and served only in secondary roles in the temples. An exception to most other ancient societies, Egyptian women achieved legal parity with Egyptian men. In theory they enjoyed the same legal and financial rights, this can be seen in art and contemporary manuscripts. The disparities between people's legal rights were based on differences in social class and not on gender. During the Ptolomeic era Egyptian women were allowed more rights and privileges than the Greek women. Women could manage, own, and sell private property, which included slaves, land, portable goods, servants, livestock, and money. Women could resolve legal settlements and had claims to up to one-third of all the community property which came after they were married. When a woman brought her own private dowry to a marriage, it remained hers, On the death of a husband, the woman inherited two-thirds of their community property, the other one-third was divided among their children From the Middle Kingdom onwards an imyt-pr 'house document', could be used as a living will. However, husbands could marry more than one wife and even married mothers, sisters and daughters. A girl did not normally get married until around fourteen although as young as eleven in royal families has been recorded. Royal family records show that children were born to girls as early as thirteen. Marriage required no particular religious or legal ceremony. There were no special bridal clothes, no exchange of rings, no change of names to indicate a marriage. Almost any reason could be used to end a marriage; legal divorces were very unusual and most marriages ended with the wife returning to her family. Although royal succession often passed through the male line the new king usually married the previous king's daughter, sister or wife to consolidate his legitimacy to the throne.

**Writing.** Some of the world's earliest writing has been found in ancient Egypt. Hieroglyphic writing dates to c3200 BC, and in early times, was composed of some 500 symbols. Hieroglyphs were a formal religious script, used on stone monuments and in tombs. (The whole of Chapter 4 is devoted to this subject).

**Xenophobia** is the Greek term used for the intense dislike and or fear of people from other countries; it was an extremely strong aspect of Ancient Egyptians culture. It all started with the king. He considered himself a living god who ruled as heir to his divine father and was the intermediary between his people and the gods. Egypt believed it was the center of the world and that Egyptians were the gods's chosen people. They believed that it was their dedication to 'maat' expressed as 'cosmic order' that set them apart from the 'barbarians' that surrounded them. They considerd themselves far superior to their neighbors in all aspects, culturally, religiously, socially and militarily. Their country was fortunate in being isolated by deserts and seas, this largely insulated them from external threats for c1500 years after the founding of the united kingdom. However this almost became their down fall when the Asiatic Hyksos people were the first of the 'hated foreigners' to capture and control a very significant part of Egypt c1650BC. The Hyksos ruled the east Delta for a hundred years and captured the Egyptian national capital, Memphis, even threatening Thebes. The Egyptians had not embraced the military advances that were occurring outside of the Nile valley at that time. When the Hyksos were finally expelled by the Theban king Ahmose I, they were driven out of Egypt and pursued into Canaan; all future references to them were prefaced by the term 'hated foreigners'. Egypt could no longer ignore their Asiatic neighbors and the rulers of the New Kingdom engaged in almost constant warfare and/ or diplomacy to control the hostile states on their eastern frontier. Later, in the twilight of ancient Egypt's authority, there were to be the barely tolerated kings of Libyan (22nd Dynasty) and Nubain (25th Dynasty) extraction. The country later had to contend, c671BC, with the hated and feared Assyrians, and their occupation. The Persians then ruled an exhausted Egypt, on and off, for two hundred years; initially the Persians respected Egyptian culture and religion and were tolerated. However the later Persian kings and Satraps were so hated that Alexander was able to take Egypt from Persia without a fight, and was even welcomed with open arms; this however was not to last. The hatred of foreigners continued right to the end. The infamous indigenous mob of Alexandria was to continually disrupt the three hundred year reign of the subsequent 'foreign' Ptolemaic dynasty even though they mostly brought peace and prosperity.

**Yuya** and his wife Tuya were very powerful members at the court of Amenhotep 3 c1390BC. They were the parents of his Great Royal Wife, Tia, and the future king Ay. Yuya served as a key adviser for the great king, and rose to the posts of 'King's Lieutenant' and 'Master of the Horse'. Yuya and his wife (right, gilded mask of Tuya), although not of royal birth, were granted the particular honor of having a tomb built in the Valley of the Kings KV46.

This tomb was discovered in 1905 by Quibell, working on behalf of Davis. Although the tomb had been entered by tomb robbers in antiquity they had been disturbed early in the robbery process, and Quibell found most of the funerary goods and the two mummies virtually intact, to huge public aclaim. The contents contained by far the the finest tomb treasures yet discovered. They were only surpassed when Carter entered the tomb of Tutankhamen seventeen years later.

**Zoo.** Towards the rear of the Karnak temple complex stands the Great Festival hall 'akh menu', built by king Thutmosis 3 c1449BC, with its unique tent pole columns. In a back room artists have depicted on the wall in the so-called 'botanical' relief, the plants and animals that the king brought back from his many campaigns in Canaan and Syria. This is the world's oldest surviving reference to a zoological collection.

**Zoser** is the alternative name for the 3rd Dynasty king best known as Djoser c2550BC. An inscription created during the Ptolemaic period relates the legend of how 'Djoser rebuilt the temple of Khnum on the island of Elephantine at the first Nile cataract, thus ending a seven-year famine in Egypt'. It demonstrates that over two thousand years after his reign, Djoser was still remembered and revered. The reason for his fame was his reputation as the first king to construct a stone pyramid for a tomb. His famous monument was a step pyramid produced by placing a number of traditional mastaba (bench) tombs on top of one another. This pioneering design led to the fully-cased, smooth sided giant pyramids of the 4th Dynasty thirty years later, culminating in Khufu's construction of the Great Pyramid at Giza; the only surviving member of The Seven Wonders of the World.

# Epilogue

The culture and monuments of ancient Egypt have left a lasting legacy to the world that is unique. Early Greek and Roman historians, such as Herodotus, Strabo and Diodorus visited, studied and wrote about the land, which in time became viewed as a place of mystery. The cult of the Egyptian goddess, Isis, for example, became popular in the Roman Empire, even as far away as England. Obelisks and other artifacts were transported from the temples and palaces of Ancient Egypt to decorate the public places and private villas in Rome and Constantinople. The Roman visitors left their Latin graffiti as evidence of this early tourist traffic. Much later in the 17th and 18th centuries, European travelers brought back antiquities, including mummies, and published stories and drawings of their journeys leading to a new wave of Egyptomania which resulted in the wholesale looting of treasures in the 19th Century. The Egyptian Supreme Council of Antiquities, the SCA, is responsible for the conservation, protection and regulation of all antiquities and archaeological excavations. Since its creation in 1858 all excavations have been aimed solely at the *'discovery of information rather than treasure'*. The council also supervises museums in Egypt and monument reconstruction programs designed to preserve its historical legacy.

The remnants of the ancient Egyptian civilization have suffered at the hands of time from local tomb robbers, Roman Emperors, indiscriminate collectors and the quarrying of pyramids, temples and palaces for their cut stone. Ironically it was because the ancient sites were slowly reclaimed by the desert and became lost, that they were largely preserved until the early nineteenth century. The surviving brilliant colored reliefs at numerous temples, is a witness to the benefits of this natural conservation process.

In the last one hundred and fifty years we have reversed this process and progressively excavated the sites, exposing them to the sun, air, flash floods and tourists. The most serious threat, however, comes from population growth and the expansion of cultivation following the construction of the Aswan high dam in the 1960s. The major consequence is that the water table along the Nile, particularly around Luxor, has begun to rise to the point that water is now constantly seeping into the foundations of those temples close to agriculture, causing erosion and worse. The ground water is moving vertically by capillary action into the stone structure of the temples themselves. The moisture then spreads slowly outwards causing irreparable damage to the surface of the stone and its decoration. We have to remind ourselves that 'eighty percent' of what we know about the history, dates, names and events of ancient Egypt has come from translating these stone inscriptions and studying the reliefs which decorated its temples, palaces and artifacts. Often they are the only historical source we have.

There is still hope. There has been marvelous work done annually since 1926 by the Oriental Institute of the University of Chicago and other research institutions. The Epigraphic Survey has accurately captured, on paper, many inscriptions and reliefs which have since faded into oblivion. Ray Johnson summarizes the challenge. 'It is a race against time to document, publish and conserve the inscribed wall surfaces of some of the most famous monuments of the ancient world. With the rising water table, increased pollution, urban expansion and agricultural encroachment threatening these priceless vestiges of the past'. It is encouraging to report, that some progress has been made in the last few years to begin to reduce the local water table in the vicinity of the major surviving Theban sites. The painstaking recording and restoration work continues; however, it is indeed a race against time.

# Appendix 1

My thanks go to the following institutions for their outstanding Egytian collections which allow those who are unable to visit Egypt to experience the Ancient Egyptian civilisation at its best.

Agyptisches Museum und Papyrussammlung,Berlin
Agyptisch Orientalische Sammlung, Vienna
Ashmolean Museum of Art and Archaelogy, Oxford,
Atkins Museum of Art, Kansa City ,Missouri
Badisches Landesmuseum, Karlsruhe
Birmingham City Museum and Art Gallery, England
Bolton Museum and Art Gallery, England
Brooklyn Museum of Art, New York
British Museum, London
Casrsten Niebuhr Institute, Copenhagen
Central Museum and Art gallery, Bolton
Cincinnati Art Museum, Cincinnati
Cleveland Museum of Art, Cleveland
Detroit Institute of Arts, Detroit
Durham Oriental Museum, England
Egypt Centre, University of Wales, Swansea
Egyptian Museum, Cairo
Field Museum of Natural History, Chicago
Fitzwilliam Museum, Cambridge, England
Hearst Museum of Anthropology,University of California, Berkely
Hermitage Museum, St Petersburg
Kunsthistorisches Museum, Vienna
Kestner Museum, Hannover
Liverpool Museum, England
Luxor Museum of Ancient Egyptian Art, Luxor
Manchester Museum, England
Metropolitan Museum of Art, New York
Museum of Fine Arts, Boston,
Musee National du Louvre, Paris
Musee d'Art et d'Histoire,Geneva
Musees Royaux d'Art et d'Histoire,Brussels
Meseo Egizio, Turin
Museo Arqueologico, Madrid
National Museum of Scotland, Edinburgh
Nubian Museum, Aswan
Ny Carlsberg Glyptotek, Copenhagen
Oriental Institute Museum, University of Chicago
Petrie Museum of Egyptian Archaeology, University College London

Pilizaeus Museum, Hildersheim, Germany
Rijkmuseum van Oudheden, Leiden
Rosicrucian Egypt Museum, San Jose
Royal Ontario Museum, Toronto
Royal Museum, Edinburgh
Staatliche Sammlung Agyptischer Kunst, Munich
Staatliche Museen zu Berlin, Berlin
San Diego Museum of Man, Califrornia
Soan Museum, London
University of Pennsylvania Museum of Archaelogy and
    Anthropolgy, Philadelphia
Walters Art Gallery, Baltimore
Wickimedia Commons for some of the images used in this volume
Welcome Museum of Egypt and Greco Roman Antiquities, Swansea

# Appendix 2

## The kings with five names

The early kings were known primarily by their Horus name. As time progressed following unification, the number of names they used expanded to emphasize their legitimacy and to underscore their royal lineage and their divine patronage. By the Middle Kingdom, kings were comonly using five formal names in their official records. In the case of Ramesses 2, in the New Kingdom, there were up to six variations for his Horus name alone. As an illustration, we will list the names of the New Kingdom ruler Thutmosis 4. Historians refer to him as the fourth king to bear the Thutmosis name, a practice borrowed from the naming of European monarchs from the past, for instance George 3 of England and Louis 15 of France. This has now become so accepted that we even refer to the number of the ruler during their life time, for example Elizabeth 2 of England. However it certainly was not the practice in ancient times to ever use a ruler's numbering.

Each of the Egyptian king's five titles would start with a standard formal introductory phase, the king would then add the ending which he believed best described his reign or how he would like to be remembered. The precise reason for the exact choice of the suffix phrase has in most cases been lost and we are left to make deductions from the major events influencing his kingdom at the time. His five names were:

1. **Horus name** – this was usually written above a serekh, an image of a royal palace, with the hawk Horus perched on top. It was the oldest name form originating from the start of the Old Kingdom.
   *'Horus the mighty bull . . . . . . . . . whose diadems are firmly established '*

2. **Nebty name** – this started to be used in the 12th Dynasty and linked the king to the two original kingdoms or 'ladies', Nekhbet the vulture of Nekheb in the south and Wadjet the cobra of Buto in the north.
   *'Lord of the two lands (or ladies) . . . . . . .stable in his kingdoms as Toumou'*

3. **Golden Horus** name - this shows Horus above a beaded gold collar. The gold expresses divinity both because of its value and its sun like color, gold never decayed and reflected his eternal life and god like status.
   *'Horus of Gold . . . . . . . .powerful of sword, destroyer of the barbarians'*

4. **Throne** name or **Prenomen** - this was the name given to the king when he ascended the throne and was the most important. Its title linked him to his ancestors as kings of the north and south realms represented by their patron icons, the sedge (nisut) and the bee (bit). This was the second most commonly used name in written records and dates from the early 3rd Dynasty.It was often used on its own.
*'He of the sedge+bee.........everlasting are the manifestations of Re'*

5. **Personal** or **Birth** Nomen or **Son of Re** Nomen -this was given to him at birth and was used commonly within his family, it was represented by a duck and the sun. This dates from the 4th Dynasty king Djedefre. It claims the king was the son of the sun god Re, it was the most commonly used name.
*'Son of Re.................... Tutmosis kha khau (born of the god Thoth) '*

Temple inscriptions could on occasion list all five names when referring to the ruler, however it was more common to see the king identified only by his two most commonly used names. Therefore, historians normally identify a specific ruler by reference to these last two names i.e. the Throne name and the Personal name. We know from the Amarna letters (Chapter 9) that when the king of the Hittites wrote to his 'brother', the king of Egypt, Amenhotep 3, he addressed him not by his personal name Amenhotep, but only by his throne name, Neb Maat Re, which distinguished him from others with the Amenhotep Personal name. Ramesses 2 used only his Personal name, Ramesu, and Throne name, User maat re Setep en re, in the inscriptions on his Abu Simble temple.During periods of strong central government people often named their children after the ruler in a display of loyalty and to obtain strength through association with an effective king. It seems to have been quite an effective tactic as many of the senior court officials through the ages bore the same name as the king, for example in the reigns of Ahmose I and Amenhotep 3.

# Bibliography

The following one hundred or so titles is a select bibliography for the reader who would like to investigate specific subjects in more detail than is covered in this concise volume. The older works are included as they are timeless classics or give a fascinating insight to the limited state of our knowledge at the time they were written.

A Description of the East, R Pococke, 1743
A History of Egypt from the Earliest Times, J Breasted, 1905
A Guide to the Antiquities of Upper Egypt, A Weigall, 1910
A Thousand Miles Up the Nile, A Edwards, 1877
History of the Giza Necropolis 1+2, G Reisner, 1942+1955
Abusir: The Realm of Osiris, M Verner, 2002
Abydos and the Royal Tombs of the First Dynasty, B Kemp, 1966
Archaic Egypt, W Emery, 1961
Akhenaten King of Egypt, C Aldred, 1998
Akhenaten:the Heretic King, D Redford, 1984
Ancient Egypt, Anatomy of a Civilisation, B Kemp, 1989+2006
Ancient Egypt, A Dodson, 2006
Ancient Records of Egypt,J Breasted, 1905
Atlas of Ancient Egypt, J Baines, 1980
Avaris and Piramesse, M Bietak, 1979
Amenhotep 3: Perspectives on His Reign,E Cline, 1998
Bibliotheca Historica of Diodorus, C Oldfather, 1933
Building in Ancient Egypt, D Arnold, 1991
Denkmaler aus Aegypten und Aethiopien, C Lepsius, 1849-59
Description de l'Egypte, Commission des Monuments D'Egypte,1809+
Die Agyptischhen Pyramiden, R Stadelmann, 1991
Early Dynastic Egypt,T Wilkinson, 1999
Egypt After the Pharaohs, A Bowman, 1986
Egypt and Nubia, D Roberts, 1845-49
Egypt's Dazzling Sun, D O'Connor, 1992
Egypt Before the Pharaohs, M Hoffman, 1980
Egypt ,the Aegean and the Levant, W Davies, 1995
Egypt, Canaan and Israel in Ancient Times, D Redford,1992
Egypt in Nubia, W Emery, 1965
Egypt of the Pharaohs, A Gardiner, 1961
Egyptian Antiquities in the Nile Valley, J Baikie, 1932
Egyptian Grammar, A Gardiner, 1957
Egyptian Mummies, B Brier, 1994
Excavation at Deir el Bahri, H Winlock, 1942
Excavations and Explorations in Egypt,A Weigall,1909
Guide to the Valley of the Kings,A Silotti, 1996

Libya and Egypt,M Leahy,1990
People of the Sea, T+M Dothan,1992
Pharaohs of the Sun, R Freed, 1999
Pharonic King Lists, D Redford, 1986
Forgotten Pharaohs, Lost Pyramids,Abusir, M Verner,1994
Mycerinus: the Temples of the Third Pyramid at Giza, G Reisner, 1931
Narrative of the Operations and Recent Discoveries within the Pyramids,
    Temples,Tombs and Excavations in Egypt + Nubia, G Belzoni, 1820
Operations Carried on at the Pyramids of Gizeh in 1837, R Vyse,1840
Pioneer to the Past, C Breasted, 1943
Saqqara, Royal Necropolis of Memphis, J Lauer, 1976
Science and Secrets of Early Medicine, J Thorwald, 1962
Seventy Years in Archaeology, W Petrie, 1933
Temples of the Last Pharaohs, D Arnold, 1999
The Art of Ancient Egypt, G Robins,1997
The Amarna Letters, W Moran, 1991
The Cambridge Ancient History Vol 1-4, 1971
The Complete Temples of Ancient Egypt, R Wilkinson, 2000
The Complete Pyramids, M Lehner,1997
The Complete Royal Families of Egypt, A Dodson, 2004
The Complete Valley of the Kings, N Reeves, 1996
The Decrees of Memphis and Canopus, E Budge,1904
The Edwin Smith Surgical Papyrus, J Breasted, 1930
The Histories of Herodotus, D Lateiner, 2004
The Hyksos, E Oren, 1997
The Geography of Strabo ,W Falconer, 1857
The Greeks Overseas, J Boardman, 1964
The Manners and Customs of the Ancient Egyptians, J Wilkinson, 1837
The Monuments of Upper Egypt, A Mariette,1877
The Literature of Ancient Egypt, W Simpson, 1973
The Oxford History of Ancient Egypt, I Shaw, 2000
The Penguin Historical Atlas of Ancient Egypt, B Manley, 1996
The Pyramids, A Silotti, 1997
The Pyramids of Egypt, I Edwards, 1961
The Pyramids and Temples of Gizeh, W Petrie, 1883
The Relation of a Journey Begun in AD 1610, G Sandys, 1673
The Rise and Fall of the Middle Kingdom, H Winlock, 1947
The Royal Canon of Turin, A Gardiner, 1959
The Royal Tombs of the the the Earliest Dynasties, W Petrie, 1901
The Sea Peoples, N Sandars, 1985
The Search for Ancient Egypt , J Vercoutter, 1992
The Tale of Sinuhe, R Parkinson, 1997
The Tomb of Tutankamen, H Carter, 1923
The Temples of Karnak, R de Lubcz Schwaller, 1999
Thebes, It's Tombs and Their Tenants, H Rhind, 1862
Travels in Upper and Lower Egypt, V Denon, 1803

Travels to Discover the Source of the Nile, J Bruce, 1790
Travels in Egypt and Nubia, C Irby, 1868
Topographical Bibliography of Ancient Egypt, B Porter, 1927+
Topography of Thebes and General View of Egypt, J Wilkinson, 1835
Valley of the Kings, K Weeks, 2001
Valley of the Kings, H Hornung, 1990
Valley of the Kings, J Romer, 1981
War and Peace in the Ancient World, 2007, K Raaflaub/L Bell
Women in Ancient Egypt, G Robbins, 1993
Who was Who in Egyptology, W Dawson, 1995
Who Were the Pharaohs?, S Quirke, 1990
X-raying the Pharaohs, J Harris, 1973

# Index (selective)

# Errata

P5      line 26  Ptolemaic
P25     line 17  Khasekhemwy
P27     line 24  Heliopolis
P29     line 21  Tutankhamen
P33     line 24  temple
P35     line 28  illustration
P42     line 4  Deir el Medina
P44     line 19  configuration
P47     line 17  Heliopolis
P50     line 21  Medieval
P55     line 31  archaeologist
P56     line 41  p57 lines 10 and 15 Abu Roash
P70     line 20  Abbe Barthelemy
P92     line 10  Fayum
P94     line 31  typical
P95     line 4  Fayum
P111    line 29  a Thutmosis 2 Deir el Bahri
P114    line 37  representation
P129    line 32  Heliopolis
P132    line 43  last commenced
P135    line 3  jubilee
P142    line 6  led
P143    line 32  mouth
P144    line 33  archaeologist
P149    line 5  Memphis
P154    line 34  statues
P155    line 23  Bintanath  line 32 (Merenptah)
P160    line 20  dedicated
P166    line 5  king of Israel
P169    line2  Assyrians
P170    line 10  towering  line 13 more aggressive  line 15 Assyrian
P172    line 44  response
P174    line 13  Ashur
P178    line 21  Artaxerxes
P179    line 33  relatively
P180    line 4  Ptolemaic
P181    line 28  Alexander's
P185    line 19  Ptolemaic
P187    line 31  calamities
P189    line 7  Senate  line 19 consensus  line 26 an effigy
P206    line 32  Egyptians
P210    line 5  Punt (Somalia)
P211    line 21  Ptolemaic